BIG IDEAS FOR SMALL SERVICE BUSINESSES

How to Successfully Advertise, Publicize, and Maximize Your Business or Professional Practice

D1280386

BIG IDEAS FOR SMALL SERVICE BUSINESSES

How to Successfully Advertise, Publicize, and Maximize Your Business or Professional Practice

Marilyn and Tom Ross

COMMUNICATION CREATIVITY
425 Cedar Street
Buena Vista, CO 81211

Printed and bound in the United States of America.
First printing 1994

Library of Congress Cataloging-in-Publication Data
Ross, Marilyn Heimberg.
    Big ideas for small service businesses : how to successfully advertise, publicize, and maximize your business or professional practice / Marilyn and Tom Ross.
    p. cm.
Enl. and rev. ed of: Big marketing ideas for small service businesses. 1990.
Includes bibliographical references and index
ISBN 0-918880-16-5 (pbk.) : $15.95
    1. Service industries—Marketing.   2. Small business—Marketing.
3. Professions—Marketing.   I. Ross, Tom, 1933-   II. Ross, Marilyn Heimberg. Big marketing ideas for small service businesses.   III. Title.
HD9980.5.R68 1994
658.8—dc20   93-27219
                                               CIP

Dedication

*To our dear parents who gave us legacies
of unconditional love, sound values, and
entrepreneurial spirits. We cherish all our
moments with you.*

Books by Marilyn and Tom Ross

Country Bound!™

The Complete Guide to Self-Publishing

Marketing Your Books

How to Make Big Profits Publishing City & Regional Books

The Encyclopedia of Self Publishing

Books by Marilyn Ross

Be Tough or Be Gone

The National Survey of Newspaper Op-Ed Pages

Discover Your Roots

Creative Loafing

How to Contact the Authors

Tom and Marilyn Ross provide consulting services for selected businesses, associations, and non-profit organizations nationwide. Requests for information about these services, as well as inquiries about their availability for speeches and seminars, should be directed to them at the address below.

Readers of this book are also encouraged to contact the authors with comments and ideas for future editions.

Marilyn and Tom Ross
Accelerated Business Images
425 Cedar Street, P.O. Box 1500-BI
Buena Vista, CO 81211-1500

Contents

PART I.   WINNING MARKETING STRATEGIES

Quick and Easy Market Research ■ Who's Your Competition?
■ Positioning Yourself for Profits ■ Niche Marketing/
Segmentation ■ Developing a Powerful Marketing Plan
■ Prudent Budgeting ■ Hiring Professional Help ■ Methods for
Measurement ■ Brainstorming to Unleash Your Creativity

Developing Personal Power and Credibility ■ Your Business
Attitude and Manners ■ The Telephone as Goodwill Ambassa-
dor ■ What's in a Name? ■ Logos and Slogans ■ Designing
Letterhead ■ Business Cards as Minibillboards

Writing Copy From a "Benefit" Perspective ■ Classified Ads
■ Display Ads ■ The "RUB" Formula ■ Free Standing Inserts
■ Advertorials ■ Placement Ploys ■ Negotiation Tips ■ Choos-
ing the Media ■ Understanding Psychographics ■ Yellow Page
Ads ■ Directories Help You Get Discovered ■ Broadcast Media
■ Signage ■ Exhibiting at Trade Shows ■ Telemarketing
■ Novelty Items

List of Illustrations

Introduction

There are those who contend service businesses are second-class citizens. After all, they don't make anything useful—like a car. This simplistic attitude presumes that delivering the car to the dealer (a service), financing it (a service), insuring it (a service), and repairing it (a service) are all unessential jobs.

New technologies, paired with a long-term shift in the U.S. economy, have transformed the service sector into one of the most exciting and fastest growing games around. Just what does "service" include? Admittedly, it's a hodgepodge of businesses. They range from health to hospitality, real estate to recreation, TV repair to temporary employment, day care to dry cleaning, interior decorating to information management. In hundreds of different ways helping hands are making fistfuls of dollars. Opportunities expand like bread dough on a warm day.

But the diversity doesn't end there. Another whole group of service firms exists. It encompasses attorneys, accountants, physicians, and other professionals such as engineers, architects, consultants, public relation (PR) agencies, executive recruiters, and financial advisors. This group may need the help offered in *Big Ideas for Small Service Businesses* the most. Practice development is paramount for stability and growth.

The landmark court decision, *Bates v. Arizona*, allowed lawyers, physicians, and certified public accountants to begin promoting their professional practices. Although the propriety and desirability of advertising and marketing is still controversial in some ranks, most professionals now realize they live in a "promote or perish" society. This book is for them.

Perhaps you wonder what we mean by "small business." Did you know over 95% of American businesses have fewer than 100 employees? That means there are over 9,872,000 businesses like yours. We're addressing the concerns of this group: from the one-person entrepreneurial venture, to professional practices, to companies with up to 100 employees. That's where the real excitement is, not in the Fortune 500 companies. Since 1973, this elite group has lost a net of 6 million jobs! Manufacturing is on the wane.

Fortunately, for every job in manufacturing that disappears, one opens in services. In fact, 90% of all new jobs and 67% of the gross national product are generated by the service sector. The Bureau of Labor Statistics projects it will account for 74.4% of the total labor force by 1995.

When manufacturing jobs vanish, livelihoods evaporate and careers disappear—people lose their sense of security and stability. However, many are turning adversity into enterprise. They're opening beauty shops, starting auto repair businesses, turning their homes into Bed & Breakfast Inns. This book is also for them. It's an invaluable business start-up tool.

The service sector is wide open. Beginning entrepreneurs don't require the big chunks of capital to start these kinds of businesses they would to launch a retail or wholesale endeavor. But because the market has low entry barriers especially attractive to newcomers (not to mention that the average service company or professional practice loses 10 to 20% of its customers/clients each year to natural attrition), existing service businesses must continually hone their competitive edge.

Seasoned players can be nudged out of the game by bright rookies—if they don't carefully mind their profits and losses. Virtually any service can be duplicated. How do you stay on the leading edge? The key answer is astute marketing. That's what this book is all about. It contains hundreds of proven ideas established businesses and professional firms can use today to excel. We'll keep you from becoming sluggish and show you how to outfox and outflank the competition.

No bland armchair theory here. This guide offers practical, innovative suggestions covering everything from how to cultivate the right business image—to designing and producing effective brochures, direct-mail packages, and ads—to the secrets of gracefully generating free publicity. There are scores of examples of things that work, plus powerful models and analytical methods that cut through the fluff and get to the core realities behind success. *Big Ideas for Small Service Businesses* is a unique contribution to business literature. It's chock-full of lessons about the very soul of the marketing process.

The dozens of individual sections serve as a written brainstorming partner, suggesting a multitude of little moves to big results. They show you how to promote for pennies. Stimulate new business strategies. Fuel your imagination. Renew your vigor. They also provide specific guidance for the person who wants to probe more deeply. The book concludes with a comprehensive section of sources and resources to make your job easier, your results faster.

So whether you're involved in a professional practice, a not-for-profit organization, a sole proprietorship, a government agency, or a well-established corporation, *Big Ideas for Small Service Businesses* will pyramid your profits. Now you can get Madison Avenue results on a Main Street budget.

Marilyn Ross
Tom Ross

Part I

Winning Marketing Strategies

1

Setting the Stage for Success

Before a person can effectively grapple with all the elements of doing business, there must be a backdrop of research, knowledge, and planning. That's what this chapter deals with. Market research—learning who your competition is—establishing your niche—developing a marketing plan—and unleashing your creativity—will help you steal the show.

Quick and Easy Market Research

Market research is simply an orderly, objective way to learn about people—the people who deal with you now or might deal with you in the future. It allows you to put or keep your ear to the marketplace. It can be expensive and sophisticated. It can also be economical, nonscientific, and usually effective if done creatively. You need to know the potential market risks and consumer biases to avoid nasty surprises. Market research is a wonderful tool to help you hedge your business bet.

Historically, research has rewarded those who do it well and heed what it reveals. It must, however, be correctly interpreted. Coca-Cola proved that even huge corporations can go astray. They interpreted consumer taste tests too literally in 1985 and replaced their traditional drink with a new, supposedly improved, one. It was a poor understudy. Within a matter of months they were forced to eat crow and rescind their decision.

Research begins with tough questions. We might call it market intelligence. Our aim is to suggest innovative, inexpensive ways you can accomplish this so someone else doesn't mine the gold *while you* get the shaft.

There are two ways to conduct market research. One is using secondary data—information accumulated by others. The second is primary data—information gathered yourself. Either can be accomplished by a variety of different forms of investigation and surveillance.

Perhaps the most obvious approach is to talk to people. Not just selected people, but anyone and everyone who might have an informed opinion on industry influences and issues that could affect your service idea. When deciding whom to approach, think about sales and support personnel from companies with complementary services. What about chatting with past employees of these companies or alumni of your competitors? Talk to distributors, dealers, and franchisees serving your potential customer/client base. How about key industry vendors, plus writers and editors from trade journals that serve your industry?

Don't stop there. If you're really serious, step up your research and seek to interview investment banking and security analysts from large financial institutions, industry fund and portfolio managers, consultants, and other industry luminaries. These people will have done their homework and can offer a better perspective on the viability of your proposed idea.

No doubt you could benefit by talking directly with consumers. Ask them what they need and want—and what they're willing to pay for it. There is a way to do this. It is called "focus groups." It's relatively easy to set up sessions with local shopping malls. However, because a typical focus group session lasts about two hours, business customers are understandably reluctant to take time from their day to participate.

If you were to hire a firm to arrange and direct a focus group, the cost would be around $3,000. With planning and chutzpa, you can conduct one yourself. One enterprising man used his church congregation as a test audience. Remember, however, it is almost mandatory to provide some sort of financial incentive or gift for participation.

An additional option is to interview prospects by phone. Although this alleviates the group dynamics, people are often more candid. They may not speak freely in a group because of the perceived "pecking order." Do bear in mind you miss the high and low ends of the economic spectrum when using the telephone. Often well-to-do consumers have unlisted numbers; many low-income families are without a phone.

A third way to glean customer input is via mail interviews. The smallest sample to consider is around 2,000 names. The more people you test, the higher the probability your results will be accurate. Here again, some incentive is called for. Be sure to include a self-addressed, stamped envelope (SASE) or a postage-paid business reply card.

Colleges and universities are another prime resource. Not only do their libraries contain useful information. but professors are a knowledgeable resource. Interview university faculty who specialize in your field. What about working through the Marketing Department professor? Perhaps he or she will make your research needs part of a course. Students can work on questionnaires, service development, market evaluations, etc. This approach can save you a small fortune compared to hiring outside professional research companies.

There is also a wealth of information tucked away in doctoral dissertations all over the United States. We recently discovered a way to access them! University Microfilms International [(800) 521-0600] offers a free subject catalog of more than one million dissertations available for purchase. Much of this information has never been printed elsewhere. A further creative way to use this bonanza is to contact the dissertation's author to get your questions answered.

Speaking of getting questions answered, don't overlook a source of local information available in virtually any town or city. That is the chamber of commerce. Their mission is to represent the businesses in the area and promote the area's economy. To accomplish this job, most have facts and figures that may prove useful to you.

What about trade and professional associations? In many cases they set the standards for their fields, take surveys, and offer assistance in research. To find out which ones operate in your specialty, contact the American Society of Association Executives, 1575 Eye Street NW, Washington DC 20005, (202) 626-2723. For an even more complete list, check the *Encyclopedia of Associations.*

A large local library will also have answers. In addition to the normal books and periodicals, there are reference works, maps, charts, audiovisual aids, and a vertical file with pamphlets and brochures covering countless subjects. A library near us has a Colorado Room where a myriad of worthwhile documents and facts are stored. Some larger libraries also serve as depositories for government documents. Did you know the U.S. government is the largest publisher in the world?

Of course, government agencies at the local, state, and federal levels can provide an abundance of useful information for little or no cost. The Department of Commerce oversees the research and distribution of economic information. Their *Survey of Current Business and Census Bureau Reports* covers changes in the nation's economy, population statistics, and other demographic data.

Many communities also have Economic Development Offices. Here you can find current statistical data regarding the economy, building activity, sales trends, community services, etc. Don't overlook the Superintendent of Documents, U.S. Government Printing Office, Washington DC 20402. They have books, reports, and government documents on a variety of subjects.

Then there's the Small Business Administration. Although their literature is typically general in nature, they have a consulting arm called SCORE. It consists of retired executives—one of whom might be a boon to your market research project.

If fast facts or competitor reconnaissance is a vital strategy for you, going on-line with a computer puts global information at your fingertips. Retrieval services such as Dialog, with over 300 databases, gives access to documents on virtually every imaginable subject. And information services like CompuServe and Prodigy offer more intelligence gathering tactics.

These services are also wonderful for studying industry trends and prospecting. A key-word or key-phrase search of trade magazines, government publications, professional journals, or consumer magazines can yield an enormous return. And you can scout for new clients among the computerized special interest groups, forums, and electronic bulletin boards.

When Marcia Layton—who operates out of her home in Rochester, New York—wants new clients, she simply logs on to her computer! Layton produces business plans. She finds potential customers through an on-line special interest group for entrepreneurs. By auditing the mail messages posted there, she can pinpoint start-ups who seek guidance. Then she goes on-line and suggests ideas and software. Should the individual need more expert help, guess who's available to save the day? She also tests new ideas by conducting electronic surveys.

Nothing beats these tools of the computer generation. They are incredibly helpful for small businesses, not only in the initial research stages but for future marketing decisions as well. Says one user, "Research that used to take me all day now takes me 20 minutes." For your convenience we've included telephone numbers of the major computer information services in the Appendix. There you'll also find a table listing state publicly accessible databases.

Sometimes phone books prove useful. The yellow pages will tell you how much competition you have. By studying the white pages in smaller towns, you can pick up on such things as the ethnic mix. For a small fee, you can order any phone directory published in this country by calling Pacific Bell directories at (800) 848-8000.

In the hope some of our readers can adapt it to their purposes, we'd like to share the following true story. During a three-day promotion, a clever discount merchandiser gave away "all the free peanuts you can eat while shopping at our store." By the end of the promotion, the merchant had distinctive litter trails that provided information on the traffic patterns within the store. Trampled peanut hulls littered the most heavily traveled aisles and heaped up in front of merchandise displays of special interest to customers. With this ingenious trick, the merchant compiled a graphic picture of what most attracted customer attention.

Suppose you need a more sophisticated measuring stick. *Findex: The Directory of Market Research Reports, Studies and Surveys* is a treasure trove of information. It contains references to approximately 11,000 studies, surveys, and reports on market and business research. They are arranged in 12 general industry classifications, then divided further into subcategories to allow quick scanning. For instance, if you are involved in banking, financial services, plumbing, industrial cleaning, computer and information systems, hospitals and health care facilities or movies and theaters, there are sections devoted to market research in each of these areas. Report costs range from a low of $13 to a whopping $12,000.

Who's Your Competition?

No matter what business you're in, it makes sense to mind your competitors' business. By employing ingenious "intelligence gathering" techniques you can monitor their activity. This gives you direction and helps you focus on what to do to keep one step ahead. There are a multitude of ways to probe what—and how—your rivals are doing. Let's start with some of the elementary techniques, then graduate to more innovative strategies.

Call or write and request information. Ask them to mail you a brochure, a company history, and letters from some satisfied customers/ clients. If appropriate, you might also ask for an annual report and a copy of any newsletter they publish. Analyze this literature to discover their strategic plans.

Now look them up in the yellow pages. Ads often reveal such things as date founded, additional locations, hours of business, membership in national associations, etc. You can also get a feel for what they emphasize. Are they touting price, service, quality, or some unique characteristic?

Once again, the chamber of commerce can come to your aid for local or regional competitors. If they are members, the chamber typically can tell you who the principals are, as well as shed some light on their reputation, history, and civic involvement.

Don't overlook the area better business bureau. They frequently have company histories on file that show the date of incorporation, who the owners are, and what the company does. Additionally, they will know if any consumer complaints have been received and whether a satisfactory settlement was reached.

What's the ideal way to glean first-hand information? Use their service yourself! Make every second count while you're on the premises. What image is projected—is the atmosphere conservative or avant-garde, friendly or formal? Are there plaques, awards, or framed letters on the walls that give clues about their reputation? Is the environment organized and sparkling or messy and dirty? What kind of reading material is placed in the lobby? How do employees act toward each other—and you? Now think about how the service is delivered. Is it timely? Of superior quality? Are any "extras" included? Did the person who worked with you make an effort to sell you additional services? Noticing what they do poorly (and well) gives you a mighty weapon for your marketing arsenal.

A trip to the biggest library in the area will also net information to help you outmaneuver the competition. For larger corporations, look in the *Dun & Bradstreet Directory* or *Standard & Poor's Registry*. Firms with a net worth of from $500,000 to $1,000,000 are listed in *D & B's Middle Market*. Those topping $1 million are in the—you guessed it—*Million Dollar Directory*.

Here you will learn when and where incorporation took place, subsidiary details, names and functions of corporate officers and directors, annual sales volume, plus the number of employees. The

Standard & Poor's reference set is even more complete. It probes capitalization, corporate background, subsidiaries, finances, and recent dividends.

If you weren't able to get an annual report yourself, major libraries often have copies for heavyweight area businesses. While on your research safari, look up the CEO in *Who's Who in America* or one of the other who's who directories. These biographical references reveal such tidbits as alma mater, accomplishments, books authored, community involvement, hobbies, and personal data. One more library assignment: research local news stories. Many libraries index the local newspaper or clip articles and file them in vertical filing cabinets. By scouring these you can harvest pertinent competitor information, plus get a feel for their advertising budgets.

Word-of-mouth can be more revealing than a sheer blouse. Talk with friends, relatives, business colleagues, vendors, sales representatives, even strangers. Listen carefully. One daring soul we know puts himself within close physical proximity to his competitor's location in the hope of overhearing useful information. He eavesdrops in nearby neighborhood bars and on buses to catch snatches of conversations.

If you don't have that much moxie (and most of us don't), consider attending trade shows and conferences. By visiting your competitors' booths, you can collect available literature, tune in to industry gossip, and perhaps get a leg up by discovering future expansion plans.

Always have your antenna out. Help-wanted ads, for instance, can yield information on your opponent's activities. Are they adding to their staff? Looking to hire a branch manager? Another place to scrutinize is trade journals in your field. Tune in to them for articles about your opponents. Specific magazine sections—such as personnel announcements, calendar listings, or news and notes—can also provide ammunition.

It may be wise to hire a clipping service. You can instruct them to pull all magazine or newspaper articles on any company, clip industry trend pieces, cover virtually anything you want to track. (If you hire one, be sure to add your own company name so they provide an overview of what is appearing in print about you.) A list of clipping services appears in Part III. Should radio and TV play a major role in your adversary's plan, they also audit electronic media.

There is yet another way to tune in to a competitor's advertising activity. Space Analysis Systems, Inc. [2300 Computer Avenue, Suite H38, Willow Grove, PA 19090, (215) 784-0404] monitors ads in over

300 publications. For a minimum of $30, they can check their database and determine which publications your competitors use for advertising.

Last, but far from least, you can read your way to a hot career. Yes, there are books, magazines, newsletters, and newspapers to help you stay abreast of trends and create exciting new business opportunities. Some suggestions for trend tracking are offered on the following page.

Positioning Yourself for Profits

When times are tough, there's great temptation to cut the marketing budget and work harder. We'd like to suggest you work easier . . . and more ingeniously. How?

By "positioning" yourself for greater success. What does this snappy term really mean? Positioning is simply looking for the hole—then plugging it. Finding ways to differentiate yourself from the pack. And many of these strategies cost little or nothing. Using traditional techniques to fight for market share makes about as much sense as a bunch of mice getting together to build a cat. Take a leadership posture rather than being a look-alike.

Do you remember who was the first man to walk on the moon? Now who was the second-person? Nobody knows but his relatives. Being first has always garnered attention. In today's world, however, most organizations don't enjoy a leadership position. As a result, they have to relate their firm and its services to the leader. That's positioning. Avis Rent-a-Car did a superb job by playing on their "number two" position.

Service businesses and professional firms position themselves in different ways.

Bob Unger and John Kupillas are attorneys specializing in real estate law in Great Neck, New York. With that, their similarity to others in the legal profession ends. Unger and Kupillas are known as The Singing Lawyers.

"We had a tough time getting clients," remembers Unger. "We handed out business cards everywhere, even in elevators. We needed a way to stand out among the thousands of law firms in New York." When they got an invitation to speak before the North Shore Real Estate Board in Queens, they decided to combine singing with their talk—certainly an attention grabber to reach the real estate market they wanted to penetrate.

"We took voice training, created special lyrics, and customized our song for that particular group," explains Kupillas. They were an instant hit. Soon their law office was alive with the sound of music . . . and

TREND TRACKING READING

The Popcorn Report, by Faith Popcorn, not only pinpoints consumer moods but is just plain fascinating reading.

Megatrends 2000, by John Naisbitt and Patricia Aburdene, details 10 new directions for the '90s.

Powershift, by Alvin Toffler, is both entertaining and profound as it serves up insights we need to survive in the future.

The Lifestyle Odyssey: 2,001 Ways Americans' Lives Are Changing, by the editors of Research Alert, pinpoints six principles—and their ramifications—that will shape our lives in this century.

The New Tools of Technology, edited by Daniel Burrus and Patti Thomsen, cites 20 key technologies entrepreneurs can use and discloses 520 of the latest advances.

Trend Tracking: The System to Profit from Today's Trends, by Gerald Celente with Tom Milton, offers a formula for trend analysis that people can apply independently for business survival and growth.

Advertising Age or *Ad Weekly* magazines help you get a feel for what new products, consumer interest trends, and ad agency advance plans are on the horizon.

American Demographics magazine forecasts consumer trends for advertising executives and other business leaders. Back issues on specific topics are also useful.

Entrepreneur magazine interviews forward-thinking small business-people and is a good idea generator.

Publishers Weekly is the bible of the book industry. By studying the spring and fall issues you can get a feel for upcoming consumer interests.

The Wall Street Journal gives an excellent overview of breaking business news.

USA Today runs cover stories plus interesting "snapshots" of statistics and how people feel about issues.

The Futurist is a journal of forecasts, trends, and ideas about the future. (Global in scope, it's available only through membership in the World Future Society.)

John Naisbitt's Trend Letter offers cutting-edge news on a variety of topics twice monthly.

client conferences. They even received an invitation to sing the National Anthem for a New York Jets game. "We've shown that music is a tool in establishing rapport," says Unger. It is also the positioning strategy that has allowed them to build a two-story law office and garner a publishing contract for a book titled *Tune In to Success: Strategies for Achieving Your Greatest Potential.*

Gratzi's, a high-end Italian restaurant located near an industrial complex in Colorado Springs, Colorado, took a different tack. It launched Fax-A-Meal using modern technology to appeal to the rushed business crowd. All people have to do is fax in their order and the time it is to be ready. Presto. They can arrive and eat in—or send a gopher to pick up antipasto, tortellini, or crispy calamari. Another positioning trend is for restaurants to deliver elaborate feasts to your doorstep. Harried two-career couples can wait until the kids are down, add candles and wine, then dine.

The Blue Frog Bar & Grill's owner, Mim Witschy, got frustrated working for someone else. So she bought this little hole-in-the-wall bistro. But how to attract customers? She and a partner came up with the idea of offering children's games to their adult patrons. Bar sales in '93 are expected to hit $500,000. Both businesspeople and yuppies love the games—for ages three to twelve!

What you're reading right now is a prime example of positioning. Successful authors position their books. When we got the idea to write a marketing guide for small businesses, we did our homework. A trip to the library and an hour or so pouring over *Books in Print* told us what was already available. What a blow! There was page after page of titles on advertising, promotion, sales, and publicity. As we studied them more carefully, however, it became evident not a single book dealt exclusively with marketing for *service* businesses. Bingo! That's how we positioned *Big Ideas for Small Service Businesses.* With some 53,000 new titles coming out each year, other authors would be wise to position their books for a specific audience as well.

How do you find your special stance for success? As we said before, know the competition. Before you can possibly position yourself ideally you must evaluate what your rivals do well—and poorly.

Next you need to understand *your* operation. What do you do better, faster, more innovatively than others? Focus on your real strength. Don't try to be all things to all people. Rather make the most of your unique resources. Build depth.

"The key point in positioning," says Unger, "is to know what your goals are and be sure they're consistent with your morals and ethics. Then every single thing that flashes across your life relates. Ask of everything you read, everything you see, every experience you have: 'how does this fit with my goal?' By doing that you're constantly looking for 'hooks'— ways to position yourself."

Then get out of *your* head and into your prospects' mindset. "What's in it for me?" is all they care about. If you put more in it for them, they'll put more in your coffers in return.

That's what happened at a Chicago travel agency. They came up with a different twist: a discount travel club that offers short-notice vacations. Discovering that traveling on short notice was the preferred mode for a fast-growing group of people, they cater to young professionals looking for exotic vacations within their budget. Retirees who consider travel an important part of their lifestyle are another large segment of their clientele. Their drawing card? Economical pricing. Members save several hundred dollars per trip.

Speaking of travel, Mighty Eagle Travel, Inc. moved their agency into a former bank building with a drive-through window. Quips owner Christopher Hinn, "If McDonald's can do it, why can't I?" This new twist on an old concept allows customers to pick up tickets in a more convenient way. One woman drives in wearing her robe and slippers. A corporate client sends a driver over for tickets while he's running other errands. And because the agency is situated between downtown and the airport, customers can get their tickets on the way to catch their flights.

And a forward-thinking Massachusetts woman by the name of Susan Berk set up sightseeing tours called Uncommon Boston, Ltd. Berk quickly built her business into a quarter-of-a-million dollar venture. "People want to feel like an insider. They want to get unusual questions answered and see unique places," she observes. Berk's firm customizes each program for the client—be it a spouse tour, reunion, retirement party, or dinner for the chairman of the board.

She has amazing resources and can pull off exceptional events. Rather than hitting the usual tourist spots, Uncommon Boston gives people an insider's view of the city. A cadre of guides whisks clients off on a tour of a chocolate factory (to learn its history, how it's made, and to indulge in a tasting party). Or perhaps a college tour for students and parents making Alma Mater selections is in order. Even private home tours for cooking lessons with renowned chefs and visits to famous area artists' studios to watch them work can be arranged. Uncommon Boston, Ltd., gives the typical tours servicing the city a real run for their money. Susan Berk has created something special. Different. Imaginative. She constantly proves small is spectacular—and profitable too.

That's also what D. Edward Jones, an unusual brokerage house decided. The brokers who work there conduct business in the boonies. They purposely shun big cities, preferring to contact well-heeled investors tucked away in the hills and dales of America. Said the late Ted Jones, the firm's senior partner, "There were a whole lot of farmers, storekeepers and small-town professionals out there that brokers weren't calling on." Now that's all changed. A lot of this firm's penetration in the marketplace results from capitalizing on a specific niche.

There are countless strategies for positioning your business. Perhaps you should investigate the hours or days you are open. One store that closed Sundays found it was their second busiest day when they opted to remain open. Or maybe an outlandish guarantee could be your claim to fame. Chances are, offering pick-up and delivery service will capture new business. In our harried world, people are especially receptive to anyone or anyplace that saves them time or makes their lives easier.

A Vista, California, entrepreneur decided to piggyback two businesses. Dubbed Clean & Lean, the concept consists of a laundromat in conjunction with a fitness facility. "We got the idea 3½ years ago," explains president Greg Trabert. "My mother noticed people wasted so much time doing their laundry."

People seem to like Clean & Lean's personalized service and the opportunity to make new acquaintances. It is very different from a big, impersonal gym where you have to sign an expensive, long-term contract. Here you choose from a menu of four options: coin laundry only, a visit to the fitness center, fitness sessions on a monthly basis, or a combination laundry and fitness deal.

Partially due to tremendous publicity (they've been interviewed by *CBS World News*, ABC, CNN, BBC, Japanese TV, the *Japanese Wall Street Journal*, *Sports Illustrated*, *Time*, *Glamour*, and *People*), things are looking anything but lean. In fact, they're "cleaning up." Several franchises are in operation now and many more are in the works.

Positioning comes in as many varieties as Madonna has outfits. Capitalizing on age to set itself apart, a Denver bank specializes in kids doing grown-up business. Junior patrons open checking accounts and take out loans while the bank makes a name for itself—and long-term customers. A doctor makes house calls from her fully equipped medical vehicle. An enterprising masseuse makes "office calls" to loosen the stressed neck muscles of secretaries and executives. The list is endless. Entrepreneurs all across America are discovering practical, profitable ways to make themselves uniquely competitive.

While it's true the only person who really likes change is a wet baby, to survive and thrive in today's economy we must be willing to change—to innovate—to plug the hole. You can try to do business as usual, or you can do business unusually well. Positioning could make the difference.

21 WAYS TO OUTDISTANCE THE HERD

1. Price point: are you expensive, moderately priced, or cheap?
2. Size: small may be beautiful; play on your personalized attention.
3. Atmosphere: are you laid back? sophisticated? hip? continental?
4. Hours: do you stay open late (or open early) to accommodate working people?
5. Days of operation: should you consider opening weekends? holidays?
6. Location: are you convenient? easy to find? handy for walk-by traffic?
7. Portability: could you put your business "on the road?"
8. Ease of purchasing: do you accept credit cards? lay away? or financing?
9. Convenience: can people get in easily? find what they want? pay quickly?
10. Do you have a gimmick: an environmental angle? a theme decor?
11. Delivery: do you offer pick up or delivery?
12. Guarantee: have you a unique money-back policy?
13. Packaging: could you use innovative, reusable, or fun packaging?
14. Giveaways: do you offer free gifts to potential customers? to purchasers?
15. Piggybacking: can you combine two businesses to better serve people?
16. Samples: could you offer samples to entice buyers?
17. Seminars or demonstrations: should your service be showcased?
18. Contests: would some form of competition focus attention on you?
19. Age segmentation: should you slant toward teens? adults? retirees?
20. Service: do you offer extraordinary assistance to your customers/clients?
21. Technological edge: will a fax, modem, or cellular phone open new doors?

Niche Marketing/Segmentation

A close cousin to positioning is niche marketing/segmentation. Perhaps using a military analogy will help you understand what we mean here. For thousands of years military leaders have used the strategy of maneuvering *around* strength, rather than *confronting* it, to win victories. They exploit their adversaries' weakness. It's the old "divide and conquer" theory.

You can carve out a niche just for yourself, doing something different or better or faster than your competition. This way you identify and serve a segment all your own, instead of tackling the major competition head on.

Let's use cookies to understand how it works. Cookie manufacturers tailor their approaches to appeal to very different segments of the population. Thus, some cookies are *chewy*. Others are *crunchy*. There are those *"like Grandma used to make"* for nostalgia buffs. And what about *nutritious* cookies pitched to the health-conscious? Then there are *gourmet* cookies for those poised on the cutting edge of cuisine. And don't forget *gigantic* cookies—or *bite-sized* miniature ones—or the just plain *fun* ones we learned to unscrew and devour—centers first—as toddlers. Get the picture? (These manufacturers are definitely not into cookie-cutter marketing! Smart cookies go after their own sweet section of the market.)

In the service sector, hospitals and health care facilities are becoming very innovative at carving out special niches for themselves. They've aborted their attempts to reach every health care patient and are dissecting and refining health care markets, focusing on specialty care. The primary objective of these niche programs is to increase market share. It's working handsomely. In an annual diversification survey by *Hospitals Magazine,* the results show overall hospital segmentation strategies add to profitability.

Dayton, Ohio's, St. Elizabeth began advertising its sports medicine center the beginning of 1987. The center, dedicated to injury evaluation and treatment of athletic injuries, had been averaging 20% growth a year. In the first quarter of 1987, growth mushroomed 100% over the same quarter of the previous year! St. Elizabeth also sponsors Body Cues, a women's health education program that features home health parties.

To court mothers-to-be, Women's Hospital in Houston offers a special "cameo" package. It features a private room, lobster dinner, and a limousine ride home. Other hospitals concentrate on physical rehabilitation, senior care, oncology, corporate wellness, even eating disorders. They specialize to help them stand out from the crowd, selecting only those service lines that blend with their community or regional demographics.

Donald C. Hambrick, a professor at Columbia Business School in New York, feels small companies are often shrewd segmenters. "Their best bet for surviving and thriving is to be niche players," he advises. Futurist Edith Weiner, president of New York-based Weiner, Edrich & Brown, agrees. She noted at the American Marketing Association's 50th Anniversary World Marketing Conference and Exhibition that niche marketing will soon become the rule rather than the exception.

In the hotel industry, which is also considered a service business, niche marketing is thriving. Segmentation is especially important here because of limitations on site availability. Some chains segment by price. La Quinta is reasonably priced at about $50, whereas the Ritz Carlton charges over $150 per night. Charles Schwab also used price to set it apart from other stock brokerage firms. It was the first *discount* brokerage and is still the largest.

Clever Bed & Breakfast inns cater to pet owners, gay couples, or vegetarians. And more and more serve businesspeople, providing in-room telephones and fax machines. Some are putting together package deals to give them a competitive edge. Fifteen B&Bs in Virginia's Shenandoah Valley tied in with a vineyard to promote a new line of wines via mid-winter getaways.

Give this concept careful thought. Perhaps you could get a toehold in your industry by appealing to the price conscious—or the well-heeled. A maid service, for instance, might put together a luxury package for affluent consumers that includes such amenities as regularly polishing the silver. On the other hand, a whirlwind budget package for those who want someone to just come in once a month could attract working mothers or retirees who can't afford weekly professional cleaning.

Cadillac applied just the opposite philosophy during the Great Depression. It was about to be liquidated because few customers were buying its expensive cars. A virtually unknown middle manager by the name of Nicolas Dreystadt rescued Cadillac. How? By analyzing who was buying their cars and why. He found a neglected market segment: wealthy blacks. Black lawyers, realtors, doctors, entertainers, and the like were buying Cadillacs (with a white person "fronting" for them). They were doing it because that was the only success symbol the affluent black could acquire in those days. Prestigious housing, luxury resorts, and other trappings of wealth were denied them. Dreystadt, in the depths of the depression, turned an obstacle into an opportunity. He aggressively pursued and developed this neglected market segment—and sold enough cars to turn Cadillac into a long-term moneymaker.

More recently, Arun Sampanthavivat also used high prices to create demand for his Thai restaurant. In the Chicago area where his establishment is located, most of the areas 90 or so Thai eateries are inexpensive and plainly decorated. His meals, on the other hand, average $35 per person. Does it work? It takes 15 employees to help him cope with the crowds that come every night.

The Marriott hotel chain appeals to different segments of the population with different needs. Regular Marriotts cater to businesspeople and meeting planners. The Marriott Marquisses are located in major markets and have large convention facilities. Their Resorts attract vacationers, whereas the Suites target the upscale market that plans longer stays.

Even movie theaters are using segmentation to boost their bottom lines. Kidpix Theatres Corporation, in Los Angeles, caters exclusively to children between ages five and eleven. Located in malls, these theaters show cartoons and shorts to youngsters whose parents park them there. You can buy up to two hours of supervision for $3 per ticket.

With freshman enrollment down, innovative colleges aren't just tearing open fortune cookies in a frenzied hunt for clues to stimulate renewed vigor. Instead, they're recruiting specific types of students or touting exclusive majors. One offers a refugee studies program, another targets entrepreneurs. Landmark College in Putney, Vermont, is the nation's only accredited college for those with dyslexia and other learning disabilities.

Advertising agencies are also finding ways to set themselves apart from the competition. New York-based Trout & Ries, Inc. is extolling a "second-opinion service." Says Ries, "You wouldn't have major surgery without getting a second opinion. So why spend $10 million . . . or $50 million on advertising without getting one?"

Certainly from all these examples you have gotten ideas on how to slant your business or professional practice to a specific segment of the population—and position yourself for success.

Developing a Powerful Marketing Plan

"Chance favors the prepared mind," said Louis Pasteur. Never was that statement more true than in marketing.

One of the best ways to prepare for developing a dynamite marketing plan is to first create a Mission Statement. It needn't be long. In 20 to 40 words capture the essence of your service. Who is it for? How will it assist them? In what major way can you meet their needs? Writing this Mission Statement will help you get—and keep—focused.

If you intend to sculpt yourself a dominant position in your industry or community, a forceful marketing plan is a must. Not to have one is like going bear hunting with a switch. A plan consists of two elements: *goals*—which is what you want to achieve, and *strategies*—which is how you expect to achieve them.

There are many things to take into consideration. You must analyze your customers or clients (assuming you are an already established organization) and evaluate your competition. What sort of growth trends might you logically anticipate? If you're in the information industry, for instance, spiraling opportunities are predicted for the latter 1990s. What are your company or organization capabilities and capacity? Temper enthusiasm with realism. Although you might like to take on the world, success often evades those who use no common sense in their business dealings.

Along with opportunity comes obstacles. Have you thought about potential threats? How can you keep a rival firm from eroding your market share? Can you preempt the disastrous consequences that could result from a shift in the economy?

For your long-term success, you will ideally construct a five-year marketing plan. Of course, you'll concentrate on drafting a vigorous annual plan, which is a detailed version of the first year of your longer-range blueprint. The foundation of your plan will be a marketing mix of such elements as publicity, promotion, sales literature, direct mail, and advertising—not to mention pricing and customer service. Each is a vital building block. Don't fall into the trap of many neophyte marketers who feel if they've placed a few ads, they have a marketing plan.

To maximize your dollars, be sure PR efforts and advertising reinforce each other. They should be engineered to build on one another, establishing a cohesive, forceful image in the prospect's eyes. PR creates excitement. Ads contribute drama. Sales presentations reinforce enthusiasm. Together, the elements add up to a big bang. Individually, they are diluted and ineffective.

Quantify your goals. Do you want to increase your market share by 10% this year? 25%? If you are a start-up business, what is your target annual revenue? One hundred thousand dollars? A quarter of a million?

A marketing plan isn't an academic exercise. It should be a living, dynamic tool. The good news is that to develop such a road map you don't have to visit a channeling medium or take a course in reading tea leaves. The process needn't be intimidating. We've included specific guidelines in the Appendix. A sound marketing plan helps you kick yourself in the assets. And it's a wonderful tool to audit your progress because it makes you really think. While it's vital to have this road map, remain flexible. As on vacation, so in business: sometimes it's the side roads that are the most exciting and memorable. Perhaps an unexpected opportunity will arise that ordains action to alter previous expectations.

Don't assume if something worked in 1992 it will work today. Rubber-stamping last year's plan will likely pound another nail in the coffin of success. Such backward thinking can be deadly. Competition continually escalates. A recent *Wall Street Journal* career poll revealed the majority of people said their dream job was to "head my own business." Today more than ever before, people are turning that dream into reality. To stay competitive you need sound marketing goals and strategies. If you fail to plan, plan to fail.

Have an ongoing strategy. It's no accident financial planner Albert B. Woodward, Jr., CFP, stays visible in the Denver metropolitan area. He meets with his wife and partner, Marilyn, on a regular basis to go over a Marketing Matrix they've developed. "I believe in structure," says Woodward. "We look at the things already scheduled, those that need to be worked on, plus future possibilities we're thinking about."

Herein lies one of the prime tenets of marketing: to establish a presence in the community and develop a successful practice, you need *consistent, ongoing effort!* Creating a flurry of activity one month, then doing nothing for the next year, is like sitting down to a seven course meal—eating the appetizer—then going to bed. You need exposure. Repetition. Momentum.

"People have to know who you are and what your capabilities are," advises Woodward. His four-week planning matrix includes public speaking to civic and business groups, conducting in-house seminars, writing articles and columns, promoting referrals by phone and by mail, and a miscellaneous column.

If you want to call the tune instead of paying the fiddler, always follow up! Be prepared to monitor the progress of your projects. While diligent follow through increases your odds for success in all aspects of business, it's especially crucial in marketing. Many sound marketing plans flounder for lack of follow up.

The squeaky wheel gets more attention. We encourage clients to be politely persistent. Stopping before you get results—or a firm "no"—is like ordering an ice cream cone, then letting it melt onto the floor. Remember the three bywords of meticulous follow through: chase, trace, and replace. With this philosophy, your marketing plans are sure to be on a firmer foundation.

START-UP CHECKLIST

Below is a list of things to consider if you're just starting your business.

✓ Accounting/Bookkeeping/Tax Preparation

✓ Advertising/PR Plan

✓ Alarms/Security Systems

✓ Answering Machine/Service

✓ Auto Renting/Leasing

✓ Banking Services

✓ Business Consulting Plan

✓ Chamber of Commerce/Other Memberships

✓ Computer Consulting

✓ Computer Equipment/Software/Supplies

✓ Computer Repair/Service

✓ Copy Machine

✓ Data Processing

✓ Delivery/Messenger Service

✓ Equipment

✓ Fax Machine

✓ Federal ID Tax Number

✓ Graphic Design/Desktop Publishing/Typesetting

✓ Insurance

✓ Janitorial Service

✓ Leasing Space
✓ Legal Services/Lawyers
✓ Licensing Requirements
✓ Loans/Start-up Capital
✓ Meeting Facilities/Conference Room
✓ Mission Statement
✓ Name Registration (dba)
✓ Office Furniture
✓ Office Machines/Typewriters, etc.
✓ Office Supplies/Business Forms
✓ Printing
✓ Sales Tax Permit
✓ Secretarial Service/Word Processing
✓ Shipping & Mailing Supplies/Service
✓ Signage
✓ Space Planning & Design
✓ Telephone Equipment/Paging & Mobile Telephone
✓ Trademark/Service Mark Registration
✓ Transportation & Moving
✓ Trash Removal/Recycling Plan

Prudent Budgeting

Is there a way to keep a modest budget from cramping your style? Yes and no. If you try to whittle costs too much you may end up watching your whole business being sacrificed at the altar of fiscal restraint. Typically, marketing is not the place to cut back. That said, let us offer some suggestions for those of you with budgets tighter than fiddle strings.

When they think marketing, most people automatically think advertising. That can be a fatal mistake. If you're the new midget on the block, publicity and promotion are the mainstays that can help you skyrocket to success. You must outsmart, not outspend, the competition.

Depending on the type of business you're in, there are many free or very inexpensive ways to promote. A music teacher, plumber, or day-care center might do well by posting index cards on supermarket and laundromat bulletin boards. A business card can be handed out to spur word-of-mouth. Well-written news releases focus attention on your establishment. A professional who gives talks to civic organizations often sees his or her practice take off. Providing a free weekly column to the local newspaper can have a similar effect. A computer consultant who offers free computer lessons for city hall employees could turn this good deed into a publicity stunt of interest to the local TV stations. These are just a few of the hundreds of ideas you'll find in the following chapters.

Marketing budgets are as individual as snowflakes. One company will only spend 1% of gross sales, whereas another will boldly allocate 12%. A further determining factor is whether you are a new or established organization. Business and professional start-ups require more financial commitment in the beginning. 10% is a wise amount for the first year. This extra investment helps focus public attention on them. There is a logo to be designed, stationery to be printed, a brochure to be created and produced, signs to be fashioned and erected, perhaps a direct mail package to be developed, etc. Many choose to hire public relations or advertising professionals to accomplish these tasks and initially devise a convincing overall plan. (More about that later.)

The majority of established firms spend 2 to 5% of their gross sales on marketing. Perhaps that's why many of them fail. Spending money on marketing is a lot like tending a fire. If you want it to roar warmly, what do you do? You stoke it! Otherwise, you shiver in a semifrigid state—perhaps not freezing to death, but never being comfy and content either.

What you spend is dependent on many factors. If you're lucky enough to be in a position where there are few competitors, you needn't allocate as much as someone who is going head-to-head with several already-entrenched opponents. On the other hand, in a saturated market, it may behoove you to match what your main competitor spends to keep your portion of the market share—or enjoy increased market penetration.

In an industry that has been previously regulated—such as banks, airlines, and telephone companies—when the restrictions are lifted, competition soars. If you are in such an industry, then you'd better fuel the fire with the biggest, hottest-burning logs you can find.

One of the questions that always comes up in the seminars and lectures we give around the country is, "Shouldn't I cut back when times are bad?" Absolutely not! Slicing your marketing budget during an economic slump is like handing your assailant a gun.

A recent issue of *Business Marketing* tells of a new study that proves the fallacy of that theory. Research conducted with some 600 companies by McGraw-Hill Inc. of New York indicated those that didn't reduce their advertising during recessions had significantly more sales growth—both during and *after* the recession—than those who cut back.

Before we leave budgeting, let us introduce one other element that will impact your financial business future. That is pricing. There are four basic pricing strategies:

1. Skim the cream off the market for high, short-term profit.

2. Compete at the normal market price.

3. Charge low prices to create a mass demand.

4. Use cheap preemptive pricing to keep competitors out.

What should you ask for your service? We've all heard the phrase, "Charge what the market will bear." Although it sounds crude, there is wisdom here. If you are targeting a luxury clientele the people aren't price sensitive. They are more interested in quality, convenience, and reputation. At the other extreme is the person who is extremely price conscious and makes buying decisions based exclusively on that criterion. Think about your operation—and your competition. Do your homework. Then you will make well-informed decisions rather than simply embarking on a witch hunt for profits.

Hiring Professional Help

If you're a novice at all this, you may decide to enlist the help of professionals. Although most large agencies won't be interested in dealing with you unless you have a sizeable marketing budget, that's no reason for disappointment. It could even be a blessing in disguise. Most small businesses do best working with a smaller agency or even a well-qualified private PR/advertising practitioner. Smaller agencies typically respond quicker and take a more personal interest in your future because they aren't trying to juggle 50 clients at once.

The first person you meet will normally be a key individual in the firm, rather than just an "account executive" (glorified salesperson) for a large agency. One of the most important elements in any client/PR relationship is for you to like one another. This synergy lays the groundwork for harmony and can lead to great things. In a healthy collaboration, the CEO, or vice president of marketing, and the prime agency person initially spend a lot of time together. They explore the business' strengths and weaknesses, hammer out the marketing goals, and get a sense of each other's style and pace.

If there are wide differences, beware. An organization that prides itself on being formal and sophisticated will quickly become disenchanted by the zany creativity of an unpretentious, laid-back agency. Suppose half of the team consistently meets deadlines and is punctual for meetings. How do you think they will feel should the other half function just the opposite? If the chemistry isn't good, the results won't be either. We refuse to accept a client with whom we don't feel comfortable; life's too short to work with people you don't enjoy.

If you have a small fixed budget, don't expect the agency to play guessing games. Tell them up front what you can spend. Why should they create a million-dollar proposal if you can only allocate $200,000 to marketing? Likewise, if we know a client has only $5,000 to work with the first year, we take that into consideration when making recommendations on how they should proceed. Obviously, large-space ads and extensive direct mail are out of the question; our challenge is to devise low-cost, high-impact creative strategies. You want an agency that will spend your money as if it is their own.

Just as there is etiquette for how to handle yourself at elegant dinner parties, there is a protocol when dealing with agencies. Don't, for instance, expect them to put together a complicated presentation on "speculation." Many have been burned by companies that did not hire them, but stole their ideas to implement themselves. The "products" of advertising and PR experts are their ideas—their creative genius. You wouldn't go into a store and ask for a free suit so you could decide if you liked the store and wanted to shop there again. So don't expect PR professionals to give you their ideas and guidance until you have drawn up an agreement and bought a ticket for the show.

Once you hire pros, please do what they say. We've become very discouraged when a client pays for advice, then repeatedly ignores it. Predictably, it is this same client who, a few months later, wonders why nothing worked.

What will it cost? Fees vary as much as people. Most larger agencies prefer putting their clients on a monthly retainer basis: $3,000, $4,000, or $5,000 a month, plus ad costs and out-of-pocket expenses. We customize total start-up marketing packages for new businesses and professional firms. The one-time cost typically runs from $3,000 to $10,000, depending on whether the campaign is regional or national and what is included. Another option is hourly consulting. Costs here range from $50 to $150 per hour. It can also be done by phone. We've counseled people from coast to coast—all from our Buena Vista, Colorado, location.

When you begin working with an advertising/PR agency, don't expect instant results. It will take them awhile to grasp what your business is about, to learn the industry politics, and plant the necessary seeds for your campaign. Magazine placements, for instance, take about six months. Although it may seem to happen about as fast as getting your teeth straightened, effective PR will be generated if you choose an agency carefully, then give them the tools and time to do their job.

There are many things you can do to make the relationship go more smoothly. First, show your own enthusiasm. If you don't give a damn about your company or industry, how can you expect them to care? Next, respect your agency's time. Don't insist on a rush job when it isn't necessary. Avoid phoning constantly over trivial things. When a person is involved in a creative pursuit, an untimely interruption can put them back to square one quicker than anything.

Lastly, when you are shown a new ad, direct mail campaign, or other print piece, remember creative types have sensitive personalities. Evaluate thoroughly. Praise well. Criticize constructively. State what you like before you go into what you don't like. Try to assist them in understanding why you feel something won't work in your community or industry. By helping these creative team members learn from this experience, you groom them for pleasing you more in the future.

Methods for Measurement

Of course, before you know if you've reached your destination, you have to know where you're going. Simple, right? Not necessarily so. When an agency begins to work with you they will create a plan customized to your needs and goals. This will serve as a future measurement tool. It must be compared with baseline figures that quantify the status quo.

It is much easier to access success in advertising than it is in PR. When ads are coded, replies tracked, and sales logged, the hard numbers tell the tale. This isn't the case in PR. Publicity and promotion have a cumulative effect. They can't be tangibly quantified and easily tracked in and of themselves.

You have every right to expect some form of reporting. In this way you can document success and learn from failure. Major projects should be summarized and critiqued. Was the objective met? Did the return on investment match initial expectations? When you are sizing up the results your PR firm generated, don't just look at the big coups. Although our business clients love to be featured in the *Uall Street Journal* or *Fortune*, we know from personal experience little placements can add up to big dollars. We practice what we preach. Our firm has a regular program of offering complimentary articles to appropriate publications. One of our biggest clients found us as a result of a piece placed in an obscure newsletter with a circulation of less than 5,000.

Brainstorming to Unleash Your Creativity

Don't just compete—create! To excel in your business or professional practice you need to think creatively—be an innovator—dare to be different. Being creative doesn't necessarily mean concocting something new. It can be the rearrangement of something old or seeing ordinary things in an extraordinary way.

One thing is for certain: you can't have a mind locked in concrete. Lord Thomas Dewar observed, "Minds are like parachutes—they only function when open." Why not open yours to new possibilities? One of the secrets of true originality is to determine what everybody else is doing, then *don't* do it. With ingenuity, chances are you can liberate yourself from mediocrity.

Is there a way you can magnify or minify your service business?

One caterer looking for expansion found it by *compressing* her business. Instead of going head-to-head with her competition to get the big banquets and cocktail parties, she specialized in catering smaller affairs. Banks celebrating new services had her prepare cookies, punch, and coffee for customers. She was on hand to do a little decorating, be gracious, and give refills. Soon other businesses that previously felt they couldn't afford a catered function were calling for bids on their special activities. She even developed a variety of "packaged celebrations" for birthdays, anniversaries, special dates, etc.

The computer field gives us a perfect example of how minimizing has led to new profit centers. From PCs that sat on our desks, they went down to portables, then to laptops, and now to notebooks. Small is beautiful.

So is big. Our aging population, for instance, will increase demand for large print books in the years to come. Can you capitalize on less or more? Some upscale beauty salons are now converting to mini-spas where a woman can be pampered from head to toe for a day. One enterprising Texan took the car wash concept and expanded it. He established a service that washes and cleans airplanes. Many private jets are kept spotless by his company.

Maybe you can outclass your competition by using a combining technique. An example of this is the laundromat we spoke of earlier with exercise equipment, for instance. Another one is a law firm that also sponsored seminars on how their corporate clients could avoid discrimination problems.

Many successful new ventures offer only a slight variation on a proven market leader—just enough to establish an identity and a profitable market niche. Look how overnight delivery services flourished once Federal Express proved it was possible.

When searching for a new idea, look from all angles. Successful businesses are often simply a different application of an existing concept. Can you reverse something? (Look at the huge new industry of fragrances for men. Twenty years ago guys wouldn't touch perfume.) When using "reverse" psychology, think about not only the opposite sex, but young to old, right-handed to left-handed, etc.

Try to improve on something for which there is already an established market when inventing your own business, rather than beginning from scratch. Reverse it. Minimize it. Maximize it. Combine it. Examine the possibilities from every perspective.

Creativity may be the catalyst for a winning company slogan or jingle as well. Remember the reverse twist used in the following TV commercial: "Listerine has the taste people *hate* . . . twice a day." How about the Marriott hotel chain's push for their two-for-breakfast weekend: "For the price of a pair of sneakers, you can be a pair of loafers." Set your imagination free and see what you can come up with.

What's a great approach to getting from the itch to the idea? One of the best ways to generate a whole host of possibilities is to invite a group of people to help you think of ideas for a business opportunity. Set an initial time period, maybe two or three hours, and explain the procedures. (See the following Brainstorming Guidelines.) Set a positive tone. You might start by reminding everyone that, "No *one* of us is as powerful as all of us."

In a brainstorming session, each participant generates as many options as possible. All ideas are welcome, even if they sound kooky, impractical, or wild. The point of this exercise is to explore a range of possibilities, not to settle on any one perspective. Brainstorming stretches the imagination and produces acres of ideas from which you can harvest the best.

BRAINSTORMING GUIDELINES

- *Appoint someone to serve as a facilitator.* It's this person's job to ensure that everyone gets a chance to discuss their ideas. It helps when the facilitator summarizes the previous participant's contributions before the next person speaks. Use a blackboard or flip chart to record what's said so it is visible to everyone.

- *Reinforce and encourage all suggestions.* Don't worry about details at this point. Concentrate on producing as many ideas as possible. Encourage people to participate quickly without evaluating their own or others' thoughts.

- *There are no wrong ideas.* Don't be judgmental. If you must comment, limit your remarks to how a proposal might be improved.

- *Listen to the full explanation of an idea.* Don't interrupt others—wait until they're finished talking.

- *Nobody has all the answers.* Group success depends upon every member sharing opinions and observations. Encourage all to contribute and avoid promoting your personal agenda.

- *Sort out the best suggestions.* At the end of the time, have the participants divide the ideas into three groups: 1) those with excellent potential, 2) fair options, 3) unacceptable suggestions.

- *Focus attention on the most promising in group 1.* Refine these ideas. Further brainstorm why they're a good match for you and how they might be implemented. Look for ways to put a more profitable spin on them.

- *Bank the best of the rest.* Keep an inventory of other potentially useable possibilities. This might take the form of 3 x 5 cards, notes jotted on scraps of paper, articles, etc. Deposit them in a manila folder, large envelope, shoe box, computer file, or whatever makes sense for you. But keep them so if times turn sour, you have a waiting account from which you can withdraw inspiration. One of them will serve as a catalyst to mobilize your creative thinking.

It isn't necessary to have a room full of people to accomplish wondrous acts though. You can take other approaches by yourself with a pencil and paper or computer keyboard. One method is called Freewriting. Sit down for 15 minutes and write anything and everything that comes into your head. No fair stopping or crossing out words. And don't worry about spelling or punctuation. The object is to lose control, to reach your intense inner thoughts so you can harness that energy.

Another dynamite doorway to your mind is called Clustering. This is a magic key for getting in touch with your secret reserves of imaginative power. Clustering is a nonlinear personal brainstorming process similar to free association. It's like writing a map of ideas, beginning with a core word or statement, then branching out with associated ideas in many directions.

Starting with the main idea in the center, give your mind free reign to radiate thoughts and images out from this nucleus. Write new ideas in circles which, in turn, are connected by lines to other circles. Ideas spill out with lightning fast speed. They form associations that allow patterns and solutions to emerge. Chaos becomes order as ideas surface in a gradual map that accesses our interior landscape of thoughts. It's an easy, flowing process. There's no right or wrong place to start; nothing is forced. While this is an excellent solo exercise, it can also be effective done as a group.

But whether you do it individually or in tandem with others, brainstorming is sure to unleash your creativity. Now let's proceed. The next chapter deals with how you can develop an image that will make a good impression and lead to more business.

2

Image-Building:
How to Create a Good
and Lasting Impression

The personal image you project and the reputation your firm, nonprofit group, or business cultivates can spell the difference between success and failure. Image building must be proactive, not reactive. Are you just starting a new business or professional practice? Or perhaps you want to change a soft-shoe, tippy-toe image into a position of power. In either case, the tangible things you can do to become a vanguard in your field are the subjects of this chapter. We'll address personal power and credibility and how to influence your clients'/customers' perception of your organization. We will also discuss the trappings of business: creating a pleasing facility; becoming a "presence;" telephone goodwill; choosing a name, logo, and slogan; and designing your stationery and business cards. And we'll show you how to manage the image you project to the world.

Developing Personal Power and Credibility

Locally rendered services rely heavily on the personalities performing the services. Many of us choose a mechanic, family doctor, or neighborhood hairdresser simply because we *like* the person. Although the 21st century will see more national franchises and chains for such things as muffler repair, teeth cleaning, and quick divorces, individual service providers will still play a key role. Consequently the entrepreneur, professional, or CEO will continue to have high visibility.

Whether we mean to or not, we constantly send messages to others. We're judged by how we dress, walk, speak, interact, and so on. In real estate, property buyers are said to build equity as they pay off their mortgages. Building equity can apply to people as well. Let's look at things we can do to increase our individual net worth in the business world.

We are judged long before we're given an opportunity to perform our services. It would be wise for us to understand the rules of the contest. Be comfortable in the role you project. Be yourself. This doesn't mean you can't change or grow . . . it simply means make sure the image is you.

We have all encountered folks who seem artificial, a bit phony. They appear as actors in a bad role. So be the best, most polished, most sincere, and most friendly *you* that can be managed with comfort.

Most impressions are formed within the first 30 seconds of meeting someone. A solid handshake makes for a good beginning. Ideally, women should extend their hands to men first. Pump the other's hand firmly two or three times.

"People take what you wear as information," says Judith Waters, Ph.D., a New Jersey psychology professor and management consultant. How we dress is a large part of our image. That is not to say men must always wear three piece pin-stripe suits nor women tailored designer ensembles.

Dress for the job. A plumber will be clothed differently than a physician. There is no excuse, however, for the plumber to wear jeans with the knees out. If he is that careless about his appearance, customers may have little confidence in his ability to repair their plumbing problems and even more concern about the horrendous mess he may leave. Especially in the service sector, wherever you go, a picture of your firm is being conveyed.

We had a big problem with one client who had written an excellent book about power and gave lectures on the subject. Her verbal message was penetrating, perceptive, and right on target. Her physical message was something else. She looked more like an unkempt housewife than an influential executive. Her unprofessional dress code made attendees question their own judgment in making her their guru.

It's necessary to wear attire appropriate to the occasion, especially when you're in the limelight. It may be conservatively corporate or uninhibitedly creative (if you're a painter, advertising exec, or design consultant, for instance). You must feel good in it. Then you can forget your appearance and concentrate on the important matters at hand. Consider accessories as well. Polished, well-heeled shoes; carefully groomed fingernails; and a fresh haircut speak well of a person.

Women should also think about jewelry. Dangling earrings are distracting. So are clanging bracelets. Contemplate whether you want to flaunt your expensive jewelry for business or save it for after-hours activities.

It may be you do want to impress clients. Perhaps the trappings of wealth and elegance are called for in your business. If so, don't just talk the talk: walk the walk. When showing a million-dollar property, pick up a prospective buyer in a Cadillac, BMW, or Mercedes rather than a '78 Ford. Wear your suede jacket and Gucci shoes; carry your alligator briefcase. When dealing with a clientele that has money and power, it is wise to project such an image yourself.

Be aware of how you sound. We've all talked with someone on the phone and formed our very own mental picture of what that individual is like. It's sometimes disappointing to meet them in person, isn't it? The voice is a wonderful tool. If yours is too shrill, people will shy away from you. If your accent is thick, this poses another problem. Consider the pace at which you speak. It's ideal to match your rate to that of the person you're trying to influence. Fast talkers quickly become annoyed by those who drag out a conversation. On the contrary, you may lose slow talkers if you whiz by them in high gear.

Speaking of whizzing by, there is one occasion in particular you do not want to hurry through. That is self-introductions. This is a great opportunity to create a favorable impression, not to mention educate others about what you do. Create a 30-second and a 60-second introduction of yourself and your services. Practice your delivery. Test it out on some acquaintances who do not know about your professional life. Be sure your remarks make crystal clear what you do for people. With slight modification this introduction works whether you're introducing yourself at a cocktail party or informally before a club or committee.

It's no secret that our body language says a lot about us. Our movements signal all sorts of nonverbal communication. According to image consultant Glen Pfau who coached Col. Oliver North before his public appearances, there are 600,000 physical human gestures. This is in comparison to 400,000 words in the English language. An astute observer can tell if someone is uneasy, defensive, or smug. There are many fine books on this subject. In conjunction with reading them, videotape yourself. It's a revealing experience.

If you must make your mark in the more educated and refined circles, be sure your table manners are impeccable. Use good grammar and proper English. It certainly won't hurt to be grounded in the arts. A liberal arts education will put you on comfortable footing with many CEOs. You can also raise your own cultural level by going to museums, art galleries, operas, and reading current good books.

Power—the ability to make things happen and to control events—is often the currency of business success. It can be formal or informal. Being named a partner in a law firm or asked to chair an important local committee represents formal power. Informal power, although harder to detect, is often more influential. It centers around such things as you taking the initiative and inviting a notable person to lunch.

Says Philip Kotler, coauthor of *High Visibility,* "Image is power." If you want to be perceived as a respected and beloved leader—one with charisma, credibility, and clout—give serious consideration to the points above.

Your Business Attitude and Manners

The philosophy of the owner or manager sets the tone for the whole organization. How will you posture your enterprise? Will you foster an attitude of caring? Mechanics do this by picking up and delivering the cars they repair. Dentists provide earphones with soothing music and interesting graphics on the ceiling of treatment cubicles. Banks offer drive-up service, stay open weekends, and make their meeting rooms available free to nonprofit groups. Real estate agents provide "get acquainted" packages to folks considering a move into the area. Appliance repair facilities arrange for rush shipping of critical parts. The list could go on and on. Some places have a knack for making you feel more like a guest than a customer.

No matter what business you're in, there are ways to show your constituents you consider them special. In the process, you become special to them. You provide a lasting value and build a genuine relationship. As you become more prominent, the resulting awareness of your existence and what you do will in itself produce more business.

Every organization is the sum of the people who work there. Employee attitude plays a big role. Be sure you consider the image your employees hold about your organization as well as your external one. They could differ. If they do, it's like trying to mix oil and water. It's imperative personnel buy into the same image you intend to portray to the world. Otherwise the disparity fosters mixed signals.

Employees impact your success in other ways too. Inattention, improper dress, and rudeness are quick ways to turn off a potential patron. Such negative impressions are hard to live down. Another thing to consider: avoid hiring personnel who are considerably above or below the educational level of most of your public.

Now let's look at our business or practice through the eyes of our clients/customers. Is the image we want to present the one being received? If not, we're opening doors to show people out instead of welcoming them in. Tour your own organization, both physically and on paper. In one hotel complex, conference rooms were hard to find. This quickly became obvious when the manager toured his own facility as a guest. Pay attention to details. You may be in for some unpleasant surprises. For instance, are the restrooms clean? Properly equipped with toilet tissue, soap, and towels? Are all light bulbs burning brightly? What kind of paper trail do you leave? Are letters being sent on proper stationery, or is a ream with out-of-date information being used? We gain revealing insights when we perceive what others receive.

The Telephone As Goodwill Ambassador

The telephone is a crucial member of the sales team in many business environments. It is an extension of your operation. In some cases, the only contact people have with a company is through the telephone. Be sure your primary phone receptionist is pleasant and well-informed about routing calls. Such things as answering promptly and not leaving people stuck on hold contribute to the image callers retain.

Having a separate business phone line is important. Although the cost may seem high for a brand-new cottage industry operating out of your home, it is certainly more professional than answering your personal line with "hello." Additionally, it allows you to get your business listed with the information operator and in the phone book.

If you don't want to install a business line, consider installing a second residential line (for grandma or the teenagers perhaps?). Or investigate the new feature that allows one phone to have different sounding rings. Because you've already established credit as a residential user, they probably won't ask you to post another deposit. Then you can answer this second line in any way you wish. Some other considerations: Putting the call-waiting feature on your phone will help absorb overflow until you can afford a second business line. Be aware that frequent busy signals tell callers you are small and/or a novice.

Suppose you are a one-person shop and you must leave to conduct business? Then hook up your answering machine. You do have one, don't you? Agreed—many people hate the confounded things, but they're better than an unanswered phone.

That brings us to an important point. Don't you get aggravated when you leave a message and the person doesn't get back to you? This is the height of rudeness. Some professionals—attorneys and physicians in particular—have honed this to an art. We were particularly impressed the other day when our doctor's nurse called to say he was in surgery, but would get back to us as soon as he finished. Sure enough, a few hours later, he called. That's good image-building!

What's in a Name?

Naming babies is easy. There are several books to help expectant parents choose unusual names, trendy names, endearing or catchy names, even power names. Christening your new company presents more of a challenge. Renaming an existing firm is even more complicated. We'll talk about that shortly.

You want something clear and concise—something with presence—a real slam dunk. It should stir customer interest. Project the proper image. Rally spectators to cheer you. Choosing a name is showing your face to the world. You want something that reflects what you are.

How do you go about blazing this trail? First, think about what you are naming. A health care facility would differ considerably from a motel, as would a dance studio from an engineering firm. To cut a clear path, ponder your main features. What is your competitive edge—your special niche?

Who are your customers/clients? If they are older and conservative, you will want a very different sounding name than if they are teenagers or successful yuppies. Identify their likes and dislikes, and think about their lifestyle.

Depending on what field you're in, it may make sense to develop a name that falls very early in the alphabet. This is especially shrewd strategy for those who depend heavily on the telephone yellow pages to generate business. TV repair shops, secretarial services, plumbers, locksmiths, and chimney sweeps, for instance, could benefit from such planning. Look in the phone directory to see what you are up against, however. A previous entrepreneur may already have AAA Auto Repair.

Another factor to consider is visual appeal. We will be talking about logos—a readily identifiable symbol linked to your company name in the next section. It is important, however, to think about whether a name candidate would easily translate into a logo at this point.

Now it's time to do some brainstorming. Jot down every idea that comes to mind (or use a tape recorder if you can't write that fast). Capture every word and phrase. Don't be judgmental now. Selection comes later. During this creative stage, hunker over a dictionary and thesaurus, or use those on your computer. Let one thought trigger another in a rippling circle of ideas.

Next begin to pick and choose. Discard those with harsh sounds. *The Book of Lists* tells us that "crunch," "gripe," "jazz," "sap," and "treachery" are among the 10 worst-sounding English words. On the other hand, people like "dawn," "golden," "melody," and "murmuring." Try combining different words and syllables to form new names. With a little ingenuity you can come up with hundreds of distinctive phrases and permutations. Use all the skill at your command to generate winning ideas.

A computer software program called IdeaFisher can boost your skill enormously. As the name suggests, this innovative program nets elusive ideas by serving as a conduit to the rich imagery in your own mind. It actually automates a part of the thinking process. A workshop containing over 5,900 problem-solving questions, it can be used to generate ideas for names, slogans, advertisements, promotions, even whole marketing strategies.

The key concepts derived from your answers to these questions, in conjunction with the 60,000 idea words and phrases contained in the Ideabank, trigger associations in your mind. In addition, this brainstormer is flexible enough you can customize it with user-defined questions and idea words.

As if this weren't enough to stimulate your creative juices, two add-on modules round out this versatile system. The Strategic Planning Module is comprised of more than 2,100 questions designed to help with goal setting and implementation. The second, a Presentation Planning Module, guides you through the creative and planning process necessary to develop and deliver an attention-getting message. IdeaFisher is user-friendly and has good on-line support. Easy to install, it runs on almost any computer with seven megabytes of available disk space.

Now develop a list of alternatives. Prioritize it with your favorite name on top. Be sure to check on your competition—you don't want to select something too similar. It's a good idea to do a little market research at this stage. Solicit feedback from others, especially your potential constituents. You might even want to conduct a focus group to incorporate a wider range of opinions.

Next comes the frustrating part. If you anticipate going national, you or your attorney should conduct a trademark search. The reason it is frustrating is that most good names are already taken. (That's why you listed several alternatives.) The search to find unique, positive names has reached almost desperate levels. Many companies rely on meaningless words they coin, acronyms, or initials. To apply for a trademark, contact the Commissioner of Patents and Trademarks, Washington, DC 20231. Thomson & Thomson in Boston or Compu-Mark in Washington, DC, can also help investigate patent and trademark records.

There is a free booklet available for the do-it-yourselfer. It includes checklists, addresses and phone numbers of sources, a section on trademarks, even a glossary and bibliography. To request one, contact Salmon Corporation, 7424 Greenville Avenue, Suite 115, Dallas, TX 75231, (214) 692-9091. They also manufacture a software program, "Namer by Salinon," which you might find helpful.

To give you a boost in the name game, we've included a list of possibilities that may be helpful. Also consider acronyms. We live in an MTV culture. Kentucky Fried Chicken recently became KFC to get away from the negative "fried" label.

Like the nicknames we get as children, some companies eventually outgrow their identities. They need something that more precisely communicates the firm's purpose. Such was the case when Sickroom Services Company evolved into the more upbeat Healthcall, Inc. a few years ago.

Perhaps you have an established company that requires a name change. A new name can send a powerful message to stockbrokers, portray a company's business or mission more accurately, and generate media attention. It also has a downside. You risk losing instant recognition among customers, investors, and other audiences. In one swoop you can reduce awareness back to zero. With the current flood of mergers, divestitures, and acquisitions, however, renaming is sometimes the only sensible option.

When choosing a new moniker, many firms encourage employee participation. Including personnel in the decision gives them "ownership" in the process. The search is often carried out in a democratic fashion with input from the entire staff, who are sometimes plied with prizes or the promise of brief notoriety. When International Harvester changed their corporate home and identity to Navistar they reportedly spent $13 million. Datsun topped that amount to become Nissan.

NAMING NOTIONS

Agency	Corner	Management	Shop
Annex	Corporation	Market	Shoppe
Arbor	Cottage	Mart	Source
Associates	Deals	Maxi	Society
Association	Design	Mini	Specialist
Bazaar	Emporium	Mobile	Stall
Beat	Enterprise	Outlet	Store
Browser	Equipment	Park	Supply
Bureau	Exchange	Partnership	Systems
Cache	Expeditions	Peddler	Trader
Call	Forum	Place	Trading Post
Camp	Foundation	Plaza	Training
Carrier	Inn	Plus	Tours
Cellar	Institute	Portable	Vendor
Center	Junction	Practitioner	Villa
Channel	Gallery	Productions	Village
Clinic	Group	Products	Wagon
Communica-	Incorporated	Provider	Wares
tions	Lodge	Rental	Warehouse
Company	Loft	Repair	Works
Connection	Lounge	Salon	
Consultant	Mall	Shelf	

Logos and Slogans

There are many subtle nuances in creating a logo that effectively depicts your company, nonprofit group, or firm identity. Sometimes the symbol is the picture of an object, such as the apple missing a bite that personifies Apple Computers. Other times it is an unusual combination of the partners' or owners' initials. Although the actual job of fashioning your unique symbol should be left to a professional graphic designer, you need some understanding of good design yourself. Only then can you provide him or her with guidance. Your logo contributes a great deal to your overall image. It gives you muscle; it must feel right to you.

A logo has four basic components: color, type, content, and size. Let's investigate each of these elements.

Strong colors—such as red, gold, and bright blue—are attention grabbers. They particularly appeal to younger people. (Note the spectrum of bright pigments in Apple's logo; then recall Apple was initially positioned as the computer for schools.) Political organizations, bands, or athletic clubs might opt for bright colors. On the other hand, pale pastels and soft hues elicit feelings of restfulness and tenderness. A psychotherapist, reflexologist, or hospice could employ such colors. Metallic gold and silver connote elegance and richness. One of them—in combination with another color—might be used by private schools, health spas, or yacht clubs wanting to appeal to an elite clientele. Have you noticed that Campbell's new line of more expensive soups carry gold labels?

Different type styles have different personalities. The Levi Strauss Company, for instance, uses a strong, square type style that looks as tough as its pants. Script, which resembles handwriting, would be a natural for a graphologist (hand-writing analyst). A circus could get extra mileage by using a typeface called P. T. Barnum. If you're a data-processing service, consider computer typeface. Kartoon works ideally for clowns; Wedding Text, for bridal consultants. A theater might do its logo in Broadway. Attorneys should stick with more traditional styles, whereas a high-tech company wants a contemporary, avant-garde feeling.

To discuss content let's go back to Apple's symbol, because most people are familiar with it. The missing bite could be interpreted as a "byte." Do you suppose the apple also connotes knowledge? Didn't kids used to take an apple to the teacher? Does the bright apple suggest a savvy, enthusiastic firm to you? There are several subtleties here.

Other well-known examples of content are depicted by the insurance industry. Prudential has its rock; Travelers uses an umbrella; Allstate's good hands promise to take care of us.

An architect might use circles and straight lines to create a structural design. A law firm or financial consultancy frequently uses the principal's initials in some way. This can apply to other types of enterprises as well. Suppose a construction company was named Johnson and Sons. A clever designer might create a child's building block with a "J," an "&" and an "S." These would be placed on two sides and the top of the building block, giving it a three-dimensional look and tying in graphically with the construction idea.

Some names cry out for movement. This can be accomplished with lines that imply speed. Notice the adjacent letterhead logo, envelope, and business card for our agency, Accelerated Business Images. Playing on the word *accelerated,* the designer accomplished a forward motion feeling by using shaded lines. The "ABI" acronym also has a clever twist. Next time you get a delivery from Federal Express, notice their logo. The words slant up as though representing a plane taking off. Ocean Spray's logo has a rocking sensation and a wave curling over the right side.

Now let's look at size. A large, bold logo makes a statement in itself. It says the company is aggressive, a pacesetter in the industry. Smaller-size logos are used by firms that want to characterize quiet distinction.

If a professionally crafted logo is out of your immediate budget, talk with your local printer about using generic emblems. There are typewriters for secretarial services, telephones for answering services, and horses for horse trainers. These universally adopted symbols are recognized by most people.

Akin to logos are slogans. A slogan is a catchy phrase used in advertising and promotion. Just as a picture is worth 1,000 words, some examples will immediately give you the idea. A florist uses a play on Budweiser's "This Bud's for You." A clever shoe repairer advertises: "I doctor shoes, heel them, attend to their dyeing, and save their soles."

The tourist industry relies heavily on slogans. A Colorado ski resort's new ad campaign taunts "Snow Ahead, Make My Day!" Back in 1969 the state of Virginia came up with the slogan "Virginia Is for Lovers." More recently, the city of Long Beach, California, declared itself the "Most on the Coast." This theme is designed to instantly convey the image that Long Beach offers the best—its port, shopping and business-es, convention facilities, and multibillion-dollar redevelopment projects.

If you decide to coin a slogan, re-read the previous sections on creativity and naming to get your imaginative juices flowing. You might also find a rhyming dictionary and a thesaurus useful. And once again, IdeaFisher can add magic to the process.

Designing Letterhead

Once you've decided on a name and a logo, it's time to have a graphic artist orchestrate your letterhead, envelopes, and business card. We'll discuss the first two here. This is more crucial for some service organizations than others. Consultants, for instance, use their stationery for presenting proposals. It is also vital to ad agencies whose print image is viewed critically by prospective clients, not to mention nonprofit associations doing direct mail fund-raising.

In fact, an effective public image means a contemporary, integrated, and recognizable "look" to all your business collateral materials. This includes stationery, cards, invoices, mailing labels, brochures, ads, even signage. (We explore the latter elements in future chapters.)

Sometimes people forget to include important information, such as the telephone area code and the full zip code. These days be sure to also list your FAX number.

Many service businesses operate primarily with a post office box. That's all right. However, also include a street address for shipments, such as UPS deliveries. Plus it makes you appear more substantial and permanent.

Another consideration is paper. Although it will boost your costs considerably to use a higher-grade paper, it's money well spent. Why go to all the trouble of creating a snappy name and stunning logo and then print it on cheap 20-pound bond? Ask your printer for advice on a better quality paper stock. Speaking of paper, if you frequently do two-page letters, order an extra ream of matching paper to use as plain second sheets. Also consider something other than white. There are pale shades in several hues that create nice business effects.

Be sure to consider the impression you leave if you want to compete successfully in the trade areas. Lopsided placement of clip art, dot-matrix computer letterhead, or—horror of horrors—handwritten notes on lined pads all smack of amateurism.

If you absolutely can't afford professional design, contact the Quill Corporation. This is a huge, mail-order office supply firm that offers several typeface choices on nice paper for reasonable prices. Write for their catalog to P.O. Box 4700, Lincolnshire, IL 60197, or call (312) 634-4800.

Letterhead Sample

Business Cards as Minibillboards

A business card is your goodwill ambassador within the community or across the land. Your first contact with a prospective client or customer is typically a handshake, a few words, and a business card. A card is the perfect networking tool, setting the tone for your entire relationship. Yet it always amazes us how many entrepreneurs don't have one. If you fall into this category, please do yourself a favor and remedy that tomorrow!

Back when Marilyn was doing a lot of free-lance article writing, she always tucked a card in every query letter. A year after getting a negative response from one editor, he called and asked if she would cover a story for him. How did he happen to think of her? He had kept her business card on file.

Not only can you dispense cards to prospects, but you can also use them socially, post them on bulletin boards as tiny advertisements, and tuck them into correspondence. Carry them wherever you go. We've handed them out on airplanes, in the market, even at gas stations. One graceful technique when meeting someone new is to ask for *their* card. Normally an exchange follows. If this is someone you particularly want to remember flip the card over and jot down a couple of key phrases to set that person in your mind. Then you have a mind jogger to use in follow-up. If this new acquaintance is more social than business, you may want to note your home phone on the card. When exchanging cards with prime contacts, give out two—one for the individual and a second for his or her secretary. We usually ask for two cards for the same reason.

How do you create a memorable card—one that will fix you and your service firmly in the mind of the other person? There are several ways to make yourself unforgettable.

Consider switching from the traditional rectangular shape. Many service businesses lend themselves ideally to particular outlines. If you're a piano tuner, an open grand piano would be perfect. A bowling alley could develop a round card or one in the shape of a bowling pin. People with surnames like Fox, Post, Sea, King, Stone, Spear, or Church have wonderful visual opportunities. There are two drawbacks to unusually shaped cards, however. The die-cuts required to produce them are expensive, and people sometimes resent odd-shaped ones that don't fit conveniently into their file. A less drastic alternative might be to run your copy vertically instead of the normal horizontal way. This works well for law or CPA firms where several individual names must be listed.

Size is another way to distinguish yourself. You might deviate from the normal 2 inches high by 3½ inches wide by designing yours 4 inches high, then folding it like a tent. That way you actually have four tiny surfaces.

You can use such business cards in one of two ways: 1) To include more selling information about your services or to list several locations. In effect your card becomes a tiny, portable billboard. 2) To provide some sort of useful freebie.

A home economist printed a handy fabric conversion chart on the back of her cards, then laminated them. Political candidates include the phone numbers of public services. You might make up a list of special events in your particular industry, do a minidirectory of useful numbers, or print a map or a calendar. A business card with a calendar often finds its way into people's wallets, their bulletin boards, or under the glass on their desks. We designed the card of a women's clothing store to a tent format, then added a mini chart inside where ladies could list their clothing sizes. That way, husbands, sons, and other loved ones were helped with gift giving. Any of these devices encourage the recipient to keep the card and remember you.

Of course, there are other ways to set yourself apart. How about a four-color card? Or one that contains your photo? This works well if you do business long-distance; people like to see what the folks they are dealing with look like. Cards designed to fit in Rolodexes are another alternative. Authors have been known to turn a card vertically, then put a thin rule around it to signify a book cover.

Is your name Black, Green, Grey, or Brown? Certainly some play on this color angle would be appropriate. Color can be used in another way. Certain services can be promoted with wildly bright florescent cards. A small appliance repair shop might produce a flashy, distinctive card using a hot-pink background with black lettering.

To cultivate a higher-quality look, many professionals prefer embossed cards. This is often done with blind embossing where the surface of the card is raised to show just a letter, word, or symbol.

If you expect to do business in a foreign country, print the reverse side of your card in the language of the place you're visiting. Although many will understand English, your thoughtful gesture will be noticed and appreciated.

One final bit of advice regarding business cards: Don't pass out dog-eared ones, they give the impression you never do any business. Also, don't try to correct old information; print new ones with the correct phone and address. Don't use your cards as scratch pads. If you don't value them, can you expect others to do so?

To find information on various card options and printers, see the list we've prepared for you under "Selected Suppliers" in Part III. Now that you have the tools to create a dynamic image, let's explore how to advertise effectively.

Business Card Samples

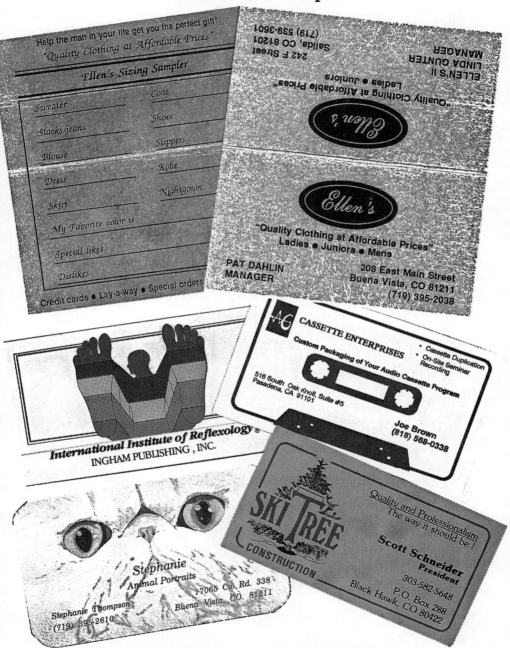

More Business Cards!

Marilyn and Tom Ross

3

Advertising's Many Faces: Which Ones Are Best for You?

We are bombarded by an estimated 15,000 commercial messages every day. The sell goes on with print advertising in newspapers, magazines, and yellow pages; radio and TV commercials; billboards; even such subtle things as matchbook covers and bumper stickers. Some of it is good advertising; most is "badvertising." Our job is to show you how to create a demand for your service without a Madison Avenue budget.

Rather than you just "doing something creative," we intend to give you the tools to achieve your advertising objectives. This chapter investigates the options. We'll explore print advertising in-depth—not to mention using commercials, telemarketing, exhibiting, and dozens of other innovative ad concepts.

Advertising revolves in two different arenas: One centers around business-to-business marketing. That is where one company (such as a bank) sells to another company (such as a building contractor). The other form most of us know more about. It is companies selling directly to the consumer.

Writing Copy
from a "Benefit" Perspective

There are a few individuals on this earth who could sell sand to a sheik. Most of us, however, have to work hard at being strong sales-people. Any time you write—whether it's an ad, a brochure, or a news release—you're much more apt to seduce prospects with a "you" approach rather than "me" or "we" or "I." All of us like personalized copy that addresses our individual needs.

When you emphasize benefits, you tell the customer/client what he or she will get: not what your service *is*, but what it *does*. Features tell what the service is. Benefit copy tells prospects what's in it for them. You give people tangible reasons to buy because you offer solutions to their problems.

First make a list of the features that make your service or product unique or better than the competition. Suppose, for instance, you have a custom-made, wooden lawn chair for sale.

FEATURES:
1) Hand-crafted
2) Made of teak and brass
3) Curved back
4) Adjustable back angle
5) Natural teak finish

Now determine the benefit of each of these. Translate the lawn chair features into benefits (things that meet your customers needs) like this:

BENEFITS:
1) Heirloom quality
2) Strong, durable, maintenance-free, naturally resistant to weather
3) Excellent back support
4) Comfortable, perfect for a nap in the afternoon sun
5) More in harmony with the natural landscape than a plastic or aluminum chair

---

Let's look at some examples. Suppose you run a catering service. Instead of listing what goes into planning a dinner party, tell prospects why their dinner party will be a smashing success. That's the result they want. If your specialty as a hypnotherapist is memory improvement, point out these techniques will have your patients astounding their friends and impressing their business associates. They'll never need be embarrassed again because they've forgotten someone's name.

Are you doing consulting on inventory control? Don't preach about how you'll set up and monitor their inventory control system. Instead, reassure them that inventory shortages and surpluses will be a thing of the past. Maybe you manage a health spa. People don't want to hear about diet and exercise. Romance them by explaining how they—and their family and friends—will see a marked improvement in their appearance and stamina. As Elmer Wheeler wisely said, "Sell the sizzle, not the steak."

To arouse a potential buyer, use punchy verbs and adjectives. That doesn't mean totally unleash your vocabulary. Terms like "miraculous," "magic," or "spectacular" usually sound unconvincing and exaggerated. On the other hand, honest, colorful words produce positive mood changes. Cut through the communications chatter with clear, memorable copy that offers prospects instant solutions to nagging problems.

According to Yale University researchers, the 12 most persuasive words in the English language are:

Save	Proven	Easy	Guarantee
Health	Discover	Results	Money
Love	You	Safety	New

One significant writing technique is to speak in specifics rather than generalities. Instead of saying you offer low prices, say "Haircuts $7." Rather than telling prospective guests your Bed & Breakfast is homey, tell them there's a warm, crackling fire, homemade cookies, and fresh flowers awaiting them. Those are amenities people can identify with.

When you are writing promotional literature, be aware of what we call "information-shaping." How a person presents information—what isn't said as much as what is—can make a big difference in the story slant. You can mold information to suit your own purposes. Statistics are often molded when taken out of context.

Classified Ads

Modest-sized classified ads have led to great fortunes. Did you know that Richard W. Sears put an ad in the *Chicago Daily News* for a watchmaker in 1887? It was answered by Alan C. Roebuck. These two later formed a corporate partnership that was to become one of the nation's premier retailers.

Thousands of other people have poured their classified ad money down a rat hole. We hope the tips in this chapter will guarantee you don't fall into that category.

Each word costs money in classified ads—sometimes as much as $8 each for large-circulation magazines. For that reason, people frequently try to cut their ads to the bare bones. That's almost always deadly. Readers need enough meat to entice them to respond. The more you tell, the more you sell, so flesh out that skeleton. Be sure the ad expresses *benefits*. Let's face it, self-interest is the strongest force in human nature. Successful ads usually lead off by promising to do something for the reader.

There are two approaches in classified ads: You can either go direct for the action/order, or use a two-step method where you advertise for inquiries. Whether you can get orders or inquiries from a classified depends upon several factors. There is the proposition, the unit of sale, the publication you use, and if you can adequately describe your offer in the space.

Another important variable is under what heading you will place the ad. You may have to choose between "Business Services," "Personal," and "Jobs Wanted," for instance.

Be sure to track your results. The easiest way to code an ad is by affixing something extra to the address. Maybe it is P.O. Box 1500-R, or you might add a suite number after your address. If people are telephoning, ask during the conversation how they heard about you.

We recommend starting with a single insertion of your ad. Don't respond to the urges from media salespeople to save money by committing to several consecutive ads initially. Sure, you will save money per ad due to a "frequency discount." But what good is that if the ad isn't pulling? Best to wait until you have a proven ad and a proven publication before agreeing to multiple placements. One of the biggest ingredients in successful advertising is patience.

Display Ads

There is a cross between a classified ad and a full-fledged display ad. We call it a "scatter ad." These are small, usually only one-twelfth or one-sixth of a page. Repetition is the key. Several of the same ads are scattered through a newspaper or magazine.

Scatter ads only work for certain things. If you can find one or two words to express the problem you solve, they may be ideal. Here are some examples: An accupressurist might say "Headaches?" An attorney "Bankrupt?" "Car trouble" might be the flag waved by an auto mechanic, whereas a doctor might say "Hemorrhoids?" The ad continues with "Cured without surgery in 15 days, call XXX-XXXX." This kind of an ad campaign can have striking results when used carefully.

Larger display ads make more sense for many service organizations. Here you have more room to tell your story. You can more forcefully appeal to your target audience's desire for quality, comfort, style, savings, convenience, fun, love, or status.

Display ads typically have three components: a headline, illustration, and body copy.

The headline is your workhorse. If it doesn't do the job, they'll never get to the body of the ad. Don't be a copycat when it comes to headlines. Thomas Jefferson's "All men are created equal" has been the springboard for numerous ad campaigns. There are takeoffs such as all calories are not created equal, all fiber is not created equal, all cigarettes are not created equal, even all gold is not created equal. In fact, Roger Butler, a senior copywriter at the Ogilvy & Mather ad agency, has an interesting collection. It includes more than 80 print ads that use the "not created equal" routine! Be original. Punchy. Provocative.

The headline and illustration have to be complementary. They make up over 60% of the ad's effectiveness. In illustrations, if you are aiming at one sex, show a member of that sex in the graphic. Presenting people doing something rather than just sitting or standing is always more convincing. Although having your own graphic artist is the optimum in developing an illustration, it is only one option. Many newspapers have clip art drawers they allow display advertisers to scavenge in. Or you can buy clip art books at art supply stores or software for your computer. You may be talented enough and have the right equipment to do an original computer graphic. Another alternative is to wrangle help from a high school or college art class. Black and white photographs can also be used, but they reproduce better in magazines than on the rough newsprint newspapers use.

Each of the elements must work with the other. We discussed how to write benefit copy earlier. Now be sure your design and copy are coordinated. You can't put together a good ad by locking the designer and the copywriter in separate rooms, then pasting together the results.

As the ad size grows, copy can be expanded to include testimonials from satisfied clients/customers. Coupons usually increase response. Perhaps a car wash will include a coupon for $1 off, or a jeweler might offer a free ring cleaning with each coupon (hoping, of course, to find the prongs holding the stones loose and requiring repair or to convince women they need a new piece of jewelry while in the store).

Always double-check your ad to be sure major points are included. Make it easy for people to see your name and phone. Be sure to include the address. Should you add credit card logos? Your hours?

If you are running more than one ad at a time, incorporate some way to track the results. One trick is to include a coupon for some inexpensive trinket. Then when they bring in the ad you know where the lead came from. When receiving phone calls, simply include a question about how they heard of you as part of the presentation. For radio, tell listeners to mention station XXXX when they come in to get their free trinket.

By the way, if your service is aimed primarily at older people, there is a free booklet available called *How to Advertise to Maturity.* You can get a copy by contacting Modern Maturity, 420 Lexington Avenue, Fifth Floor, New York, NY 10170, (212) 599-1880.

Another type of ad is the institutional advertisement. It isn't designed to evoke a direct response. It's purpose is to establish strong recognition within your industry. Such professionals as insurance agents, architects, and financial planners can use this very effectively. In the institutional ad the goal is to "humanize" the firm and build trust. A personal picture helps people feel they know you and tumbles barriers.

There are many tricks to make your ad stand out on the page. One is to use a *screen* which means a lighter color of the ink will be used as a background. Screens are usually done in 20% so the lettering over them can be easily read. Another technique involves using a distinctive *border*. A border adds impact to even tiny ads and gives instant recognition. It could be a larger rule line than usual, or it might incorporate a symbol that ties in with your service or message. A string of hearts might encircle a florist's ad for Valentine's Day. Dollar signs could serve as the border for a loan company, a set of false teeth for dentists, flags for political advertisements, even shoes or boots for shoemakers.

Many ads are too busy. Using a small amount of type and lots of *white space* helps make your ad stand out on the page. Another technique to set you apart is called a *reverse*. With this approach, you have a black background with white lettering. Don't try this if you have a lot of copy, however. Copy is harder to read when reversed.

The "Rub" Formula

Once you've created a good ad, keep with it. Use our RUB formula.

R = Repetitive. To generate outstanding results you need to be seen over and over again. Repetition is what implants your service or professional practice firmly in the prospect's mind. (It has been said repetition is reputation.)

U = Uniform. If you do one kind of ad this week, another next week, and a completely different one the following week, you look as confused as a hillbilly in Manhattan. Previously we talked a lot about image. Your ads need an image—a steady, consistent presentation that people begin to recognize as you. Keep it uniform.

B = Basic. Our motto might be "Nothin' fancy, ma'am, just the basics." Cutesy, flippant ads are not the kind that endure. You want something clear, uncomplicated, and easy to understand.

Free Standing Inserts

Most newspapers offer another kind of advertising option: It's called a free standing insert. What that unusual term refers to is a loose flyer inserted in the newspaper. Flyers are nice for several reasons. They stand out more than ads in the paper and are easier for prospects to set aside for future action. Another big plus is you can typically target specific zip codes. That way if you know your potential buyers are located in just one or two zip codes—or you feel only people in your immediate area will patronize you—you can target just them. This is cheaper than trying to reach everyone. Of course, you also have more space to develop your message.

Advertorials

An advertorial is a bit like the offspring from a horse and a donkey. It is neither an ad nor an editorial. It is space that is paid for, but it looks more like an article. The term *advertising* in tiny letters across the top is the only giveaway that this isn't a normal article.

Why bother with such subterfuge? Says ad magnate David Ogilvy, "Roughly six times as many people read the average article as the average advertisement." In the competitive ad game that can mean dramatic results! These ads couched in the guise of editorial text and public service communication pieces are definitely catching the eyes of the public. They are an ideal vehicle for the service organization seeking a low-key advertising profile.

Placement Ploys

One way to be distinctive is by seeing that your ad is placed in an advantageous location on the page. This is called a "preferred position." Most newspapers and magazines charge about a 10% premium for it. At least that's what their rate cards say. We know for a fact this is a negotiable point. If you are a new advertiser or a very good account, they often waive the extra fee. The best position is on a right-hand page, above the half-way mark. That's what you want to request.

While we're talking about placement strategies, here's another idea. Suppose you want to advertise in the *Wall Street Journal, Time, McCalls*, or *Industry Week*. The costs for their full readership would be prohibitive for a small business. However, each of these publications, and several others, print regional editions. This is called a "split run" or "zone edition." You can advertise just in the western edition of the *Wall Street Journal*, for instance.

By the way, reprints of such ads make impressive handouts to clients or customers. They build your image and give you more credibility. One firm reproduces their ads from the *International Herald Tribune* and the *London Financial Times* to "get across awareness of our international capabilities," says a spokesperson. Sometimes reprints generate more long-term results than the ads themselves.

Many service providers and professional practitioners run a couple of ads, then say, "It's not working, let's quit." In so doing, they defeat themselves. Frequency is the name of the game. It is much, much better to run several small ads than one large one. People seldom make a decision based on seeing one or two ads. Experts say it takes three or four months before you experience a notable outcome from ads. That's because most people who see your ad this week don't need your service right now. You want to advertise often enough though, so when prospects do need your service, they think of you instead of the competition.

Negotiation Tips

Yet another tactic to trim ad costs is to buy what is termed "remnant" space. As a piece of leftover cloth is called a remnant, so too is ad space that is unsold just before press time. This happens when another advertiser takes some, but not all, regions or when a magazine has had a bad month and hasn't sold its quota of ads. This space can often be bought for 25 to 50% below the rate card price. If you hope to cash in on this bonanza, have your ad already typeset and ready to go. Time is of the essence; you'll have to get them the ad by overnight mail.

Some advertising agencies have success in negotiating not only price, but other benefits. By talking to the magazine's salespeople (or directly with the publisher if it is a small, entrepreneurial operation), you may be able to arrange other considerations. Perhaps you can talk them into a two-color ad for the price of one color. Or maybe they will give you an additional ad at no extra cost. You might even ask for a complimentary list of their subscribers on labels if the readership is directly targeted to your service. (Many magazines rent these lists, by the way.) Also remember to ask magazine ad reps about merchandising aids, such as easel-back cards, ad reprints, or decals with the name of the magazine. They can often be used as signs, display pieces, or in direct-mail programs.

If ads play a large role in your overall marketing mix, it may be worthwhile to establish what is called an "in-house" advertising agency. You simply set up another company name, address, and phone. In most cases, this will save you 15% for anything listed as "commissionable" on a rate card.

One last thought is "PI" or "PO" ads. PI ads mean per inquiry; PO, per order. Simply stated, you don't plunk down a cent for an ad. Instead you negotiate a deal with the magazine or newspaper where they get a portion of the profits on all activity. In effect, they gamble and provide the ad space free with the idea they will get anywhere from 25 to 50% of all business generated by the ad.

While this works much better when there is a product involved, certain service businesses may be able to take advantage of the approach. It would work with a coupon when selling spa or athletic club memberships, for instance. A dry cleaner might be able to swing such a deal with an entrepreneurial-minded publisher. Likewise, a hotel or motel owner might offer a kickback for each coupon they received from the publication.

Choosing the Media

Media analysis will be different if you are dealing on a regional basis around your hometown, rather than in a national arena. If your sphere of influence centers around one community or area, the print ad choices are less confusing. (We'll be talking about radio and TV shortly.) There is probably one major daily paper, plus several smaller neighborhood newspapers and a free shopper or two. In large metropolitan areas, there may also be an alternative newspaper that appeals to the more "hip" crowd, a New Age publication, a senior citizen paper, maybe even an ethnic publication. Often there is a regional magazine, such as *Arizona Living Magazine, Chicago Magazine,* and the *Ann Arbor Observer.* If you plan to use print ads, these are your options.

Newspapers have an immediacy that can be a real advantage. Because of their short lead time, you can run an ad the beginning of the week and be getting calls from it by the end of the week. This allows you to capitalize on timely events or situations. If your city has just been hit with a heat wave, advertising your air-conditioning repair service would be a stroke of genius. (Better gear up to cope with the onslaught, though!) A locksmith might want to plug in some quick ads to counteract a local wave of burglaries. You could also synchronize your advertising with the payroll days of large local industries.

It may be best to avoid Wednesdays and Fridays. These are the "clutter" days when papers are chuck full of grocery and entertainment ads. (Ignore this if you are in the amusement or entertainment business.) Sunday is a good day as people spend more time perusing the paper. As with magazines, a few big metropolitan dailies—such as the *Los Angeles Times* and the *Houston Chronicle*—publish zoned editions. Remember there is one distinct disadvantage with newspaper advertising: tomorrow there is a new paper. The life span of your ad is very short.

One possible way around this is to consider supplements. These are special sections that newspapers run occasionally. They typically deal with targeted topics of interest to specific groups: seniors or job seekers, for instance. Or they cover a generic subject like health or real estate or automobiles. Since these stand alone, they are often pulled out and saved if the topic interests an individual.

Magazines are kept around for months, so your message keeps selling. There is also prestige value to having your ad next to that of some Fortune 500 company like Ford Motor Company or AT&T. Also ads simply look better in magazines; photographs reproduce well on the slick paper.

Obviously, price is going to be a prime consideration. But don't just take that at face value. A more expensive ad may be a far better value. Here's how to find out: For both magazines and newspapers, you need to determine the cost per 1,000 (CPM) formula. It tells you what it costs to have your ad seen by 1,000 people in each publication.

For newspapers, divide the cost of your potential ad by the paper's circulation in thousands. In magazines, the cost of a full black-and-white page is the standard. Divide it by the net paid circulation in thousands. Let's do a little math to make that more clear. Say ABC newspaper has a circulation of 40,000, and your ad would cost $400. The CPM would be 400 divided by 40—$10 per 1,000 subscribers. Now suppose you're considering an ad in XYZ magazine with a circulation of 100,000. But the price here is $800. That figures out to be $8 per 1,000 subscribers. Other things being equal, the magazine is a better deal even though it costs more. Before plunging into an advertising commitment, figure the CPM for each publication on your list to determine the best bargain.

Of course, price is only one consideration. You may decide to pay a higher CPM because a particular publication is positioned ideally for reaching your market. A funeral director or convalescent home may elect to advertise in a senior citizen newspaper. A reflexologist will fare better in a New Age or alternative newspaper than in the traditional press. An art gallery, reducing salon, or financial planner might choose a very different advertising medium. They would be wise to consider the print program put out by a symphony orchestra, for instance. Here they can reach a captive upper-crust audience.

If your prospect territory is greater, perhaps a region of the United States or the whole nation, your challenges are elevated. Now you have national consumer magazines—some with zone editions—plus special-interest trade journals all vying for your advertising dollars. To learn about your options, go to the main library and consult *Standard Rate and Data Services*. It is broken into two main sections: "Consumer Magazines" and "Business Publications." Study the appropriate magazines, using the CPM formula plus your good common sense.

Understanding Psychographics

It used to be advertisers talked about "demographics," information about the age, income, and sex of prospects. Over the last decade, however, a more definitive way of measuring potential customers/clients has emerged. Called "psychographics," it evaluates the lifestyles, interests, and behavior of people. This system classifies people according to what motivates them. Do they prefer the tried-and-true, or are they trend setters?

A fascinating book, *The Clustering of America* by Michael J. Weiss, looks at our nation as 40 different types of neighborhoods or clusters. He ties these psychographics in with specific zip codes to determine what kinds of buyers live where. Each one has its own lifestyle and values. There are the Blue Blood Estates (Beverly Hills, CA, and Scarsdale, NY), Shotguns & Pickups (Zanesville, OH, and Molalla, OR), and Money & Brains (Princeton, NJ, and Palo Alto, CA). Then there is Gray Power (Sun City, AZ, and Sarasota, FL), Black Enterprise (Capital Heights, MD, and Auburn Park, IL), even the Bohemian Mix (Greenwich Village and Haight-Ashbury), to name a few.

Now this may sound like so much gobbledygook. Yet it has exciting implications. Let's say a PBS station is launching a fund-raising campaign. Clustering shows that Suburban Elite Business Buffs (SEBBs) are strong supporters of public television. By finding out which zip codes in their area are comprised of SEBBs they could practically hand deliver an invitation to support PBS via a direct-mail campaign.

Could not an inventive insurance agent make use of such information as well? With a little detective work, he or she could track down the area zip codes where affluent, forward-thinking young couples live who recently had babies. Wouldn't a larger proportion of them than usual be receptive to taking out an insurance policy on the little one? Certainly health care providers can use clustering information to target their efforts to the most likely potential patients. The possible connections are most intriguing.

Yellow Page Ads

Statistics show that people refer to various yellow pages 49,000,000 times on a typical day! Did you know 50% of these references result in the purchase of a product or service? For many service businesses and professional practices, this is the smartest place to put your advertising dollars. People don't let their fingers do the walking unless they are actively interested in buying something. Consequently, they literally prequalify themselves.

What kinds of establishments can most benefit from this medium? W. F. Wagner, in his excellent *Advertising in the Yellow Pages,* lists the most often looked up headings for residences. In order of inquiries, they are cleaners, physicians and surgeons, department stores, television dealers and service, taxicabs, beauty shops, and air-conditioning contractors and service. All but one of these are service providers!

Businesses also use service firms. In the top five of their most often looked-up categories are plumbing and electrical contractors and sign companies. You may want to consider business-to-business yellow pages. Chicago pioneered the first of these several years ago. Today more than 20 large metropolitan areas sport such editions. They go to business phone locations and carry headings of interest to—you guessed it—businesses. Rates for business directories are comparable or slightly higher than for the consumer directories.

Others apt to find this an especially viable advertising medium include tanning salons, videotape and disc renting, computer system design and consulting, auto renting and leasing, carpet cleaners, florists, insurance agents, typewriter and computer repair facilities, temporary help agencies, and travel agencies.

Many lawyers choose consumer yellow pages as competition increases and advertising in general has become a more accepted marketing tool in their industry. The yellow pages are also a comfortable marketing strategy for dentists, chiropractors, and physicians who make use of personal photographs, colored graphics, and slogans.

What should your yellow page ad include? Your name and phone number in large, bold letters, your logo, and your address. The idea is to establish trust. Citing years in business, size, family management, or association memberships helps confirm your reliability. Be sure to note special features or unique qualities that separate you from your competition. Of course, you will phrase these things as *benefits,* not features. Always remember you aren't selling you or your business—you are selling solutions to people's problems. The following list of points will stimulate ideas applicable to your ad.

YELLOW PAGE AD POINTERS

Convenient location	On-call 24 hours
Credit cards accepted	Free estimates/exams
Awards you've won	Caring concern
Extended hours	No muss/no fuss attitude
(evenings/weekends)	On-site service
National brands you work on	Certified employees
Rush service available	Mobile unit
Free pickup and delivery	References furnished
One-stop/full-service establish-	Satisfaction guaranteed
ment	Confidential help
Free initial consultation	Preventive care
Personalized service/custom work	Always on time
Special financing arrangements	Special rates for seniors/others

There are other considerations too. Ads appear in a given section according to their size. Thus, half-page ads precede quarter-page ads, which precede eighth-page ads, and so on. If you feel yellow page advertising is pivotal to your success, invest a large portion of your overall marketing budget here. It might be wise to consider cross-reference under several headings as well. A secretarial service, for instance, could also list itself under "Stenographers-Public" and "Data Processing Service." Some unusual businesses and professionals will want to run ads or listings in books for adjacent communities as well.

It may not be necessary to purchase a large display ad. Half-inch type-only ads, and even bold listings, help set you apart. If your budget allows it, a way to really stand out on the page is to incorporate a second color into your ad. Studies done by Donnelley Directory indicate including red in an ad attracts the eye and gets faster recognition. The jury is still out, however, on whether color is really worth the extra money.

With the divesture of AT&T, some communities now have as many different phone directories as they do churches. There are more than 6,000 of these directories sprinkled around the country. Many of these privately published books go to extreme lengths to look like "the real thing." Interestingly, some of them are actually better, because they contain a wealth of community service information. Find out which is the most popular book in your area, then go with it.

Directories Help You Get Discovered

Besides the yellow pages, there are many other specialized and regional directories. Virtually every industry has one. They are typically divided into categories, arranged like dictionaries, and updated annually. If you don't know about these opportunities, go to the library and look in *Directories in Print*. Some of these listings are free for the asking. What could they do for you?

Let's use ourselves as an example. As consultants, listings in appropriate directories figure prominently in our marketing mix. We know that approximately one-third of our inquiries are attributed to this one strategy! This parallels the national average. A study by the Association of Industrial Advertisers found that when buyers look for sellers, 35% find them in business directories. This category leads all others (literature on hand, sales calls, periodicals and direct mail, recommendations, and yellow pages) by a significant margin.

Here are some tips for appearing in free directories: Use every bit of space the listing forms allocate. If they give you five lines to describe your services, use all five lines. This will make you appear stronger on the page. When a firm puts down only their name, address, and phone, their listing looks far less impressive. Choose your words carefully. Stress the benefits and your diversity of services. Many people are attracted to a one-stop-shopping concept. Code your listing by using a department number or some other address devise. Or use a different contact name to differentiate this listing.

When people use a directory, they are in a buying frame of mind. Rather than being lookie-lous, they intend to make a purchase. Your task is to influence them with your reputation and supply detailed information showing how you can meet their needs. You want to appear the dominant company or firm on the page.

Free listings are becoming more scarce. Today smart directory publishers are going after paid appearances. There are three considerations when developing directory ads: which directory, what heading, what advertising level. If you were an industrial supplier, you'd have more choices, but for most service providers, there is only one prime directory. Within its pages, however, await many tempting options. Evaluate the headings to determine which ones are appropriate for you.

It is better to place several small ads under each possible heading than a large umbrella one.

As to the advertising level, most directories have several alternatives. There is often a plain vanilla free listing, a chocolate variety where the information appears in bold, and a strawberry option that also includes your logo. The gourmet flavors offer various-size display ads.

The headline and copy for a directory ad differs from that of a magazine or newspaper. In this case, you aren't so concerned with grabbing their attention; they wouldn't be here if they weren't interested. Sell the inquiry, not the service. Your goal is to get them to call or write. Provide information. Draft a list of your sales points (refer to the list we provided for the yellow pages), giving prospects many reasons to contact you. Then you have a better chance of hitting their particular "button."

As in all advertising, it is essential to track results. Most of your inquiries will come by phone, especially if a toll-free number is included. For more sophisticated monitoring, there is remote call forwarding. With this tracking method, calls go to a different number, then are automatically routed to your regular switchboard. The customer/client never knows the difference, as there is no interruption. You get a bill each month with the time and date of each call. To get this exact record of the number of inquiries, you'll pay around $40 per month plus 12 to 27 cents per call, depending on the vendor selected. Another interesting approach is to connect your toll-free number to a dedicated key phone that records who called, for what, and when.

Broadcast Media

Broadcast media—the world of radio and television can lead to a huge influx of business. The power of the airwaves is an effective advertising tool. The downside, of course, is that it's expensive. There is little point in buying a few commercials. In most cases, you have to commit to about three months before you can anticipate striking results.

Radio spots are a good solution for many service businesses and professionals. They allow you to reach a small geographic area at an affordable price. Unlike TV, most stations don't tack on production costs.

To begin investigating radio, think about the format of your local stations. They will probably range all the way from country to classical, easy listening to heavy metal. Some service businesses can be matched to the type of listener who tunes in different stations. A golf course would do best advertising on the classical or easy listening station, a bowling alley on the country station.

Contact the station and ask to have the advertising sales manager call on you. If possible, insist on the sales *manager*; that individual can help educate you. Many sales reps are new to the job and still unfamiliar with the particulars of radio advertising. Although they'll be happy to write up a contract, they won't offer much helpful advice.

Radio spots can be purchased in one of two ways. Either as run of station (ROS) or for specified times. ROS is cheaper because they can plug you in to undesirable times, such as late at night. Ideally, you want morning drive time (7:00 A.M. to 9:00 A.M.) or afternoon drive time (3:00 P.M. to 6:00 P.M.). People listen to their radios while they commute to and from work. This is a prime advertising period for most services. Of course, if you're trying to reach teenagers, it's a different story. Then you want early evening and Saturdays. Spots are 15, 30, 45, or 60 seconds long. We usually advise clients to get 30-second spots. We've found them to be the most sensible over the years.

Now let's talk about what will be said during the commercial. This is a place where professional copywriting can be very cost-effective. There is an art to writing strong radio copy. It isn't something you master overnight. If you insist on being a do-it-yourselfer, here are a few tips: As we've preached before, write from a *benefit* rather than a feature perspective. Include your company name and phone number three times. Don't tell people to look you up in the yellow pages. Why direct them to where your competitors advertise? Instead suggest they check the *white* pages!

The script should be typed double-spaced in all capitals. For unusual names or words, spell them out phonetically. Indicate where any sound effects should be used. By the way, the station will have various sounds on records or tape that you can add for special effects. Consider using background music to accompany your commercial. Remember psychographics. If you are appealing to Young Urban Self-Help Buyers, for instance, they are jazz fans—so let that be your accompaniment.

It pays to tune in to the psychographics of your targeted audience. Merrill Lynch discovered that a few years ago. You may recall they used to show a herd of bulls galloping to financial success on their TV commercials. They learned, however, that the herd concept was a turnoff to the achievement-oriented people they sought to attract. Now they show a solitary bull that is a "breed apart."

Often an announcer simply reads your radio script. If the announcer articulates well, reads coherently, and has a dynamic, variable delivery style, you're in luck. If not, you're better off taking a different approach. Pay a few hundred bucks for talent, go to the studio, and "direct" the commercial until it is right. That way you end up with a proven product and have quality control.

Television may not be out of your reach, especially if you sidestep the network affiliates for cable TV. Here a prime 30-second spot that reaches perhaps 40,000 households costs less than $100. One of the reasons you pay less is you reach a smaller area, which is desirable for an advertiser wanting to pinpoint only a 20-mile radius. Cable also allows you to target your audience. The upscale viewers of Cable News Network (CNN), for instance, are perfectly suited to services aiming for intelligent, affluent consumers. Cable networks dealing exclusively with sports and music offer other opportunities.

Gerald LaFrance, a cleaner in Florence, Massachusetts, decided to use cable TV after he purchased a new machine to press shirts. He bought 150 spots for $7 a piece (less than radio would have cost) and spread them over a three-month period. When asked how his shirt business fared, La France reported, "I ended up tripling the volume in three months!" He had to stop advertising, because he couldn't handle any more business.

It used to be higher-priced items couldn't be sold successfully via TV. Today, however, the barriers have been crossed, and products and services worth several hundred dollars are being merchandised this way. TV is especially viable for services that can be visually demonstrated. An insurance company might show a house burning down, then being rebuilt for the happy policyholder. A burglar alarm firm could enact a scene where a potential intruder is scared away when the alarm goes off. A river-rafting company might show footage of an especially exciting trip. Some attorneys who have adopted TV as a primary advertising medium cite 50 to 75 new cases each month attributed to television commercials. Doctors are also turning to electronic advertising as never before.

Sometimes good values can be had at unusual times on regular TV. We used to run very successful 30-second spots on a late-night wrestling program. They promoted a vocational school specializing in welding.

Don't overlook the fact you will be charged for production. Prices typically range from $200 to $1,500. Of course, if you hire nationally known talent and directors, costs will skyrocket.

Speaking of prices, the published rates are not cast in bronze on either radio or TV. Naturally, stations are not going to discount rates just before Christmas, during prime times, or for especially popular shows. They are often open, however, to negotiation with savvy advertisers. You have nothing to lose by asking.

Your local movie theater is another possibility. On-screen advertising lets you reach area consumers. Companies using this medium typically reach 5,000 to 30,000 people in one weekend at a single theater complex. Costs range from $75 to $700 per week, based on the previous year's attendance.

Signage

Most businesses require signs of one sort or another. The most obvious is the one identifying a store or office. A day-care center might opt for something big and bright, whereas an attorney wants a sign that is professional and dignified. If your business is easily recognized by a symbol or emblem, you may want a sign cut in this shape. A bicycle shop could do this nicely, so could a library or a saw sharpener.

Think about the character of your organization and the image you want to portray. A dude ranch would use rustic wood, with bold, routed lettering. On the other hand, an upscale hairdresser might use calligraphy (swooping letters that look like handwriting) on a gold background.

Signs can do wonderful things. We're reminded of the little store that was located in the middle of a rundown minimall. The adjacent businesses were remodeling and wanted to buy the owner out, but he held steadfast. As all the others revamped their facilities, they tried even harder to squeeze him out—all to no avail. Then opening day arrived. There over the door to his store hung a banner that read "Main Entrance."

Signs do indeed have far-reaching possibilities. What about removable magnetized ones for you and key associates to put on your automobiles? Speaking of cars, personalized license plates are another way of advertising. So are bumper stickers. We saw a provocative one the other day while traveling in Washington, DC. It read "If Con is the opposite of Pro, what's the opposite of Progress?"

Harvey Mackay, best-selling author and CEO of MacKay Envelope Corporation, says the "easiest, least expensive and most neglected form of advertising is painting *on top* of your truck." Then all those people who work in tall office buildings and look out from time to time will see only your advertising. Mackay Envelopes has been doing it for 25 years and swears by this technique.

An Ohio man who operates a gas station asks customers to let him put bumper stickers on their cars and trucks. Everyone who agrees gets a free gallon of gas then and with each refill of 10 gallons or more. The bumper stickers read "I buy my gas from Jim Breeson—5th and Marlowe." So far over 1,000 people are driving around advertising for Jim.

On a more casual basis, some merchants have been known to promote their ventures via sandwich boards or picket advertising. Of course, tee shirts, jackets, and caps are popular advertising vehicles. An amusement park might use inscribed balloons; an association, decals; a theater company, posters. Is an adjacent storefront empty? You might pay the owner a few dollars a month to put a small sign and display in the window. This is a cheap way to promote a timely special or event. If you believe in doing things in a "big way," what about skywriting, blimps, or banners towed by an airplane?

For museums, golf courses, swimming pools, churches, etc., street or highway signage may also be a consideration. Each city, county, and state has different regulations, so be sure to check with the proper authorities before commissioning a sign to be built or erected. In some instances, public funds may be available for state tourism signs. Talk with your state senator about this.

While we're on the subject of signs, outdoor advertising may be appropriate for some businesses. This not only includes billboards, but also bus stop ads and messages on the sides of buses and tops of taxicabs. A prominent local hospital might use this method of communicating with the public, as might a political organization or hotel.

Exhibiting at Trade Shows

Trade shows, exhibits, and trade fairs provide a viable opportunity for certain types of service businesses. To be properly exploited, however, there are tricks of the trade show. First, you need to know why you're there. Seems like a dumb statement, doesn't it? But many businesspeople fail to recognize their prime objective is *to generate leads.* While developing a better image, reinforcing customer contact, being there because the competition is, or getting a feel for the market are nice, they simply don't justify the costs involved.

First, let's differentiate between a local or regional trade fair—where area businesses ply their products and services to local consumers—and a full-fledged national trade show. We'll discuss the local event first. It will more likely apply to your needs and budget.

These kinds of exhibits are often sponsored by chambers of commerce. We had one here in Buena Vista, Colorado, recently. There were such enterprises as photographers, travel agents, insurance brokers, banks, upholsterers, construction/remodeling firms, hairdressers, and nonprofit organizations, even a hypnotherapist exhibited.

At such events, each entry is usually allocated booth space of about 10 feet by 10 feet, a table, and maybe a couple of chairs. The rest is on you. One effective way to establish a versatile backdrop is to create a three-fold (or "Z"-shaped) screen out of corkboard (or pegboard) with a lightweight wood frame. On this you can affix photos, signs, or lightweight objects. Additionally, it will fit in the back of a pickup or van.

How do you inexpensively make your display stand out from the others? One way is color. Bright, fluorescent posterboard; balloons; or streamers attract attention and dress things up in a hurry. Another tip is to include motion. Perhaps something could be hooked up to a small motor so it revolves or sways back and forth.

Of course, people always take heed of freebies. If there are no restrictions, some unusual finger food (be more creative than cookies please) will have people rallying around. There are hundreds of small novelty items that can be given away. (See Selected Suppliers in Part III for more details.) Try to be more original than an imprinted key chain. Ideally, select something useful that ties in with your service.

Many companies have a free drawing for what they do. A cleaner offers a complimentary dress or suit cleaning; a beauty salon, a free haircut. A chiropractor could provide an adjustment; a bowling alley, two free games; a music teacher, a complimentary lesson. Of course, this has an added advantage besides attracting show attendees. You also get a mailing list from the entry forms or business cards collected.

Is there something you can do in your booth to focus attention? Maybe you could give a demonstration of some sort. We noticed a hairdresser was giving manicures. Charlotte is a clever businesswoman. Being new in a small community with more than its share of beauty salons, she sought a way to get acquainted with people. By giving manicures, she literally held women captive while getting acquainted and subtly promoting her services.

Perhaps your sights are set higher than local events. If so, choose carefully. National trade shows involve travel expenses, accommodations and meals, plus a commitment of several days away from your business. We haven't even begun to talk about booth rental, designing and furnishing your exhibit, shipping charges, and union setup fees. Nothing is free here.

Do your homework. Gather solid advance information about your show. Is it the biggest and best in your industry? Where is it being held? Party towns like New Orleans and Las Vegas, for instance, water down the amount of business you can expect to do. Are there any restrictions that would limit what you'd like to do? Ask the show sponsors for a list of last year's exhibitors; call and talk with a few. Was it worth their time and money? Also consult with attendees. Their feedback can be very revealing. If you are one who really plans ahead, consider attending this year's show as a spectator so you can make a truly informed decision about participating in the future.

Much of your success is determined before you ever leave home! According to a study by the Trade Show Bureau, "exhibitors who don't take specific, positive action to get on a prospect's schedule of exhibits . . . may let up to 40% of their target audience slip by." Contact potential customers/clients several weeks ahead. Tell them your booth number and try to pin down an appointment with them. Often mailing lists of conference registrations can be rented. Check with the show management to see if free admission tickets are available.

Be sure to give your travel wardrobe careful consideration. Take comfortable shoes. Trade shows have been dubbed "the agony of de feet." Plan to dress in layers. Then if the airconditioning gets overtaxed or the heat is skimpy, you won't be miserable. Always wear something with pockets so business cards can be easily handled. Your own cards go in the right pocket; calling cards you gather from others into the left.

Although generating leads is your primary task, trade shows afford other opportunities. They are supreme networking opportunities. Here you are shoulder to shoulder with everybody who is anybody in your industry. We've been successful in personally approaching important people who are normally protected by gatekeepers on their own organizational turf. You'll meet colleagues here you won't bump into for the rest of the year. Perhaps you can explore a way to work together for mutual benefit.

Trade shows are also fertile ground for detecting what the competition is up to. Many shows sponsor educational sessions for the attendees. By monitoring some of these yourself you can get a better grasp of your prospect's mindset and needs.

There is that old saying of all work and no play and what it does to Jack. Never fear. Every trade show has a social whirl surrounding it. In addition to taking care of business, they allow you to take care of you. Some of the parties and cocktail receptions will be sponsored and open; others are invitation-only gatherings. If you remembered to pack some relaxing cassette tapes and lotion for sore feet, you may also find pleasure in retreating to your hotel room. If time allows, why not enjoy the sights of the city you are visiting? If what you do is unique and of interest to a national audience, you may be able to capture some media exposure and really make the trip pay. (We tell how in a future chapter.)

Renting a booth at a good show is akin to leasing space in a shopping mall. At a carefully targeted trade show, you can accomplish more in two, three, or four days than you could in six months selling on the road, and it's a whole lot cheaper. A recent study by the Laboratory of Advertising Performance/McGraw Hill Research estimates each sales call costs approximately $230. A qualified trade show lead costs $107. Of course, it's paramount these leads be worked promptly after the show.

Although we can't possibly cover the subject fully here, do establish written goals. Is your objective to write $50,000 worth of business? How many new customers/clients do you intend to secure? With careful planning, definite goal-setting, and diligent follow-up, trade shows or regional fairs may open lucrative new doors for you.

Telemarketing

There is no doubt about it. You can ring up extra results with telemarketing. Now don't tune us out until you hear us out. Telemarketing is much more than the obnoxious salesperson who calls during dinner to hawk something you don't want. It can enhance your profits in six different ways. When Mr. Bell invented the telephone over 100 years ago, he couldn't possibly have envisioned the impact it would have on business at the turn of the century.

First, it is a cost-effective way to follow up leads. (Perhaps the ones you got from exhibiting at a regional or national trade show.) Over the phone you can quickly qualify prospects to determine who's hot and who's not.

Second, the telephone allows you to stay in contact with existing customers/clients. You can use it to herald the arrival of a new service you know they might like or to canvass active accounts on behalf of a special offer.

Third, it provides a quick way to activate old or forgotten accounts. Because it is far cheaper to do more business with an existing account than it is to find a new one, this is a key point. One phone call may reveal a simple problem you can quickly resolve, thus bringing the person back into the fold.

Fourth, how about using your telephone as a goodwill tool? In today's busy high-tech world, few firms ever call and thank a patron for their business. Nor do they tactfully suggest the individual might want to mention this service to a friend, relative, or colleague. Because word of mouth is a top motivator, such referrals can quickly boost the bottom line.

Fifth, the phone can be used for prospecting. In the business, this is termed "cold calling." At its worst, it is done indiscriminately by low-paid individuals who work in "boiler rooms." At its best, it is handled by skilled professionals who actively *help* targeted prospects procure things they need.

Using your telephone in lieu of personal sales calls often makes perfect sense. Current estimates place an in-person call at a whopping $180. Yet it's important to stay in touch with many accounts. The telephone is a reasonable substitute for face-to-face appointments. And some companies use the phone to supplement personal contact. They check back monthly to make sure all is well and service their customers.

Because the banking industry has been freed of the restricting government binds that tie, Citicorp has employed telemarketing very successfully. They decided to introduce The Home Equity second-mortgage loan in the Baltimore area. The problem was they were not well-recognized beyond their home base of New York. Using a detailed script, bank representatives were able to launch the new product triumphantly.

Having a script as a guideline is helpful. Parroting it like a dummy is disastrous. Find a happy medium between something that sounds phony and memorized and completely freewheeling it. Train your associates by using excerpts of actual phone conversations that require their reactions. List possible objections and develop ways to overcome them. If you call only three people a day, at the end of a year you will have contacted over 1,000 new prospects.

Sixth, treat inbound calls as telemarketing possibilities. When someone has phoned you, they are in a receptive mood. Yet we usually conclude the call with no effort at suggestive selling. This is an ideal time to trade up. Train yourself, your telephone operator, customer service people, technical specialists, every associate who comes in contact with a phone to suggest more expensive options or complementary services. And actual selling can be as simple as, "Mr. Jones, we have a special offer this week just for our phone customers . . . " Every inquiry is an opportunity.

Telemarketing in its various forms can work well for such service providers as health spas, athletic clubs, schools, insurance executives, nonprofit fund raisers, and many others. Another plus is its speed. While your competition is trying out various ads and direct-mail approaches, you can be reeling in their customers. Telemarketing may well prove a major component of your marketing mix. Remember to "reach out and sell someone."

Novelty Items

You've collected dozens of these over the years. They are the pens, thermometers, litter bags, match books, combs, bottle openers, and key chains various merchants pass out. These advertising specialties can be both a goodwill builder and a useful sales tool. The intent of such gifts is that they generate a feeling of appreciation and favorable remembrance of the giver. Most do tend to ingratiate recipients to patronize firms that offer them.

What are the requirements of such novelties? They are inexpensive: 90 cents a dozen, $3.50 per 144, $55 per 1000. They must be useful—in the office, home, car, or for fun. They represent reminder advertising, such as the calendar mailed at year-end by banks, insurance agents, and real estate offices. They should tie in with the giver, either symbolically or because they're imprinted with the firm's name, logo, etc.

Over the years we've observed astute companies use novelties in conjunction with direct mail. One temporary help service sent a mailing each month to other businesses. Each was different and contained an inexpensive gift cleverly matched with the copy in the letter. One we recall was a jar opener. The letter talked about how they could "open" our employee horizons by providing qualified temporary personnel. We received this letter over a decade ago. Add to that the fact we're on more mailing lists than Heinz has varieties of soups. Yet this campaign still sticks in our mind. By adding a novelty item, Kelly Services made their mailing memorable. You might use this same technique.

Where would you find suitable enclosures? The U.S. Toy Company, Inc. [1227 E. 119th Street, Grandview, MO 64030, (800) 255-6124] has an incredible catalog of cheap treats. They also have branch locations in California, Texas, Kansas, and Illinois. Novelty companies that carry more elaborate gifts are listed in the yellow pages under "Advertising Specialties."

Let's allow our imagination to run wild. The U.S. Toy company has "goo goo eyes" for 90 cents a dozen. What fun an inventive optometrist could have with these! Their coin eraser is a natural for banks or mortgage companies that want to help patrons erase their money/loan blues. A locksmith might purchase a quantity of their locks, a dentist the "goofy teeth." They have assorted badges you could include with a mailing or pin on a youngster who has been a good patient. Thirteen-inch back scratchers are available by the dozen. If you depend on referral business, this is a natural. Send one with a note saying, "Thanks for scratching my back. Now I want to return the favor." (You may choose to wrap a $5, $20, or $100 bill around the handle, depending on how valuable the referral was.)

Your advertising choices are as varied as wildflowers in spring. It might be a classified ad, full-blown display spread, an advertorial, trade show participation, or telemarketing, but keep one thing in mind. There is an old expression that says "out of sight, out of mind." We'd like to take that statement one step further: "Out of mind, out of purchase." Don't depend on advertising to solve all your marketing problems. Do let it play a supporting role in the drama of your business. Use it, monitor it, revise it.

Now on to probe another aspect of merchandising that is far from an understudy—the secrets of direct mail.

4

The Secrets of Effective Direct-Marketing

By some it is called a science, by others an art. All agree, however, it is a carefully conceived and executed way to get businesses or consumers to respond to your advertising message. A powerful medium? Yes. An easy one? No. Someone once observed a successful direct marketer must have a hog's nose, a deer's legs, and an ass's back.

Direct-marketing masquerades under a variety of similar names: mail order, direct response, and direct mail. Many people refer to it as "junk mail." This sales technique can be tailored to nearly any budget. Its mastery depends on imagination, common sense, and diligence in following the rules. Many fortunes have been made in the direct-marketing field.

Although it does not apply to all service businesses and professional practices, some find it a dazzling device for increasing earnings. It is often the lifeblood of nonprofit organizations. The insurance industry uses it with much success. So do certain lawyers—now that the Supreme Court has ruled attorneys have the same First Amendment right as everyone else to use direct mail to solicit business. Some barristers send targeted mailings to personal injury victims and those accused of crimes or traffic violations.

High-ticket items such as memberships in athletic clubs or specialized schools can be merchandised this way. Direct mail has also been successful for hunting guides who prospect for affluent outdoorsmen stalking a good chase. An imaginative architect or building contractor could obtain the names of people who just bought residential lots, then send them a solicitation package.

According to a Pitney Bowes survey, only 40% of small businesses in the U.S. actively use direct mail. If you're in the remaining majority that don't make the most of this marketing tool, we have some surprising news for you. Based on this national survey, over 85% of the small businesses that use direct mail are happy with the results! What's stopping you? Here are proven strategies to make the mail work for your firm.

Components of a Successful Campaign

A direct-mail campaign needs to succeed in several areas. First, it must present the right *offer*. Next, the *copywriting* of the package must be strong. Finally, the *list* must be good. Let's dissect these components and see what we have.

Your offer is the stimulus that creates the decision to buy. It needs to make sense for the prospect. Service providers will want to develop targeted offers rather than mass appeals to the public.

A smart offer fills a need. Take, for instance, what the Disabled American Veterans (DAVs) came up with. They targeted new homeowners. Why would a new homeowner be responsive to an appeal to raise funds for DAVs? Enclosed with the appeal were gummed address labels with the homeowner's name and new address, that's why! Recipients were inclined to donate because they received something of value to them. The clever marketer behind this program took it one step further. Only a small quantity of labels was included. A second mailing with an order blank for replenishments—and a petition for another donation—was sent soon after.

Other aspects that effect offers have to do with whether you provide a discount, offer a money-back guarantee, include a free gift, or suggest a deluxe alternative.

Package Contents

The typical direct mail package consists of an outer envelope, a letter, a brochure, an order form, and a business reply envelope. More elaborate packages may include additional pieces. Companies on small budgets can use self-mailers that wrap all these elements into one piece of literature.

If you hope to hit the Yellow Brick Road to direct-marketing success, you'd better pay a lot of attention to your *outer envelope*. If you fall there, it doesn't matter what's inside. Most marketers feel a little like Dorothy at the gates to the Emerald City. Just how does one go about baiting the mail box?

There are three schools of thought. One says, in essence, "if you've got it, flaunt it," another goes for elegant simplicity. The third advocates being a sneaky Pete. Let's look at the sneaky Pete approach first.

The object is to develop a "blind" mailing, thus camouflaging any resemblance to junk mail and stimulating recipients' curiosity. Rather than a company name, you use a person's name and street address in the return address. This is either typed or handwritten, never typeset. These envelopes carry a postage stamp rather than a postage machine symbol or bulk-mail indicia (not practical if this is a large mailing, of course).

The *pièce de résistance* is a handwritten note to provoke the receiver's inquisitiveness. You might have your secretary write, "Thought this would interest you" and conclude with your initials.

On the other hand are envelopes that shout for attention. Most of them sport a "teaser message." Clever teaser copy can do an excellent job of provoking the curiosity of people who receive your mailing.

An accounting firm seeking new business-to-business clients might print on their envelope "Good News for Calculating Businesses . . . " Inside a flat cardboard calculator tells how the accounting firm can multiply client's efficiency, subtract from their taxes, and add to their bottom line. There could also be an offer of a free calculator with each initial consultation. A health spa might titillate prospects by saying "Here's your personal invitation to change tomorrow today." Inside could be before and after photos showing the results of using their spa.

First Pennsylvania Bank used the following as their teaser message: "If you're paying more—pay it off with a line of credit up to $10,000. And pocket the savings." Inside was a Visa card with a 14% interest rate.

A word of caution about such teasers: Don't give away the punch line. If you reveal the entire sales pitch on the envelope, people have no incentive to go inside.

Although there is no surefire way to get an envelope opened, color also makes a piece outstanding. Employ either bright inks or colored paper. Today many direct mailers are using simulated telegrams or mailgrams to set them apart. Another trick is distinctive borders. A travel agency, for instance, could print baggage tags around the envelope or a pencil thin line to simulate a jet plane trail.

Window envelopes are the stock and trade of some direct marketing experts. If you decide on these, check with envelope manufacturers to see what their standard sizes are. Another possibility is to discuss with the manufacturer about piggybacking on someone else's order. This can save up to 50%.

Some ambitious projects take this window idea to the extreme. They use glassine to allow appealing graphics to show through. When the Stars & Stripes was qualifying for the America's Cup race, skipper Dennis Connor and the Sail America Foundation sent out a plea for funds to buy new sails. A four-color photograph of the ship, autographed by Connor, peaked from inside the mailing. The results were exceptional. Three thousand units were sent out at a total cost of $4,050. They produced a 10% response.

Many business-to-business mailers must get through a secretary before obtaining a response. This can be tough. In this case, you need elegant simplicity. Competent secretaries are shrewd gatekeepers. They screen for executives in nearly 87% of the cases. Studies show top executives get an average of 20 mailings per day, only half of which reach the executive's desk. How to position yourself in the winning half? Be so sharp looking and so distinctive that you command attention. Look legitimate and professional.

A less expensive alternative to standard preformed envelopes are the form-it-yourself variety. They are usually a simple 8½ x 8½-inch sheet that the customer forms by folding.

Once you've got people inside the envelope, the *sales letter* is of primary importance. This is one place where more is usually better. A two-page letter will out-pull a one-pager; often four pages prove even stronger. You're asking people to part with their money. This takes information and persuasion. It isn't done with a brief message. A good sales letter should be like a woman's skirt: long enough to cover the subject, but short enough to create interest.

To create an effective sales letter, you need a plan. This doesn't mean sifting through reams of information. There are three main things to keep in mind: the exact objective of the letter—who the prospect is—and the important characteristics, features, and especially benefits of your service. Use the following checklist for developing your letter.

If might be smart to re-read Chapter 3 on advertising to refresh your memory about writing from a *benefit* perspective.

How does the average recipient react to a direct-mail letter? First, he or she looks at the headline. Be sure it packs a wallop. When appropriate, using an unusual number—such as 23 or 106—sparks added attention. If the headline provokes interest, the signature line is examined next. While there, readers also soak up the P.S. Smart marketers don't arbitrarily tack on a postscript. Rather, it is a carefully crafted enticement. It can restate your most important benefit, be a testimonial, or provide an inducement to act now—a free gift or time limit, for instance. It's a good idea not to tell too much in the P.S. If you've done your job well at the beginning and end of the letter, most people will go back and read the entire piece.

DIRECT MARKETING SALES LETTER CHECKLIST

✓ Does the headline attract attention by promising an important benefit?

✓ Is interest built quickly by enlarging on the promise?

✓ Have you appealed to the emotions to arouse a desire to possess?

✓ Have you emphasized the unique features of your service, but stated them in benefit terms?

✓ Is one central idea emphasized so strongly it avoids confusion?

✓ Have you included believable testimonials (either here or in the brochure)?

✓ Do you offer a guarantee?

✓ Is your letter organized and designed to be inviting and easy to read?

✓ Have you closed with a clear call for action?

✓ Is a postscript included?

Many direct-mail letters go wrong because they fail to clearly and repeatedly ask for the order—or in fund-raising, the contribution. A strong letter will not only request a contribution, it will specify in precise terms exactly how much money to give. It will include step-by-step instructions on how to make the donation.

Involvement devices often boost responses. These include such things as surveys, questionnaires, and yes/no stickers. They warm up readers by encouraging them to take part in the process.

Another factor that determines your acceptance rate is how the letter looks. Be sure it resembles a normal letter. This means typewrite it and leave uneven right margins rather than having it typeset with justified right margins. If it is crowded, overwhelming, and pretentious, forget it! People want open, airy letters with easy words and short sentences. The pros keep paragraphs down to six or seven lines.

Many readers only scan letters. To aid in this, highlight pertinent thoughts with underscoring, CAPITAL LETTERS, or a second-color ink to make key words and thoughts stand out. Sometimes you see handwritten messages in the margins. If you use two ink colors, black and blue are the favored. That way most of the text is in black as a letter would normally be. The company name and logo is in blue, as are key highlights, plus your signature. (Remember to sign the master art before you take it to the printers.)

As an attention grabbing device, some mailers affix a small object to their letters. An aspirin glued to a letter might correlate with a headline that says, "Remedy your headache about which retirement plan is best . . . " A rubber band fastened to a letter could be the lead in for "Stretch your payroll dollars by using our qualified temporary help workers."

Appealing to the senses also has advantages. Sound can be used as an inducement. During a recent election year, a vinyl record containing two versions of a political radio advertisement was sent out. The accompanying literature asked "Which ad do you like best?" It went on to request that recipients back up their choice with a special contribution to help put the ad on the air. What a dynamite combination: market research and fund-raising in one fell swoop! Scent—previously the domain of perfume companies—can add a new dimension to mailings. A hunting guide, for instance, might use paper treated with the out-doorsy smell of pine to build his or her outfitting business. Interior designers could include tiny swatches of material for clients to feel.

A financial institution might appeal to our sense of taste by including a fortune cookie with their letter. We had a little fun writing copy and came up with a variety of possible accompanying messages: "Don't leave your future to chance." "We can't guarantee you a fortune—but we can show you how to increase your savings by 10%."

Some folks utilize more extreme measures. A 19-year direct-mail veteran sent a 250-piece mailing printed in his own handwriting to names from the *Who's Mailing What* directory. At the top of the first page bright red letters shouted "Crazy Jim's Crazy Offer." Chicago's Crazy Jim Mantice promised to create a mailing piece that would beat the response on their test mailing by at least 30%—or he would create a new package free. As of this writing, we know of four new assignments he had obtained.

If you intend to send your mailing to different target markets, the sales letter is the place for customizing. You can easily create two or more versions slanted toward a certain buyer profile. Although it would be costly to print differently worded brochures and order coupons, you can target the sales letter to various segments of the population with minimal expense.

The letter is the most important factor in making your sale. It is your salesperson. It accounts for 65 to 75% of the orders you get. The brochure is responsible for 15 to 25%; the order form from 5 to 25%.

Although some direct-mail packages contain huge, elaborate, four-color *brochures,* this isn't usually necessary for service providers. An 8½ x 11-inch or 8½ x 14-inch sheet, printed on both sides and folded, should do nicely. We discuss how to create a winning brochure in detail in the next chapter, so we'll only touch on the high points here. Put your selling message on the cover, it works like a headline. If "you" are the service, include a biographical sketch. Ask for the order. Tell specifically what you want readers to do. The brochure is an ideal place to tout your testimonials; they add credibility to your offer.

Stress customer/client satisfaction by offering a money-back guarantee. It reassures people. Many organizations are concerned about the number of returns they will get. There is a peculiar paradox here. The stronger the guarantee, the less likely you'll get returns. Surprisingly, a lifetime guarantee draws fewer returns than a 14-day one. Perhaps this can be chalked up to human inertia; if we think we have all the time in the world to send something back, we never quite get around to it. Assuming your offer is a sound value, returns are typically only about 1%. Yet offering a guarantee boosts sales considerably.

Develop guarantees and other incentives that add value to your offer and reduce your prospects' risk while rewarding them for responding. Create urgency by giving prospects a reason to respond *now*.

Incentives that reward response:

- Free merchandise or gift
- Free demonstration
- Newsletter, catalog, or useful reference information
- Technical assistance
- Lifetime membership

Incentives that reduce risk:

- Free trial offer
- Money-back guarantee
- Quantity discounts
- Cash discounts

Pretend you're writing to one person. Talk in specifics, rather than saying this is "an inexpensive investment." A bank or financial consultant might tell prospects it "costs less than you spend for lunch each day." A health provider could describe in precise ways *how* its facility is caring, instead of simply stating "we care." Get the idea? Talk in benefit-oriented specifics. Often the brochure picks up where the letter left off, going into more detail about the benefits prospects will gain.

Order forms are often treated like Cinderella. They are ignored and unadorned, while the rest of the mailing package goes to the ball. As in Cinderella's case, this can be a grave mistake. Busy people often scan your letter and—if the proposition interests them—go directly to the order form. Never stop selling. Use a benefit-laden headline on the order form—one that encompasses your offer. Then clearly state the offer's essential terms and conditions, reminding readers about free gifts or time limits. Put opportunities before obligations, rewards before restrictions.

If you're offering a money-back guarantee, now is the time to reinforce it. Developing and maintaining customer/client confidence is a never-ending job. Do everything you can to confirm your reliability and build trust. If possible, restate your guarantee on the order form. This is the final reassurance you are an organization people can have faith in. Consider including the handwritten signature of the president to enhance this perception.

We believe order forms should be cleanly engineered to make it *easy* for people to respond. Strive to make it simple for the customer to say yes. Provide distinct instructions: call our toll-free number (display it prominently), fill in the form, check the boxes, stick the sticker, mail the card, etc. Encourage people to "act now," "respond today," or "call immediately." To be sure your order form is user-friendly, try tearing it out, filling it out, inserting it into the envelope, and mailing it yourself.

There are people, however, who believe order forms should be busy, cluttered, and important-looking. They feel a "bells and whistles" approach will reel in more orders. It has something to do with a sense of involvement and interaction between the customer and the mailing piece. In our opinion, expecting a busy prospect to pick their way through an order form akin to a mine field is likely to explode in your face.

Think through your order form carefully. Do you need a street address for UPS delivery rather than just a post office box? It's a good idea to include a place for their phone number even if you don't really need it. Then you can call if the address is unreadable. Are you offering a credit card option? Use the logos rather than just the names of Visa, MasterCard, American Express, etc. They are more quickly identifiable. Be sure to include not only a place for the card number, but also the expiration date, plus a signature line.

Did you ever stop to think that your order blank is like the candy and magazine racks in a supermarket checkout line? It's a place for impulse buying. Once people have arrived here, they are committed. You may want to consider using this space to merchandise another similar service or related add-on item.

Before we leave the order form, let's look at two other points. Some mailers use a *business reply card* (BRC) rather than a separate order form and return envelope. As long as no check or money order must be enclosed, this works fine. If you are designing your direct-marketing package as a self-mailer, why not put the address section back-to-back with the order form? That way you can code the label with information that will be useful in tracking the results from various mailing lists.

The *business reply envelope* (BRE) is the last piece in your mailing package. Once again, you are making it easy for the prospect to respond. This is a smaller envelope that has your mailing address in the middle. Although some people prefer postage-paid envelopes rather than having to add their own stamps, this may not be practical. It requires extra fees beyond the actual postage costs. Talk with your postmaster about this option. One interesting sidelight on fund-raising: Some donors seem to feel you should *not* provide postage. Contributions have been known to dwindle when postage is included in fund-raising pleas. If you don't supply postage, be sure to print a box with the words "place stamp here" in the upper right-hand corner of the envelope.

Procuring Mailing Lists

Your mailing list is every bit as important as your package. Some say even more so. There is no point in creating a superior package if it is sent to disinterested people or businesses. You need selective lists of prime prospects.

First, define your objective. Is the aim to increase your number of sales or contributions, or do you want to sell a service with a higher profit margin? Is the purpose of the mailing to secure direct inquiries or orders? To obtain qualified leads for sales reps? To introduce a new service? For market research?

Now define your geographic universe. A neighborhood dry cleaner will only be interested in the zip codes around his or her establishment. That's easy. A certified public accounting firm with national branches would be looking at the whole country, whereas a large real estate office specializing in farm properties might be concerned with a region, such as western Kansas.

Perhaps you are doing business-to-business marketing. This is the bailiwick of advertising/public relation agencies, secretarial services, research and development firms, consultants, employment agencies, and office machine repair facilities. It also encompasses many attorneys, accountants, and engineering and architectural firms.

Specify the size of the organization that will benefit most from your services. A firm that sells small pension plans might pinpoint prospective companies with from five to 19 employees. Although a Fortune 1,000 corporation likely has an in-house repair department, a typewriter and computer repair service could find fertile ground in companies with annual sales between $200,000 to $400,000. A fledgling advertising agency may want to concentrate initially on mom and pop operations.

For those who work within the business rather than the consumer arena, be aware that there are Standard Industrial Classifications, commonly called SIC codes. These divide economic activity into 10 major divisions, then into more definitive categories. Finance, insurance, and real estate services are in the 60 to 67 range; Business Services, 70 to 89. A librarian can show you how to research this information for your business.

Mailing lists come in three types. *Occupant* lists include every household in a given geographic area. They are fine for barbers, small engine repair shops, and other businesses that depend on nearby patronage. *Response* lists are made up of people who have already bought related services or products. They usually pull best, because these people have a propensity to purchase via mail. *Compiled* lists are derived from phone books and other directories.

How do you find such lists? You can do the legwork yourself. In major libraries you'll find *Standard Rate and Data's Direct Mail List Rates & Data*. It provides detailed information on who rents what lists. You can also look in the *Direct Marketing Market Place* or *Target Marketing's Who's Who in Direct Marketing*. However, there is really no reason to go to all this trouble unless you're a confirmed do-it-yourselfer.

List brokers make their living by matchmaking. They introduce mailers to appropriate lists. How do you increase your chances for wedded bliss? Educate your list broker about your service. Then ask for his or her help on recommending lists to rent, ways to track results, advice on quantity, etc. Because the broker's fee is built into the mailing list cost, you pay no extra amount. They get a 15 to 20% remuneration from the list owner. Names typically rent for $50 to $90 per 1,000.

Frequently you will use more than one list. In this case have a "merge/purge" done. This process has two primary functions. It locates and eliminates duplicates. Perhaps more important, however, is the fact it also pinpoints repeat buyers. When the same name appears on two or more lists, this is a really hot prospect and should be identified and wooed.

Go slowly and test. Rent a list of from 2,000 to 5,000 names at first. Your broker can supply these by what is called "nth name selection." For example, if the list you are considering has 200,000 names and you want only 2,000, request that the test order be made up of every 100th name on the list. This gives a good random sample and avoids misleading geographic results. A list that pulls well in Los Angeles may be disastrous in New York. Once you've discovered a good list, its time to "roll out" with all the names.

Lists are *rented* on a one-time basis. They may not be photocopied. When a person or business responds to your mailing, however, you can legitimately add them to your own list.

Some sophisticated mailers involve three or four list brokers in their project. They get a multiplicity of opinions that way. No one broker becomes privy to the total extent of their mailing strategy. If you are involved with fund-raising, reaching an ethnic audience, or some other specialized pursuit, search out a list broker who specializes in these markets. Do you have a list that has worked in the past? Seek others that are similar in nature.

A further way to develop a mailing list is from inquiries drawn by your own ads. The names of people who respond become the core of your personal mailing list. By the way, it will typically pull better than anything you can rent. Keep it updated and add the names of customers/clients you get from your direct-marketing program, phone inquiries, referrals, and any other means. You can get a free useful book *How to Compile and Maintain a Mailing List* from the Quill Corporation, 100 South Schelter Road, Lincolnshire, IL 60069, (708) 634-4850.

If you get into this in a big way, a computer with a good database program is a must. We've found Borland's dBASE IV, Version 2.0 to be an excellent software program. Once you've captured from 350 to 50,000 names, the U.S. Postal Service will clean up your computerized list at no charge! They will validate and correct five-digit ZIP codes, update them to nine-digit codes, even standardize spelling, abbreviations, and formats. Even in a "clean" list, from 2 to 20% of the ZIP codes are incorrect. To participate, contact a local customer service rep or write USPS Address Information Center, 6060 Primacy Parkway, Memphis, TN 38188-0001, or call (800) 238-3150, extension 80. Eventually you may gather enough names to go into the list renting business yourself. We cover how to do that in a future chapter.

Planning and Profits

Before you embark on a direct-mail program, spend a lot of time planning—especially your budget. Consider your cost factors. This includes cost to provide the service (including payroll, rent, overhead, etc.), promotional expense (fixed costs including professional creative development of the package, art, and mechanicals, plus variables, such as paper, printing, and postage), list rental fees, costs of any premium gifts, and order processing. Revenue from sales minus cost factors gives you the order margin. Ask yourself if it is reasonable. The order margin divided into the promotion costs (perhaps an average of $400 to $500 per 1,000) provides the response rate you need to break even. Naturally you don't want to go to all this work and merely break even; you seek a profit.

Not all services warrant using direct marketing. You must consider the price point. Is your service priced high enough to make this approach worthwhile?

Clients and students frequently ask us what results to expect. Although it is a good question, 'tis not easily answered. If you're selling Mercedes-Benz automobiles, ½ of 1% would be acceptable because these babies are very expensive. If you're pushing karate lessons, a return of 2% may not be enough. A dental lab may need a 4% return to be profitable. We favor a different formula. You need to make at least 2.2 times the money you spend for the mailing-including costs of design, printing, list rental, postage, and mail-processing.

Timing is something else to consider. If you hit the mails during the wrong period, you could be as out of luck as a carpenter without a hammer. Some months are simply better than others. January, February, and September are traditionally good direct-marketing months. June, July, and August are poor because many people are on vacation.

If you are using first-class mail, you have greater control over your package. Avoid having it arrive on Monday, as there is extra weekend mail competing for attention. Likewise, circumvent arrival just after a holiday. On the other hand, putting things in the hands of prospects around the 15th and 30th of the month coincides with payday for many folks.

Bulk-Mail Pointers

Who uses third-class bulk mail? Organizations large and small. Political candidates solicit ballot support and financial contributions. According to *Business Week* magazine, the Republican and Democratic National Committees raised a combined $52 million by direct mail during the 1984 election. Charitable and cultural fund-raising accounts for another large chunk.   Many businesses ply their trade through the mails. Approximately 60% of direct-mail sales are made to consumers, whereas 40% is business-to-business trade. Since government deregulation loosened the stranglehold on financial services—banks, credit card companies, brokerage houses, and insurance institutions also find direct-marketing a lucrative merchandising strategy.

Serious mailers typically use third-class bulk mail because it offers a considerable savings. Present bulk rates are 16.5 or 19.8 cents per piece for profit organizations, from 9.8 to 11.1 cents for nonprofits. The range in prices depends on how fine a sort is done. Doing a significant amount of preparation is reflected in lower rates. The more work you save the post office, the more money you save yourself. On top of this, there is a one-time application fee of $75 if you choose to use a permit imprint on your mailers, plus $75 per year. The post office requires special ZIP code sorting and bundling and a minimum quantity of 200 identical pieces.

There are a few disadvantages to using bulk mail. The handling of this class of mail is done on a deferred basis. That means it is delivered after all other classes have moved through the system. During peak workloads this can involve delays of several weeks, although the average time lapse is 9.2 days. Some firms have had entire mailings disappear from the face of the earth. This is a rarity, however, and something we've never experienced in many years of bulk mailings. After all, it is to the post office's advantage to make every attempt to deliver the mail. The more they deliver, the higher our response rate, and the more revenue generated from the first-class stamps attached to the orders.

Undelivered third-class mail isn't returned to you. Instead it is trashed without your knowledge—unless you provide for special handling and pay excess rates. We periodically clean and update our lists by having the following printed on the envelopes: "Forwarding & Return Postage Guaranteed—Address Correction Requested."

Sometimes pieces go undelivered for a good reason. One mailer broke all rules by redesigning his bulk rate indicia (the standard imprinted, boxed designation that appears in the top right-hand corner in place of a stamp or postage machine marking). The sophisticated postal equipment couldn't "read" what he did. In another case, a direct marketer using window envelopes failed to make sure addresses were visible through the windows.

Let us suppose, as is usually the case, your bulk mail is delivered. Here is some revealing post office research on what happens to it: 40 to 50% of the recipients read their mail right away. Twenty to 30% barely look at it, while 8 to 10% put it aside for later reading. Ten to 15% of bulk mail is immediately discarded. Some other interesting statistics: readers respond most to companies they know. The average household receives 17 pieces of all classes of mail per week.

If this is something you plan to invest a lot of time and money into, there are a couple of free publications we'd suggest you get. The U.S. Postal Service puts out *Designing Business Letter Mail*. Write to the Marketing Department, Regular Mail Services Division, U.S. Postal Service Headquarters, 475 L Enfant Plaza SW, Room 5541, Washington DC 20260-6336. They'll also provide you with a handy locator gauge/template to use for your BREs. *Memo to Mailers* is a free monthly newsletter. To subscribe, write to the U.S. Postal Service, Box 999, Springfield, VA 22150-0999.

Using a Mailing Service

If your mailings run into several thousand pieces, you'll want to use a mailing service. (These are typically called "fulfillment houses" or "service bureaus.") Whatever the name, using one will save you countless hours of sticking, stuffing, and sorting—the boring three S's. We discovered early it is poor pay to do large mailings yourself. An automated service makes short order of it.

When choosing a mailing service, look for several things. Do they meet deadlines? This can be paramount to your survival. Ask about references to decide for yourself if they are reliable and professional. Do they guarantee security so your names will be kept confidential? What about price? Is it fair? Free pickup and delivery may be another consideration. Do they offer list maintenance? If you don't want to manipulate data in-house for your own list, choose someone else who can do it efficiently.

After you've chosen a mail service, find out about their specific needs and preferences concerning folds, packing, delivery, and label format. Label choices run a wide gamut. There are gummed, four-up, three-up, one-up, pressure-sensitive, heat-sensitive, even Cheshire. (And you always thought Cheshire was a cat!)

When instructing your printer about your mailing, be sure to indicate specifically where the material is to be shipped or delivered. The shipment should be directed to the attention of an individual. You need a contact at the mailing house so things don't get buried in a warehouse for days.

Repeat, Repea, Re . . .

Seldom will a one-shot mailing shake loose the desired results. You need a concerted, ongoing plan. Sales and Marketing Executives

International did a study that indicated 81% of all sales are made on the *fifth* or later call. Remember, as we said earlier, direct-marketing takes the place of a salesperson.

The amount of third-class mail has escalated dramatically over the last few years. More and more mailings fight for consumer or business attention. Add to that the fact your audience forgets 90% of what they see and hear within two weeks, and it quickly becomes obvious why repeated mailings corral greater sales. If you can't talk to your prospects in person, promoting your offer on a continuing direct-marketing basis makes a lot of sense. It may make sense, even if you can speak with people directly. One form of advertising reinforces another, creating an ever-widening ripple of impact.

Failure to consider the "back end" has cheated many organizations out of increased revenue. When someone buys from you or makes a contribution, they become of special value. Think about other ways you can capitalize on their interest. Politicians do this with aplomb. Once you've donated to a political campaign, you receive appeals on a regular basis. An ad agency that puts together a limited campaign for a client would be foolish not to pursue that client for additional advertising or PR work. A temporary help service or employment agency that places a worker in a company should use a systematic direct-mail approach as a constant reminder they remain ready to solve other personnel problems.

For those who use direct mail as the key thrust of their marketing plan, there are several publications we recommend. The first two are available on a complimentary basis. Simply write on your letterhead to request a subscription. *Target Marketing* is at 332 Eighth Avenue, 18th Floor, New York, NY 10001. Also contact the Circulation Department, *DM News*, 19 West 21st Street, New York, NY 10010. The "bible" for this industry is Bob Stone's *Successful Direct Marketing Methods,* which recently came out in an all-new fourth edition.

For your convenience, we make this volume—and many of the other hard-to-find resources mentioned in this book—readily available to our readers. All books listed in our Recommended Reading section on pages 269 to 281 may be ordered from us. See ordering instructions in that section.

Well, we've spent a lot of time learning the ins and outs of direct-marketing. Now let's move on to a collection of other ideas on how to score more sales.

5

How to Score
More Sales

There are countless ways to stimulate business. In this chapter we'll address how to create a compelling brochure, use suggestive selling techniques, and make it easy for people to say "yes." We explore the power lunch/breakfast and offer tips on using this deal-making tool. Professionals and service providers will master the art of cultivating testimonials and referrals. You'll learn why taking services "on the road" is the competitive edge for many entrepreneurs. Additionally, we'll look at that hot new frontier of capitalism called "franchising." And that's only the beginning.

The 80/20 Rule

Statistics show the bulk of our business (or donations, in the case of fund-raisers) comes from a small minority of our customers, clients, or patrons. This is valuable information. It tells us we are wise to concentrate our efforts on the 20% who represent our substantial profit base, rather than spinning our wheels trying to woo the other 80%. This is a shrewd way to leverage your time, energy, and advertising dollars.

If you're involved in an enterprise where repeat business plays an important role, knowing who your major clients/customers are is pivotal information. This applies to graphics designers, health services, accountants, theater playhouses, or consultants. These are the accounts you want to concentrate on now. The return on investment is bound to be better than pursuing lesser accounts.

Those who are computerized could have a program designed to print out their customer base top-down. Thus, the accounts who spent the most money with your firm last year would be on top; smaller accounts follow based on dollar volume. Now determine who falls in the top 20%. This is your prime target audience.

Instead of spending money to mail 1,000 pieces to everyone on your list, why not prepare a really snazzy mailing for the top 200? If your customer base is smaller, pick the top 20 out of 100 and create personalized letters to each. By targeting only the cream of the crop, more advertising strategies become viable. Telemarketing, for instance, would be prohibitive if a small firm were trying to reach all 1,000 accounts. However, 200 calls becomes manageable.

Another way to apply the 80/20 rule is using it to evaluate what you offer consumers. Gregg Rapp runs The Menu Workshop, a firm that helps restaurants evaluate what they offer on their menus. Menus are much more than just price lists. "We come in and help a restaurant focus on what makes them money," Rapp says. Without paying his hefty fee, however, any restaurateur can apply some of his wisdom. For instance, determine what are your most profitable items. Maybe it's margaritas or nachos or cinnamon rolls. Put these profitable items high on the top right of a two-page menu; at the top of a one-pager. Tell about it before you list the price. That way patrons will be convinced to order prior to being influenced by costs. Include a graphic. Now look at the other end of the spectrum. What are your *dogs* (And we don't mean hot dogs.) Drop these low-margin items that don't sell well.

By stressing the things that offer you the greatest pay-back, you structure your menu for real profit. Another lesson we learned while in the restaurant business is to keep our menu lean and mean. Instead of carrying a wide variety of dishes, we narrowed the focus to the most popular and profitable items and cut our waste by more than half.

Establishing a Swipe File

None of us have all the bright ideas; nor can we hit the bull's eye every time. But there is a way you can substantially increase your success ratio. How? By mining the treasure trove that surrounds you!

Every day we're inundated with hundreds of good ideas. They masquerade in the form of direct mail packages, commercials, print ads, posters, articles, jokes, quotes, catalogs, newspaper stories, greeting cards—even as conversations. Because they wear such unlikely costumes, however, we often overlook them. Unmasked, many are naturals for marketing; others lend sparkle to your writing; some furnish just the right touch to a speech. Why not begin capturing these kernels of wisdom for future use?

This is done via a "swipe file"—or more accurately, several swipe files. The term "swipe file" originated because you swipe (actually borrow) an idea from someone else. Naturally, you also give appropriate credit.

We have many such collections. Most reside in file folders. One houses interesting brochure designs, unusual folds, and remarkable headlines or copy. Another contains stunning direct mail packages. Still another is comprised of literature on competitive books. (How can we effectively highlight the benefits of our own titles if we don't know in what ways they are better or different from their rivals?) And file card boxes hold quotes, jokes, phrases, and sayings. Of course, much of this can also be organized on a computer.

When it's time to develop promotional materials or put together a new talk, going through your swipe files will add verve and variety. And many a book or article has been given pizzazz by a phrase, joke, or quote collected over the years. Don't use things from your swipe files verbatim. The idea is not to plagiarize or play copycat, but to let them serve as an inventive resource, inspiring your own creative juices.

Once you tune into developing swipe files, every place you go and every contact you make takes on exciting new dimension. Ideas for your files are everywhere: at the post office—in the library—as you peruse newspapers, magazines, and newsletters—while watching TV and listening to the radio—as you chat with friends or attend networking events. The possibilities are endless. Just be sure to collar the information in written form, then place it in the appropriate archive. By using this technique to cull the best from others, you can excel yourself.

Developing a Powerful Brochure

Virtually every organization needs promotional literature to convince prospects or contributors of its merits. Having a quality brochure or capabilities piece is the first step toward grabbing the brass ring.

Although a few businesses—laundry and dry cleaners, bicycle repair, and seamstresses, for instance, don't need such an instrument, most do.

An architectural service, museum, retirement home, charm school, consultant, and graphic design studio cry out for such a printed piece. Many services that might appear to have initial marginal use for such a piece ultimately find it quite helpful in soliciting business. A chimney sweep, for instance, could develop a brochure cautioning people about the dangers of leaving their chimneys unattended. A picture framer might show before and after photos and different matting options.

Shouldn't you learn how to develop a brochure that stands out from the pack? You'll use this piece of literature in a multitude of ways. It's a fast and effective way to respond to daily inquiries from potential customers/clients. You can hand it to prospective patrons whom you meet in person. It makes an ideal direct-mail piece to use when prospecting. Or you can routinely stuff one in packages and letters you mail. It can also be placed on tables at conventions, exhibits, trade fairs, and networking meetings.

Your brochure has additional functions. A well-crafted one serves a peripheral promotional purpose. Attach a copy of it to other paperwork when talking to your banker. Pass it out at stockholders' meetings. Share it with potential employees.

A good brochure is to a service firm what a scalpel is to a surgeon—not a substitute for skill, but a tool to increase success. Think about how you plan to use yours. Will it be to promote an existing service? To announce a new one? To impress someone? Is there an advantage to coding or folding some differently than others? Who is your target audience? What are their likes and dislikes? Of course, it never hurts to study the competition. Learn from what they do well—and note things to avoid.

We spent a lot of time explaining about writing compelling copy in Chapter 3 on advertising, so we won't duplicate that here. But remember, as Samuel Johnson said, "Language is the dress of thought." Be sure your language reflects thoughts consistent with your public's expectations.

One other word of caution: avoid terminology or information that "dates" your brochure. Rather than saying you've been in business for five years, say since 1985. If you must include information that will soon change, consider adding an insert sheet in the regular brochure. (This trick also allows you to customize it for different markets or geographic areas.) An insert sheet is much cheaper to produce than redoing the whole thing. Also, watch photographs so they don't show faddish clothes or other tip-offs that build in obsolescence.

There are three types of brochure readers. The *casual reader* spends a few seconds scanning the headline on the front panel. The *interested reader* opens your brochure and reads the headlines, but nothing more. The *serious reader* devours everything. Your aim is to convert casual readers to interested readers, then to serious readers. What this tells us is we'd better concentrate some mighty creative effort on headlines and subheads. They are the carrots dangling before prospective buyers.

We're not talking about thousands of dollars to create a brochure. You needn't be that ambitious. Although four-color photographs reproduced on glossy paper and cut into unusual shapes makes for an impressive piece, this isn't necessary. There is a happy medium between that extreme and black ink on cheap white paper. It is important, however, that you project a quality image. Your brochure is your salesperson.

Think of an 8½ x 11-inch or 8½ x 14-inch (legal size) piece of paper, printed on both sides and folded to fit into a normal No. 10 business envelope. This is an ideal size as it easily slips into a man's inside jacket pocket or a woman's purse. Folding the paper creates six or eight (depending on which size of paper you use) surfaces. Each of these is a panel.

As a loaf of bread needs flour, liquid, yeast, and other ingredients, a successful brochure has standard elements. Form follows function. Conclude what the contents should be, then think about design. If you try it the other way around, you'll feel like you've been caught in a thunderstorm with a leaky umbrella. The design should grow logically out of the subject matter. We'll be talking more about design specifics later.

First, you must grab the potential buyer's attention. This is usually done with a headline and an eye-catching graphic on the front panel. Its sole purpose is to lure the reader into the brochure. Next you have introductory copy that describes your service and addresses the specific needs of your prospects. For sales sizzle express things as benefits, not features.

Professionals should include a brief biography. Tell why you're qualified; mention appropriate affiliations that contribute to your credibility. Include a photograph. People appreciate seeing what the folks they are dealing with look like. You can use either a head shot, which is the typical head and shoulders photograph, or an action photo of you doing something. Photo captions are a good place to emphasize key benefits. They are one of the most read parts of a brochure.

Of course, impartial third-party accolades are a key element. Testimonials inject clout into your overall message (more about how to get them later in this chapter). Aim for a diversity of comments. Think about your target audience and include quotes that will appeal to different niches of potential patrons.

If you're responsible for writing a brochure for a nonprofit organization, be sure it doesn't smack of a charity with its hat in its hand. A recent United Way media contest found the majority of materials lacked clarity and direction. Sometimes the directors' egos outshine the organizations' philosophies. If you want to attract big-money contributors, you must be forceful and credible.

You may want to include a money-back guarantee if you offer something appropriate, such as carpet-cleaning or appliance repair. Give prospective customers every reason to trust you. Guarantees are sales stimulators. If you're providing quality, dissatisfied customers will represent a tiny fraction of your sales.

Ask for the order or the contribution. Just as a good speech has an introduction, body, and conclusion, so does a brochure. You must close the sale. Tell readers what you want them to do—call your toll-free 800 number or send in the information form. You can create a sense of urgency by encouraging them to act "today" or "right away."

Your company name and how to reach you should appear several times. If the brochure is constructed as a self-mailer, naturally an outer panel must be devoted to the address section.

Designing for "Aye" Appeal

Graphic design is the body language of a brochure. As you grapple with this issue, there are several questions to answer. What tone will you set? Friendly? Elegant? Humorous? Professional? Avant garde? Decide on the feeling you want to convey. Of course, this is not exclusively the domain of design. Copy must work with graphics to establish a harmonious whole.

Unlike ads, which tell your story on one flat surface, a brochure allows the reader to see only the front panel initially. Your headline must seize attention. Be pithy and benefit oriented. The front photo or graphic should actively support and correlate with the headline. Together they make a forceful statement to attract readers inside.

One trick to give a brochure variety and focus attention on key points is to use "call-out" boxes. These are frequently employed in magazine articles where the editor extracts a sentence or two from the text and runs it in larger type. This gives you another shot at interested readers. If the headlines don't capture their interest, perhaps the call-out boxes will.

For visual diversity there are other options besides photographs. Illustrations can be tailored to your needs. They add zest to an otherwise dull brochure. If you can't afford to hire an artist, use clip art. Check at an artist supply store for information on what's available or contact the companies we list in Part III, Sources and Resources to Help You Prosper.

When you're planning how to put the various elements together, give special consideration if you want to include a form for people to return for more information. It should be on an end panel and face out for writing convenience. It's easily clipped and doesn't destroy the rest of the brochure when removed. This also allows for greater flexibility. If you need a brochure for strictly institutional purposes, simply cut off this form and you have it.

If you're doing a self-mailer, plan the address panel back-to-back with the order coupon. This is especially important if you plan to conduct a lot of direct-mail campaigns. That way when people return the form you have the coding for their address label on the back and can track which mailing list is pulling the best.

Also consider what you want on the address panel if you're heavily into direct-marketing. Do you need a bulk-mail permit number? Should you be printing special forwarding and address correction instructions to clean your mailing list? It's a good idea to check with the post office to make sure what you're planning satisfies all postal regulations. A reminder when using a logo: work from an original piece of artwork rather than taking one off a business card or letterhead. This is considered a second generation image and sacrifices sharpness.

Let's talk a moment about type. Unless you're going for a specific effect, stick to standard typefaces. Don't mix several different styles. The most you want is one face for the text and another for headlines.

Did you know capitalized words are difficult to read, not to mention less pleasing? In fact, lowercase text is read 13.4% faster than copy set in all caps. So be wary of putting many headlines in all capitals. You can have the right-hand margins justified (meaning all the same length) or kept ragged. The latter gives an open feeling as there is more white space.

Also consider how the brochure will fold. There are several options. Most good books on printing show samples. Just be sure to avoid unusual sizes that require a customized envelope. This drives costs near the stratosphere. Also special cutouts, called "die-cuts," cost *mucho dinero*. If you let a designer talk you into either of these, you'll feel about as unlucky as the person who just moved into a new town . . . and was run over by welcome wagon.

Cost-Effective Production Tips

Perhaps the best advice we can give you here is to proofread carefully. Then do it again! Nothing is more aggravating—and costly—than getting 5,000 brochures from the printer, only to discover a glaring error in a headline or an incorrect phone number. Mistakes at this point are as unwelcome as ants at a picnic. In addition to diligently proofreading regular text copy, carefully examine addresses and phone numbers, and the spelling of names and headlines. Double-check every detail. Get someone else to inspect things too; one person can repeatedly overlook the same error.

Two colors of ink are preferred, but even one color used creatively will do the trick if you must be very budget conscious. Please don't settle for plain old black ink. Going to a color only adds about $15 and will energize your literature. Look at PMS color swatches at an artist supply store or your printer's shop. There's no need to settle for the standard blue, red, green, etc. You can put new sass 'n flash in your next print job very economically. Plan your brochure for two colors. By the way, studies show younger people prefer bright hues, whereas older folks respond to soft colors.

To get more mileage out of ink, talk to your designer about using screens of 10, 20, or 30%. This lays down a lighter shade of the color, over which you can print text in the full-strength ink color. If you do use a color photograph, in addition to boosting the actual printing price, you'll also need to have a color separation done.

While we're discussing color, there's another option for variation. How about using a colored paper stock? (Just be sure to consider what will happen when you add the ink color. If you were to use a yellow paper with blue ink, for instance, you'd end up with green!)

Nowadays paper is a large part of the expense of any printing job. Consult with your printer to see if he or she stocks a paper in quantity that will work for you. Coated stocks that appear glossy will cost more, but add an elegant look. They come in various weights. Beware of one too flimsy as its lack of substance will downgrade the feel of your brochure.

Get a written price quotation (not an estimate) from several printers. You may be surprised at the wide variance in charges. Be sure you think through your project first and determine the points the bid should include. What quantity do you need? Most people print at least a year's projected supply. How many folds? Are halftones required for photographs? Any trims? Bleeds?

What is their turnaround time? If they say 21 days, they mean over four *working weeks,* not three calendar weeks. Encourage your print rep to make suggestions for cost-cutting measures. Ask about "down-time"—when they are less busy and might give you a better price to keep their equipment running. At the completion of the job, we recommend getting the camera-ready art back. Then there's no question about who has it when you're ready to go back to press. If you plan on producing many promotional pieces, invest in a copy of *Getting It Printed* by Mark Beach. It's a treasure for amateur designers and people responsible for printing decisions. (See Recommended Reading.)

A compelling brochure is a surefire way to cultivate client business, consumer purchases, or patron donations. Without one, you resemble a turtle in a horse race. These tips will enable you to get swiftly out of the starting gate and create a winning brochure.

Some firms find it enhances their position to produce additional literature. Corporate histories or biographies convey a feeling of stability. Lists of clients add to your credibility and reassure individuals or businesses contemplating using your service. Just make sure all communications to your customers or clients have a coordinated look. Then you are consistent in the image you project.

Effective Lead Handling

Generating enough interest to get a person or business to contact you is, of course, an important step. How that lead is handled spells the difference between success or defeat. We devote an entire future chapter to providing outstanding service and assuring customer/client satisfaction (Chapter 8). It is paramount that people be treated well initially. They should be made to feel good in a convincing manner.

When working with prospects, use their names. This makes people feel special; it also sets you apart. Few businesspeople bother to employ this simple approach. How do you get their names? That depends on your individual operation. In professional circles, it is natural to introduce yourselves. If they are paying for repairing their vacuum or for alterations on a suit, you have a natural vehicle to discover who they are. Their name will be on their check or credit card. If all else fails, ask.

In some instances, a show-and-tell technique will help you score. A carpet cleaner could have samples demonstrating before and after cleaning; a picture framer might display the same painting or portrait with and without proper matting and framing. Of course, remodeling contractors need a portfolio showing interiors and exteriors before and after their handiwork. Ditto for plastic surgeons. Such visual statements say a great deal.

Nothing takes the place of knowledge. When we speak with potential clients they can sense immediately whether we know what we're talking about. People also know when you are bluffing. No matter whether you deal in such divergent things as chimney-sweeping or engineering services, educate yourself so you can guide those you wish to influence.

As Earl Nightingale told us in many of his dynamic motivational presentations, If you study your profession only one hour per day . . . in only five years you will be the country's foremost expert. Read trade journals—listen to tapes—attend seminars—watch videos—become that expert!

Be prepared to handle objections. When Marilyn was the director of marketing for the West Coast's largest vocational school, she trained the salespeople how to overcome resistance. How? First, you determine what the standard objections are. Then you think about ways to surmount them. This kind of preparation allows you to be one step ahead of your prospect. She literally scripted each objection with a written description on how to handle it. This resulted in a dramatic increase in business.

One vitally important aspect of handling leads is to ask for the sale. Does this seem like a stupid bit of advice? It is surprising how often this crucial selling step is overlooked or bungled. Naturally, you don't want to be crass about it.

There are several graceful ways to ask for the sale. One superior approach is to give the prospect two alternatives—either of which is acceptable to you. For instance, don't ask if they want to purchase your service. Instead say, "Would you prefer to handle this by check or credit card?" or "Which would be more convenient for our service representative to come out, Tuesday or Friday?" For institutions or firms where contracts must be signed, some people favor asking the person to "write your name here" rather than saying "sign here." Also, be careful you don't go too far and talk a prospect out of a sale. Once they indicate the answer is yes, stop selling!

Before deciding to move our company to Buena Vista, Colorado, we contacted several chambers of commerce in potential locales. We were impressed when a letter arrived from the bank president of Moffat County State Bank in tiny Craig, Colorado. The letter invited us to make them our financial institution. That's asking for the order in spades. Had we moved to Craig, that bank would have had our accounts.

Another sales strategy is to make it *easy* for the person to buy or participate. Credit cards facilitate sales. So do toll-free 800 numbers. If applicable, a free trial period will also reassure people; so will a money-back guarantee. Postage-paid business reply cards increase the results. If you're writing people asking them to do you a favor, including a stamped, self-addressed envelope (SASE) will bolster results.

Follow up. These two little words will have a big impact on your success. If you promise to do something, do it. If you expect someone to do something for you in a certain time frame and they don't, get back in touch. If you feel you have a hot lead and nothing comes of it, contact the person. Try to get them talking and discover what the obstacle is. The person with good follow-through techniques doesn't let business slip through a crack.

While we're on this subject, should you borrow a follow-up tactic used by dentists? Remember the friendly reminder to get your teeth cleaned about every six months? This same strategy can be applied by veterinarians (It's time for Rover's shots), physicians (Your last physical was . . .) and optometrists (You haven't had your eyes checked since . . .). It would also work for plant nurseries (We just got in our annuals for this year or it's pruning time), beauty shops (for a permanent), and chimney sweeps (avoid fire hazards). Carefully worded, timely reminders stimulate business and give you a perfect excuse to follow-up.

Suggestive Selling

Try to think of ways to entice your customers, clients, or patients to buy more. Suggestive selling can turn a marginal operation into a profitable one. This is done all the time in better clothing stores. When you purchase a dress or suit, the salesperson brings over accessories to complete the "look."

Why not make it a part of your service strategy? A car wash could feature special interior leather cleaning and hand wax jobs. An answering service might trade up a client to include coverage on weekends and evenings. A dentist also pushes add-ons by suggesting special fluoride treatments with teeth cleaning. An upholsterer could reap extra business by suggesting a footstool or matching pillows.

Some firms offer employees perks to inspire them to help with suggestive selling. They give a bonus when workers write add-on business. A carpet cleaner, for instance, might pay the men and women who go into homes and businesses an extra reward when they also sell the customer on cleaning drapes or waxing floors.

Service people are often in ideal positions to build greater sales numbers. By listening to customer comments, they are tipped off to new needs. The person who repairs air-conditioning and refrigeration, for instance, should be trained to recognize the potential when a customer says, "Our house is often uncomfortable." This may well be an invitation to upgrade registers, duct work, or air-conditioning units.

We were tickled by another form of "suggestive selling" that came to our attention. The owner of a document shredding service on the East Coast developed a real knack for attracting customers. He roots through trash bags collected from the local dump by two young helpers. When he finds sensitive pieces of correspondence, he sends them to the place of origin with a note saying, "Should I be reading this material? If not, why did your company make it public by throwing it away in one piece?" It typically takes less than 24 hours for a response.

Expand Your Market

Many companies miss lucrative opportunities for capitalizing on what they already have. Yet there is a proven method for expanding your market. With this technique you look for ways to get individuals or businesses to use more of what you offer. Kodak, for instance, switched from advertising film to promoting photography.

If you clean windows, is there a way to create a higher demand for this service? How about encouraging businesses to paint their windows for various holidays? Then after Christmas, Easter, and Halloween, you have a world of glass that requires cleaning! A bicycle repair shop might mount a local campaign to encourage using bikes as a cheap, nonpolluting form of transportation. A museum might spur interest in cultural activities.

Another way of expanding your market is thinking about others who are already reaching your target group and forging an alliance with them. We did this for our previous book, *Country Bound!™ Trade Your Business Suit Blues for Blue Jean Dreams™*. This is a guide to escaping the big city rat race, choosing the right relocation spot, and earning a good living in small town USA. We reasoned that United National Real Estate, which has some 300 offices around the country specializing in *rural* real estate, would be a good partner. They also produce a catalog twice a year. We met with President Lou Francis in Kansas City, Missouri, and put together a win-win proposition.

We provided him with a half-page ad which he would run in his nationally distributed catalog at no charge to us. In return he gets $5 for every book sold. We've merchandised over $5,000 worth of books this way so far and also get their names for our mailing list. Of further interest to him, is this book shows people who want to leave the corporate culture—but need a livelihood—how to earn a living in rural areas. Thus it helps his potential customers realize their dream.

Diversify to Multiply

Diversify your business and multiply your dollars. It's a result of synergy: the combined effect of two or more things working together. Have you thought of expanding your business with sidelines to create multiple income sources? That's what Luce Press Clippings did.

They offer a new option to their clients, most of which are public relations (PR) firms. The new wrinkle is dubbed Comparative Ad Costs. It provides comparable advertising figures for clippings Luce cut from magazines and newspapers. This way PR agencies can show their clients how much they *would* have spent for the exposure, had it been placed as a paid advertisement. With little extra expense or effort, Luce added a whole new spectrum to their services.

Let's examine fresh approaches for any organization that wishes to develop a new revenue source. You can set a course for a significantly improved bottom line by spinning off peripheral revenue centers. Offering complementary services or coming up with other creative combinations adds excitement and diversity to your business. More importantly, it augments your income stream.

An additional bonus is that many times doing something different is an outstanding traffic builder for your flagship service. It pulls in prospects you wouldn't normally attract. Gary Beals, CEO of Beals Advertising & Public Relations Agency, is a perfect example. One reason his San Diego-based agency prospers is because he also developed a product called *Finderbinder*. Besides being a freestanding revenue source, this news media directory positions him as THE expert on area media.

"It's the large tail that wags our dog," says Beals. "It pulls attention back to our company." Conceived as a worthwhile diversification while reinforcing the company image of being the power agency of communication services, Beals confides it's "an excellent tool for finding and landing new business. Its value is as much for the visibility as for the income," he remarks. His directory builds company identity and prestige.

Beals is an ideal example of how adding a new spin to your business can turn into increased publicity. Such activity gives area newspapers, TV, and radio a reason to focus attention on your enterprise. You're suddenly "news." This clever businessman doesn't stop there though. He has franchised the concept and now has *Finderbinders* in some 20 other cities. And he has diversified further, both to publicize his agency and create a new income stream. Gary is a speaker who specializes in doing 60 to 90-minute break-out sessions for national conventions. To date he has given some 500 talks. New business is a natural fallout from these speaking engagements.

Multi-function is a key to the future. Faith Popcorn, in *The Popcorn Report*—her book about trends—writes that multi-function is important in the streamlined '90s. This means products or services that accomplish two or three things at once, or allow you to get more than one job done at a time. "The biggest idea is *cluster marketing*," Popcorn says. "Why should we have to make one drop at the dry cleaners, another at the tailor, a third at the shoe repair, and so on?"

Innovative merchants can sub-contract some of these functions. Let's say you own the dry cleaners. Why not team up with a shoe repair person and a tailor . . . both of whom could work out of their homes using your facility as a pickup and delivery point? Everybody wins.

Time is perhaps *the* most precious commodity of this decade. To conserve it, and avoid unnecessary stress, consumers will patronize establishments that help them combine shopping and errands. Marketers who capitalize on this need will thrive.

Without incurring any expense for facility development or additional start-up costs, other businesses can benefit by thinking through how to use their existing structure more effectively. A beauty school, for instance, could embellish their traditional curriculum. A refresher course—including updating of new styles, cuts, and techniques—might be of interest to operators and salon owners. This type of instruction holds special appeal to those who haven't worked for awhile and want to get back their manual dexterity. What about a salon management course that teaches the business side of hairdressing: purchasing, accounting, marketing, plus personnel selection and supervision. Cosmetic merchandising might be another subject to offer. This is a natural as more shops become boutiques with cosmetics, jewelry, and other accessories for sale. Shopping malls have tuned in to this *diversify to multiply* concept. Many now sport driver's license renewal booths.

John Nale owns the Evergreen Cafe in Buena Vista, Colorado. Now in his eighth year as the proprietor of this restaurant, which was formerly open only for breakfast and lunch, Nale admits, "I'm not an evening person myself." But it was a waste for the place to sit idle every night, so he and a friend got creative. They put together a deal where Mary Lou Morgan uses his facilities and equipment to operate her own business.

During the day the Evergreen serves health-conscious breakfasts and lunches. At night it metamorphoses into Italian cuisine that even includes nine tempting vegetarian dishes. "There were many details to work out," reminisces Nale. "At 5:00 P.M. there's a total transition with candles, nice place mats, cloth napkins, and fancier dish ware." Operatic music serenades diners.

Are there challenges in running two different restaurants out of one facility? You bet. Storage space was one. Mary Lou bought her own freezer, two-door cooler, and salad prep table. Orders come in on separate invoices. John explains how he handles the utilities: "I contacted the gas and electric company and got the monthly totals for the last three years, then came up with an average for each month. She reimburses me for any additional costs over that average."

The Evergreen has become a popular evening dining spot with locals and tourists alike. John now receives a percentage of Mary Lou's receipts, while she has little overhead. Both score a knockout with this ingenious approach! Of course, a dinner house seeking to make better use of its facility could reverse this idea.

Lisa Carlson of Upper Access, Inc., Hinesburg, Vermont, believes, "Being open to creative diversity allows you to be much more sustaining." She and husband, Steve, started as writers. After receiving rejection slips from 26 major publishers, they became intrigued by independent publishing and decided to take the do-it-yourself approach.

Next they saw a need for a mail order bookstore specializing in hard to find books. So the Carlsons launched a catalog called Big Books from Small Presses, which specializes in selling works by small publishing houses and self-publishers. They design and distribute 70,000 catalogs a year.

Lisa and Steve looked endlessly for affordable computer software to manage all these book orders and found "there was a crying need." Not being shy folks, they spent $60,000 to develop PIIGS (Publishers' Invoice and Information Generating System). It is an industry-specific program that handles everything from invoicing to statements, royalties to mailing lists. It not only solves their problem but adds a whole new tier of profit to their enterprise.

Another add-on is an 800 service which publishers can use to promote their books 24-hours a day via Visa, MasterCard and American Express credit card orders. "The synergy is wonderful." observes Lisa. "People who order through our 800 number get the catalog, then come back to us for additional purchases."

Their latest outgrowth is sub-contracting shipping for another firm. They pack and ship UPS orders of odd-shaped special contractor tools. "This, coupled with our in-house shipping demands, has given us enough volume to now hire a warehouse foreman." explains Carlson.

Upper Access is an ideal example of what we call "LinkThink." They watch what's happening, audit consumer trends, then capitalize on complementary new needs that pop up. In the process their business has become like the interlocking parts of a chain that, when forged together, form an invincible whole.

You too can think progressively. Inventively. Outrageously. As you resist conformity you reach new heights. By boosting the ingenuity with which you view your organization, it becomes possible to turn niches into riches—to diversify to multiply—to go around roadblocks and discover exciting new profit centers.

Cultivating Testimonials and Endorsements

Testimonials from others are almost as good as money in the bank. Most service firms sell intangibles rather than something a prospect can see and touch—such as a car, dress, or lawn mower. Selling intangibles is harder; it requires a much greater degree of trust on the part of the buyer. That's why third-party endorsements are so valuable. Instead of

SPIN-OFF BUSINESS IDEAS

- Real estate office that also has a corporate relocation department and a property management division.
- Child care facility that also offers elder care.
- Child care providers that furnish creative day care programs for the children of parents who are attending seminars, conventions, or participating in adult vacation activities.
- Beauty shop that includes a sun tanning parlor and carries cosmetics and jewelry.
- Gardener who also sells fertilizer, plants, etc., plus offers window washing, gutter cleaning, and hauls large items to the dump.
- Small ranch or farm that turns a pond on the property into a for-fee fishing establishment or encourages "do-it-yourself" picking of fruits and veggies.
- Hotel or motel that puts together entertaining tourist packages.
- Campground and riding stable combination that offers trail rides, hay rides, guided horseback hunting trips, moonlight rides and steak dinners, etc.
- Butchering company that also does taxidermy work.
- Laundromat in conjunction with a dry cleaners and tailoring/alteration service.
- Laundromats also team up with bars, restaurants, tanning rooms, video rentals, exercise equipment, electronic games, you name it.
- Funeral home that doubles as a wedding chapel.
- Bookstore that also sells greeting cards and church supplies.

you saying how great you are, it is an impartial outsider reciting your praises.

When someone compliments you, the first thing to do is write back thanking them and request in writing their permission to use what they've said. We've devised a standard letter for such purposes. A sample follows. Notice it gives you unlimited leeway to do whatever you please with their comments. (Run this by an attorney to be sure it covers all contingencies in your situation.) Only once in the 15 years we've been in business has anyone refused to sign such a release.

After you have their written permission to use the material, think about how to capitalize on it. We've put together a leather notebook of the original copies of letters we've received. When prospective clients come in, we invite them to look through the book. This is a presell technique that builds trust and credibility. We also include photocopies with proposals.

People are more likely to compliment you verbally than in writing though. What to do then? Take your courage in hand, again thank them for the kind words, then say something like, "Jim, I wonder if you'd do me a favor? Would you take a couple of minutes and put that in writing for me? It would really be helpful." Once you've received Jim's correspondence, proceed as above.

The Power of Referrals

Although testimonials may be as *good* as money in the bank, referrals *are* money in the bank. Once you've honed your referral approach, we can almost guarantee your bank balance will blossom. A referral is simply one happy client or customer telling another. It is word-of-mouth praise. (To help you stimulate this area, pay close attention to Chapter 8, Providing Outstanding Service and Customer/ Client Satisfaction.)

A recent Whirlpool Corporation study showed Americans are six times more likely to rely on the judgment of others than on advertising when making a buying decision. By some accounts, a whopping 80% of all consumer choices are the result of personal recommendations. The individual who refers once will do it again and again. Because the average person has a sphere of influence of 52 people, these kudos can create dazzling momentum.

Begin today to develop a referral mindset. You get referrals by asking for them. A "Think Referrals" poster will focus attention on this thrust. (You have provided business cards to all key associates, right?)

Testimonial Letter

HOMESTEAD DESIGN, INC.

P.O. BOX 1058 • BELLINGHAM, WASHINGTON 98227

(206) 676-5647

January 2, 1991

Marilyn Ross
Accelerated Business Images
P.O. Box 1500
Buena Vista, CO 81211

Dear Marilyn,

I wanted to start the New Year off right by letting you know how much we at Homestead Design appreciate your expert advice. When it comes to publicity and advertising, you're a real "pro".

The PR work you've done for our books was excellent, and your prices were quite reasonable. In fact, since each publicity mailing was "keyed", we were able to keep track of the response in actual book orders.

According to our records, your work paid for itself ten times over in increased sales ! After getting results that good on two different projects, you can bet we'll hire you again and watch the sales soar.

Best regards,

Craig Wallin

Craig Wallin

Permission to Quote Letter

ACCELERATED BUSINESS IMAGES

PHONE (719) 395-2459 · (800) 548-1876
PO. BOX 1500 · 425 CEDAR STREET · BUENA VISTA, CO 81211
FAX (719) 395-8374

Thanks so much for your kind words. You really made our day! I hope you'll agree to allow us to share the feelings you expressed in your letter with others by signing and returning this permission form. For your convenience, I've enclosed a self addressed, stamped envelope.

Best regards,

Marilyn Ross

Permission to Quote

I hereby give my consent for Accelerated Business Images or their assignees to use the comments in my letter dated _____ in any manner or form, or for any medium, without restriction or limit for the purposes of nationwide publicity, advertising, or display. I understand I will receive no payment or compensation for this permission.

Signed_____

Printed name_____

Dated_____

Address_____

City/state/zip_____

Instruct service technicians to give two cards to each customer with the following request: "Would you please pass these along to anyone you know who we can help?" Ask for the sale. People need to be alerted to your desire for referrals. A physician, architect, or financial planner might post a discrete sign that says "We appreciate your referrals."

Start prospecting for referrals with the folks who gave you testimonials; they're obviously on your side. Now think about your existing and recent client/customer base. You know who is especially high on you—and who isn't. Target the accounts where you excelled. Contact them and explain you find people are reassured when a satisfied client/customer shares a happy experience. Explain that you would appreciate their mentioning you to some of their friends or associates.

Don't overlook nonclient contacts. Individuals who are influential in their fields can further broaden your referral program. What about attorneys, accountants, association executive directors, insurance agents, certified public accountants (CPAs), politicians, bankers, even those who have worked for you previously? Several of these people might be glad to put you together with someone who can use your service.

Engaging others to market your services with their clients is a wonderful way to expand your market reach. Establish relationships with other professionals who deliver services to the same or similar organizations as you, but who are not in direct competition with you. Educate them about why this will be beneficial. You may trade referrals with one while providing a referral fee to another.

When someone gives you a referral, promptly recognize their contribution. This can be done in person, by phone, or via correspondence. Notice the adjacent postcard used by some dentists. If it doesn't violate your professional code of ethics, a small thank you gift may be in order. We often send flowers or gift baskets to individuals who go out of their way to do nice things for us.

In some industries, paid referrals (finders fees) are an acceptable way of doing business. If yours falls into this category, be sure your record-keeping is accurate. No one will shoot you down faster than a contact who gave you a referral, but never received the agreed-upon remuneration.

Referral Thank You

The Business Breakfast/Lunch/Tea

The days of Macho men swilling down martinis, gorging on red meat, and taking three-hour lunches are as extinct as dinosaurs. They have been replaced by men and women who often prefer nonalcoholic beverages, grilled chicken and fish entrees, and more disciplined time constraints. Today's executives are more health-conscious, more time-conscious, and more price-conscious.

In many circles the power lunch has given way to the power breakfast. It can be as light as a croissant or as hearty as a breakfast buffet. Even in the priciest spots of New York and Los Angeles, costs hover well below lunch. Shoptalk over flapjacks is gaining ground in several hotel restaurants. Early-morning business pow-wows can be seen at the Polo Lounge in the Beverly Hills Hotel, the Skyway in Chicago's Hyatt Regency, and the Edwardian Room at New York City's Plaza Hotel.

Doing business over food and drink is nothing new. Business people wrapping up deals over tea is. At Chicago's Drake Hotel, the Palm Court blossoms with attache cases perched with lids at full attention each afternoon beginning at 3:00 P.M. They are in sharp contrast with the delicate tea service and the clink of wafer-thin china. Yet here, and in other high-class hotels around the country, tea is often the choice of executives who shun the old liquid lunches.

If you want to use any of these culinary methods to score more sales or do serious networking, here are a few tips. Act rather than react. You do the inviting. If someone says goodbye with, "We've got to get together for lunch sometime," take advantage of the opening. Call in a few days and suggest two alternative times you are free. (Remember to give a choice between something and something, rather than a choice between something and nothing.)

How the conversation is orchestrated varies with different individuals. Sometimes rather than real conversation, it's nonstop kibitzing. The real "meat" of the meeting doesn't get approached until you are parting company. In some situations the serious talk is conducted on the way to the parking lot or walking back to the office.

The setting you choose says things about you. If eating out plays a large role in how you develop business, it makes sense to cultivate a close rapport with a couple of outstanding local establishments. Then you will be personally greeted, your reservations honored, and your service top drawer.

One final suggestion: watch the salt. Yes, believe it or not, there are those who judge you by how you use salt. If it is important to impress the person who shares the fare, always taste food before applying salt. Some people believe if you salt without tasting, it's a sign you don't evaluate information carefully before making decisions.

Offering Financial Incentives

There are several ways a creative business or institution can use monetary inducements. The restaurant industry pioneered two-for-one dinners years ago. This is perfect for recreational facilities. Movie houses, theaters, miniature golf courses, amusement parks, bowling alleys, and race track operations could easily employ this tactic to attract new guests. So could a dance studio offer two-for-one lessons, or a museum admit two people for one fee.

On a similar bent, some places offer family discounts. Currently there is heavy competition among dentists. Because winning patients is like pulling teeth—and it's projected to continue through the year 2000—some offices offer family discounts when two relatives schedule appointments. Chiropractors and other health professionals sometimes adopt this plan as well.

Frequent guest programs are the bread and butter of major hotel chains. The business traveler now comprises the hotel industry's largest customer group. Consequently there is a veritable war to capture corporate business. The financial incentives offered here take the form of points. They are earned for each stay in a hotel and can be redeemed toward free vacation stays, air fare, car rental, even merchandise. There is no reason why an individual hotel or motel could not concoct a similar program to encourage repeat business.

Car washes already give a free wash after so many paid ones. Airline frequent flyer plans are more popular today than ever before.

Prepayment arrangements are cropping up in some unusual places. Colleges and universities are structuring "pay now, learn later" plans that are especially attractive to parents caught in the squeeze of ever-escalating tuition costs. Washington University lets families freeze tuition at the freshman level when they pay for all four years up front. The University of Pennsylvania's Penn Plan provides a menu of prepayment and installment options to choose from. Duquesne University in Pittsburgh recently allowed a family with alumni connections to enroll their six-year-old daughter for a complete college cost of $6,450. When she reaches college age it is estimated the four-year tuition will be $60,000. Meanwhile the school has the money to invest.

Prepayment alternatives find a place in other service industries as well. Innovative funeral directors have long offered prepayment plans. This kind of financing might also work for a health club or spa membership. Forward-thinking owners and executives can often come up with financial incentives when they really concentrate on looking for ways to help customers/clients partake of their services.

Nonprofits Use the Auction Block

The folks at Trinity Lutheran Church in Detroit definitely have a sense of humor. They decided to stage an Ugly Art Show and Auction to raise money for the church's restoration. Over 100 Detroiters paid $25 per couple to inspect and bid for absolutely atrocious pictures and sculpture. (Was there a "Worst of Show" award we wonder?) In keeping with the evening's theme, refreshments consisted of Cheez Whiz, hot dogs, and Twinkies.

Mile Hi Church of Religious Science took the opposite approach for their expansion fund-raiser. This Lakewood, Colorado, church put on a gala "Fancy Affair." Tickets for the buffet and auction went for $10 each. In addition to international cuisine, there was entertainment, free gifts, and door prizes. The auction preview began at 4:00 P.M., followed by a silent auction. Items were displayed on tables in rooms around the perimeter of the church. Each room was decorated to represent a country and to organize the objects for sale into logical groupings. Japan had garden items; America, sports. Furniture and household things were displayed in Germany, while Mexico offered a potpourri. Artwork could be found in France; antiques and jewelry, in England.

Those interested in supporting this cause could either place absentee bids using the auction catalog, participate in the silent auction via written bid, or cue the auctioneer during the oral raffle. Items were donated by church members and friends. They ran a wide gambit. There was a wood icebox, Wedgwood china, valuable coins, a bronze sculpture, an antique quilt, even English Hallmark sterling silver with pearl handles. One of the more inventive things to go on the block was Bronco football tickets for two and dinner with the nationally known head minister and his wife.

Take Your Service on the Road

Want to get your wheels rolling instead of spinning? An old business maxim says *drive* is what gets you to the top. That can be so . . . literally. Inventive entrepreneurs—and even some professionals—are making extraordinary livings by putting their expertise on wheels. They're clobbering the competition by offering the ultimate in service: help at your doorstep. This concept, a lifesaver for harried two-career families, single parents, and mushrooming businesses, involves work performed where and when it is most handy for the customer.

Services such as hair care, massages, video delivery, and auto tune ups are ripe areas for portable profits. Convenience is all-important. Busy working men and women patronize service providers who come to them. And innovative business-to-business companies are finding ways to serve the commercial sector as well. Coupled with this public need for better service is the small business owner's desire to avoid hassles and trim overhead. Going mobile offers a galaxy of advantages.

In the majority of cases, your entire operation is in your van, truck, bus, or car. No longer is there a need for expensive office, store, or shop space. Strangle-hold leases and crippling mortgage payments are a thing of the past. The old requirement of "location, location, location" becomes a moot point. Your ideal location is wherever you park! And you bypass zoning problems and bureaucratic red tape for building permits.

George Louser's brainchild is Wash on Wheels. Louser encountered one problem after another when he tried to build traditional car washes over 25 years ago. His solution was to design a portable pressure washing system that enables the operator to bring the cleaning system to the client. In addition to doing individual automobiles, he expanded to include truck fleets. Initially, Louser even restored buildings and removed graffiti, using a liquid sandblasting technique.

Now Wash on Wheels specializes in servicing the residential market with up to 14 different cleaning services in one visit. With today's "don't move, improve" philosophy, homeowners like the fact his franchisees wash carpets, ceilings, upholstery, drapes, driveways, roofs, pools, patios, even the entire house exterior.

Another entrepreneurial type saw an opportunity to clean up (pun intended) back in 1977 when he conceived an idea to open an airplane cleaning service. Unable to obtain typical financing, he bought a pick-up truck, got credit for the necessary cleaning equipment, and launched Fly Clean, Inc. This Houston-based operation, headed by president Dic Maxen, banishes dirt and grime from some 40-60 commercial airplanes a month. Not only do they handle exterior wash and polish, but also interior inspection, maintenance, and replenishment.

Maxen runs four mobile units and a crew of 10 to 20. Although Fly Clean originally worked single-engine planes and privately owned airliners—today they've signed lucrative commercial contracts and specialize on 727s, DC10s, and 747s. Maxen, whose annual receipts are just under $1,000,000, admits, "You can get started with a pick-up and a $1,000 pressure washer. But be sure to use cold water and low heat," he cautions, "or you'll likely ruin a $75,000 paint job." He points out that research and investigation into FAA chemicals is also important.

Personal services is a ripe area for portable entrepreneuring. In the Dallas/Fort Worth area, Timothy Terry has a fleet of mobile computerized offices dubbed Terry's Financial Express. More than 300 clients pay from $85 to $1,000 a month for on-site bookkeeping services and tax preparation. Surprisingly, Terry gets many referrals from CPAs who don't like to keep books.

Tamara Mattson's slogan might well be "Have Clippers, Will Travel." Mattson has launched a mobile animal grooming business in tiny Excelsior, Minnesota. Her van is equipped with water, a water heater, supplies, and equipment. This clever young lady prospects for dogs and declawed cats to groom by blanketing the area with flyers and checking to see who has registered a pet with city hall.

Dr. Jane Summers is carrying on a family tradition. Her grandfather used to make house calls by horse in the early 1900s. Today she rides a red Jeep to the rescue of busy Denver, Colorado, executives who want physicals and sick moms who can't readily get to the doctor. She also offers a less expensive alternative than an ambulance ride. Her practice, Pioneer Internal Medicine, is strictly mobile and very high tech. Until recently, it wouldn't have been possible to offer portable doctoring. But today's technology provides equipment compact enough to fit in a vehicle. With this unique twist, Dr. Summers offers personalized care and a closer physician-patient relationship. She feels seeing patients in their own setting is a real advantage. It gives her a holistic overview of how their condition might be affected by environment and care-givers.

Jan Robbins, a certified massage therapist, founded Corporate Stress-busters. This San Francisco company provides 15-minute upper body Japanese Shiatsu massages to office workers at their desks. "Massage is the only thing that's addicting . . . and *good* for you," quips Robbins, who followed her vision to help people avoid suffering. When she began, individual workers would hire her at $18 a session, with a discount of $3 for a series of five treatments.

Today she has contracts with four companies who provide her services to employees as "perks." With stress being so widespread, Robbins hopes to get her therapy accepted as a standard health benefit. She is currently breaking ground with the Workers' Compensation Insurance Agency.

Another woman who has turned her personal skills into financial thrills is Caryl Barday. Her Corporate Cuts Unlimited, Inc. provides in-office haircuts for busy Denver executives. The first in the nation to legally conduct such a business, Barday overcame tremendous opposition from the state health department to acquire her cosmetology license. "It took me a year and three months of intense work," she reports. Her average income? Thirty-five dollars a person including the tip. "I make two or three stops in a day and do five to six men at each place," says the savvy stylist. She sets up in the conference room and makes an appointment on the spot for two weeks hence before she leaves. An assistant carries her customized case, which contains her own chair. He also shines clients' shoes as she grooms their hair. Barday, who has been flown around the country to counsel others who want to get licensed, has been shearing the locks of Rocky Mountain businessmen for several years now. Her best customers are real estate developers, stock brokers, and county commissioners. When asked why she has been successful, Barday replies, "Professionalism and consistency." These are certainly virtues in any business.

An Olympia, Washington, woman—Yvonne Conway—is another hairstylist who goes to her customers. Rather than operating in the corporate arena, however, she typically calls on local nursing homes, jails, mental institutions, and private homes. With over 100 regulars, Conway has more business than she can handle—sometimes cutting a husband's hair while his wife sits under the dryer. For the last eight years she has taken shampoos, haircuts, color services, perms, manicures, and pedicures on the road.

Clients use her services for one of two reasons: either they like the convenience or they are in poor health. She has concocted ways to clean and style clients' hair even if they are confined to bed or in a wheelchair. "I find very little competition in offering freelance beauty services," she comments. Conway has even written a book, *Mobile Hair & Beauty Services*, which explains how other beauticians can put themselves in the driver's seat.

And The Dent Doctor also makes house calls . . . well, actually car lot calls. Rather than carrying a little black bag, he arrives in a mobile van. Through a secret process, he smooths out small dings and dents without ever doing traditional auto body work or aiming a paint gun. Those who purchase on of these franchises minister primarily to vehicles ailing from hail damage, minor parking lot incidents, shopping cart dings, or tools dropped onto the body by careless mechanics.

Perhaps you can "plus" an existing site-specific business with a mobil unit. By making it easier for customers to do business with you than the competition, you remove their resistance. Additionally, putting a part of your business on wheels often gives you a new reason to be news, thus generating valuable publicity.

Offshore Sailing School, which is headquartered in Fort Myers, Florida, has 30 new opportunities for such public relations, not to mention a new gimmick to increase sales and help their customers beat recessionary prices. They've introduced Learn to Sail vacations in 30 U.S. cities. By taking their 20-hour course on the road, they offer an action vacation minus the hassle and expense associated with long distance travel. Participants can now enjoy a weekend getaway close to home. "We're pleased with the response," reports vice president of marketing, Kirk Williams. "It has a snowball effect and is increasing in popularity."

Talking about popularity, Bob the Bankwagon enjoys enormous fame in Amarillo, Texas. This bright-red double-decker bus, which was imported from Britain, chases down customers for First National Bank of Amarillo. "It offers full-service banking," explains Jerry Polvado, senior vice-president at First National. "We can foresee a lot of benefit," he continues. "There are a number of areas in our city where there are no bank branches." In addition to servicing these locations via an established route, Bob also travels to county fairs, fun fests, retirement homes, hospitals, and company parking lots. Here again, a mobile unit focuses attention on the parent facility. "The PR value is very important," relates Polvado.

California-based EnvirOzone Technologies, Inc. is another example of a business to spin off from an existing enterprise. An environmental engineering firm that specializes in wastewater management, it has won success in a crowded marketplace. To save customers extra expense and hassle, it has developed a mobile unit that can drive to a site and perform necessary clean-up.

Bill Cherkasky, president of the International Franchising Association (IFA) cites one of the main reasons for the ever increasing mobile franchising trend is that it is filling a real need. "People will do anything to have their cars tuned without having to drop them off somewhere," he explains, pinpointing one particularly successful element of franchise mobile mania. Quick-lube and tune-up vans service vehicles wherever their owners have them parked. They also often offer oil changes, maintenance checks, plus customized interior and exterior detailing.

The IFA also notes that consumers pour billions of dollars into a wide array of home-delivered franchise services each year. They range from pet care to physician's visits. Doctors to Your Door is a referral service headquartered in Louisville, Kentucky. It scheduled about 20,000 house calls in 1990, bridging the gap between the at-home patient and the community of physicians. Doctors treat elderly shut-ins and others who are confined to home. With our aging population, health help on wheels is a wave of the future.

It's been said that moving targets are the hardest to hit. But in today's business world, moving targets are some of the biggest hits!

Consider Selling Franchises

Franchising has been termed the hottest form of entrepreneurship. A study done by the Naisbitt Group for the International Franchise Association stated that franchising has long been at the forefront of the service sector. Fast food's share of the franchise pie has shrunk. In its place has emerged instant printing, business support services, real estate agencies, personal computer rentals, diet centers, and maid and janitorial services. Additional strong candidates include signmakers, auto lube and tune-up operations, pet service businesses, photofinishing, and remodeling firms—plus recreation, travel, and entertainment companies.

Service franchises are growing for two reasons, contends Bill Cherkasky. They're filling a need, and they are relatively easy to start. Futurist John Naisbitt says that in the next 25 years almost any service imaginable will be franchised.

Why should this interest you? Franchising is a sensible, lucrative way to expand a business. It allows you to go regional, national, even international, with very little capital. Yet returns can be great. Your income is based to a large degree on royalties computed from the franchisee's gross sales. Not profits mind you, but *gross* sales. These are easier to monitor than profits. With franchising you're not limited by your own capital or your ability to develop various locations. Additionally, you're relieved of day-to-day direct management responsibilities.

There are several criterion for a successful franchise operation: First, you must be profitable. No one wants to buy a piece of the action unless there is indeed a track record of proven action. Second, your business needs the ability to be replicated. This means a prototype that isn't too costly, nor the knowledge so specialized the average person couldn't learn it easily. Your profits will be eroded if you can't train franchisees in a reasonable length of time. In a word, it must be simple.

Third, you must have positioned yourself so you fill a specialized niche. There must be a point of difference from other similar enterprises. Fourth, the cost of buying a franchise must be affordable. Don't price yourself out of the market. If all of the above are a "go," consult an attorney or franchise consultant to get assistance in meeting all the federal regulations. Additional franchise information resources are listed in Part III.

Many service providers have already jumped on the franchise bandwagon. Mr. Sign Franchising Corp. is based in Bohemia, New York. Adia Personnel Services is headquartered in Menlo Park, California. In 1992 their net income grew by a whopping 45.3%. Omaha's The Maids International Inc. has 89 franchisees with 210 units. (It's safe to say "they've got it maid.") Dynamark Security Centers is a Hagerstown, Maryland, chain that markets residential and light commercial systems. Video Data Services is one of the nation's fastest-growing franchises. The Pittsford, New York, franchisor has 250 units.

Typifying Naisbitt's comment that virtually anything can and will be franchised is Gene's Canine Waste Removal Company. It has expanded from Syracuse, New York, to franchises in Rochester and Binghamton, New York, to Portland, Oregon. You might know their phone number would be (800) 876-DODO.

Although government regulation inhibits strong growth for franchising in the health industry, specialized areas still show promise. Private-duty nursing, dentistry, optometry, and dermatology will lend themselves to franchising.

Additional Innovative Ideas

Want to attract customers like bears to a honey pot? Following is a potpourri of ideas for capturing more sales or making your patients, customers, or clients feel better.

Did you realize the local newspaper may be your route to increased business? Why not read 'em and reap? A diaper service scours the paper to learn of new births. How better to find a fresh list of perfectly targeted clients? A bridal service picks up leads by reading the engagements section. Wiley real estate agents might determine likely people to list their houses by watching the divorce or obituary columns.

All of us like recognition. Are you looking for ways to make those you help feel important? A school could give a diploma or certificate of completion—then take a photograph of all graduates and submit it to the newspaper. Speaking of pictures, how about snapshots of your patient? Many clever health professionals have a "rogues' gallery" of beaming patients decorating their waiting room or office walls.

Maybe you can make your customers or clients feel important by providing them with a collector's item. Artists offer special limited editions—numbered of course. Authors can do the same, plus provide personally autographed copies of their books. This also works well for speakers, who can autograph books they sell at the back of the room.

A few health care institutions sponsor clubs. Over 10,000 people belong to Health Express at Lee Memorial Hospital in Fort Myers, Florida. Members get a card, discounts on certain outpatient services, and a steady stream of mail from the hospital.

In some cases, sales representatives extend the merchandising arm of service providers. This is more true in business and industrial settings. Aggressive reps have been known to change a lackluster operation into a sell-raising outfit. Salespeople, however, can turn their energies on and off like a water tap. They must be constantly stimulated. We talk more about this in Chapter 9, Employee Motivation: Crucial to Your Success.

Although many business-to-business companies use cash or merchandise to tantalize other firms, there are more innovative ways to kindle responses. KBIG radio in Los Angeles bills its easy-listening format with an "Unwind and Relax with K-BIG" theme. To woo advertising agency personnel, it distributed large, brass, wind-up keys to media buyers. These made attractive paper weights. In addition, the keys were consecutively numbered and packaged in attractive leather pouches. Accompanying each key was an invitation to join the K-BIG Unwind Club. Recipients were not obliged to buy anything, simply complete and return the cards, which entitled them to be eligible for periodic prize drawings. There was a 100% response, plus most recipients either called the station to express their appreciation or thanked the sales rep in person!

Certainly you've gleaned many ideas on how to boost your sales in this chapter. Now let's move on to examine the world of publicity. There awaits a myriad of choices to focus free attention on yourself and your services.

6

Publicity: Dozens of Free Ways to Attract Media Attention and Gain Clout

Many service providers think advertising is the answer to their prayers. Those who subscribe to this theory miss the most viable business-generating medium of all. Remember the phenomenal success of the pet rock years ago? Not a penny was spent to advertise this product; it was all accomplished through publicity!

An article in *Business Marketing* points out editorial coverage is typically at least twice as credible as advertising. In most cases, the public relations cost of placing the story is about one-third the cost of equivalent advertising. Yes, for organizations with budgets as tight as shrink-to-fit jeans, the answer is publicity.

Men and women in professional practice are recognizing this is the way to bring home the bacon. Once viewed as a questionable activity by many CPA firms, public relations has—according to the firms themselves—evolved into a necessary function in today's competitive business environment. Law firms are exchanging country club selling for more creative forms of business development. Those who market nonprofits are also sensitive to public relation's (PR's) merits. The beauty is anyone who knowledgeably and methodically goes after media attention can share in the windfall.

In this chapter we provide the know-how; you have to consciously apply it. You'll be given tips on how to master the art of creating effective news releases and press conferences. Articles, columns, and "op-ed" pieces give you instant visibility and credibility. Discover here how to work this facet of PR. And we reveal success secrets for booking radio interviews—then show you how to make listeners want your service. Creative networking activities are also probed. So is preparing a company-sponsored book to focus public attention on your organization. We can't teach you to charm the lard off a hog, but we can give you the skills to competently publicize what you do.

We'll look at a variety of PR techniques. These are free or inexpensive ways to get your organization noticed. A good PR practitioner approaches his or her task like a good plumber. The same tool isn't used for every job. One time a plunger might do it; the next it takes a snake or even an air jetter. But one way or another, the blockage is eliminated and the flow reestablished. That's the purpose of public relations: to accomplish a constant flow of exposure for you.

News Releases
That Add Pizzazz Without Puff

Editors readily admit the majority of what you read in newspapers and magazines is the result of information provided by outside sources. They depend on "news releases" (also called "press releases") to keep them abreast of industry happenings. It's estimated 70% of all news is planted. Releases can also lead to articles, a subject we treat later in this chapter.

The first ingredient of a news release is news. Although this sounds like a simplistic statement, it pinpoints the reason many never get into print. When information is old, it isn't news. It is history. When a piece is too self-serving, it also isn't news. It's puffery.

What are some newsworthy topics? Openings, expansions, moves, new services added, community activities, contests sponsored, awards received—even election to regional or national office of one of the principals. Company milestones—such as a 10th, 25th, or 100th anniversary—are appropriate for stories. If a company official or firm partner gives a speech, this can often be parlayed into news. Another angle for coverage is studies or surveys conducted and trend forecasts.

Such pieces solidify your credibility. They provide an ideal, low-key reason to get in front of prospects and should be used as a mailing for anyone you're trying to woo. Also send copies to current clients or customers. Use them as enclosures in virtually everything you mail. And when soliciting additional publicity, include what has already been done. This helps establish your newsworthiness. Some firms even have prestigious articles matted and framed to hang in their offices.

Using the written word in other ways can assure you of more windfall visibility. How about Letters to the Editor? These are well read platforms for getting your message, and your name, into the public's consciousness. Op-Ed pieces, which are run in larger newspapers opposite the editorial page, do the same. These are essays about area concerns or timely topics. Or you may want to develop a flyer, quiz, or booklet of self-help information to be used as a giveaway. Professionals often find newsletters to be viable PR tools.

TOPICS FOR NEWS RELEASES

✓ The opening of your store, firm, or office

✓ Announcement of new management

✓ An anniversary

✓ The hiring, or promotion, of a key staff member

✓ Being awarded a new contract

✓ Business expansion or remodeling

✓ Adding a new type of service(s)

✓ The owner receiving an award, accreditation, or other honor

✓ Timely tie-ins with national holidays

✓ Demonstrations, open houses

✓ Appointment or election to a board of directors

✓ Financial news

✓ Having an article or book published

✓ Special event or contest announcement

✓ Trend evaluations or reports

✓ Controversial rebuttals

When writing releases, there are several things to consider. You never know how much of what you submit will be used. For that reason, it is important to get the primary details at the beginning. The five "W's"—who, what, when, where, and why—should be contained in the first paragraph or two. When editors are short on space, they cut releases from the bottom up. Although some editors rewrite releases, many are too harried to do so. A good release will be printed virtually as is; a bad one hits the round file.

This medium demands short, snappy copy. If you can state a problem or concern with which the editor and readers can identify—and how you can solve it—your chances for acceptance are better. Begin with an intriguing statement, startling statistic, or provocative question. Add supportive information in a descending order. The goal is to get your message across no matter how much is sliced off the bottom.

One workable way to give your release fresh pizzazz is to use quotes. To make a release sound like promotional copy is to announce its death. However, a health care official or law partner, for instance, can present material in a quotation that wouldn't be acceptable in normal text. This lends variety and believability.

Carefully hone a headline that commands attention. We suggest doing your headline at the end because after you've written the whole release, it will be easier to come up with a punchy headline. Put it in capital letters and add the other elements as shown in the accompanying example.

With computers, it is easy to customize releases for different media. Doing a versioned news release only entails altering the headline and first paragraph. Then you have a message specifically tailored for each recipient.

Presentation is important. Type your release on letterhead, or have it printed on stationery. Use the format we've shown. News releases, by the way, should not exceed two double-spaced typed pages; one-pagers often are better. (We sometimes cheat and use 1½ spacing to keep them on one page.)

There are things you can include to increase your chances of being selected for publication. One is an appropriate photograph. (We will talk more about that in a minute.) Another is a clip sheet of reproducible art work. This might include your logo, an illustration, or other camera-ready art. Two excellent books on writing releases and working with the press are *The Publicity Manual* by Kate Kelly and *The Publicity Handbook* by David Yale. Both can be ordered from us. To help our readers obtain hard-to-find books, and the many useful resources we talk about in this volume, we offer easy one-stop shopping. Just turn to the Recommended Reading section.

News Release Sample

NEWS RELEASE   NEWS RELEASE   NEWS RELEASE

For Immediate Release
Contact: Ann Markham
719-395-8659

Urban to Rural Paradigm Shift Captures Imagination of Millions

A movement is afoot. As the stress of urban living continues to escalate, more Americans are opting for the safety, serenity, and quality of life in Small Town USA. Cashing Out to the Country is one of the top 10 trends of the decade. While not practical a dozen years ago, today's technology cuts the financial ties that traditionally tethered people to big cities.

Information Age entrepreneurs and professionals are footloose "lone eagles" who need only a computer and access to an airport to make a living. This new breed of Americans includes stock brokers, manufacturing reps, software companies, writers, telemarketers, consultants, and others who live by their wits—anywhere they choose.

A one-of-a-kind book, *Country Bound!*™ *Trade Your Business Suit Blues for Blue Jean Dreams*™, shows them how to make that choice—and the ensuing transition—painlessly and profitably. Co-author Marilyn Ross says, "The once protective corporate umbrella is in tatters. Jobs are unstable and mediocre. Downsizing is a curse that cuts across all lines. Each month almost 40,000 jobs are lost to cutbacks, mergers, and acquisitions. Sadly, most of these corporate rejects are capable, intelligent people in the prime of their careers." Tom Ross observes, "Many are turning adversity into opportunity by moving their families where they can live better on less and launch exciting new careers."

For people who hunger to put down roots and feel a real sense of community, *Country Bound!*™ serves as a lifestyle guide as well as a business resource. No other book addresses the specific topic of earning a living in the country. Its 433 pages are chock-full of advice on how to liberate yourself from the crushing metropolitan madness. The Rosses should know. They made their pilgrimage from southern California to a quiet Rocky Mountain town in 1980. They write of their mistakes and their triumphs, providing readers with rare insight into what works—and what doesn't. The book is available in bookstores or for $19.95 + $3 shipping from Communication Creativity, Box 909-N, Buena Vista, CO 81211. Call credit card orders to 1-800-331-8355.

NOTE: Rural relocation experts Tom and Marilyn Ross are provocative interviewees.
Call the above number to schedule them. Book and author photos available on request.

P.O. Box 909, 425 Cedar Street, Buena Vista, CO 81211-0909 ● (719) 395-8659

To whom do you send this package? That depends. If you offer business services, the business editor of the closest major daily would be appropriate. A window-washing business would do better contacting the scene, women's, or lifestyle editor. If in doubt, go to the managing editor. Spend time updating your mailing list before embarking on a campaign. The most carefully developed release is useless unless it is delivered into the hands of the proper people.

We've discovered an excellent way to obtain the names of appropriate newspaper editors. One of our associates created a questionnaire she faxes to various newspapers. (See adjacent sample.) They have been most gracious in faxing us return information. In fact, the response rate is an astounding 55%. This allows them to respond at a time convenient for them—and gives us current names for key people to contact.

Our technological age has now made possible video news releases (VNR). This allows you to spread the word visually. Because of costs, these are beyond the reach of most businesses. They can run as little as $2,000, or as much as $25,000 to produce. By the way, some companies are now using videos as sales tools. In just 11 or 12 minutes they can provide prospects with more information than if they filled volumes with print. And its an exciting and little used medium.

If you decide to consider this alternative, before choosing a producer, look at demo reels that relate to your industry, service, or objective. Finding one individual who can write, direct, and produce a VNR is the perfect combination. It is also helpful if he or she has a background in broadcast news. There is no point in creating a spectacular VNR if it never airs. A VNR must be designed not only to inform, but also to promote, influence, and motivate. A list of VNR companies appear in Part III.

Photographs Help Emphasize Your Importance

Photographs are prime tools in a clever PR effort. Let's look at photo releases, which are closely related to the typical print news release. They consist of an attention-grabbing photo combined with a tightly written caption.

There are tough editorial standards here. Editors want quality pictures that project clarity, simplicity, and creativity. They prefer action and human interest shots. In some cases using a visual element to establish size and scale will win their favor. Suggest the photographer add new interest by changing his or her point of view. Shoot down from a ladder or up from floor level. This adds a fresh perspective to your presentation.

Fax "Facts" Form

ACCELERATED BUSINESS IMAGES

Abi

PHONE (719) 395-2459 · (800) 548-1876
P.O. BOX 1500 · 425 CEDAR STREET · BUENA VISTA, CO 81211
FAX (719) 395-8374

FAX "FACTS"

From: _____   Fax #: (719) 395-8374   Voice phone: (719) 395-2459

Date: _____   Time: _____AM / PM   Total number of pages: _____

PLEASE PROVIDE OR VERIFY THE FOLLOWING INFORMATION BY RETURN FAX
If you have this information available in another format, feel free to submit it rather than filling out this form.
Name of Paper:
Mailing Address:

Telephone Number:_____**Fax Number:**_____

Name of the Following Editor: **Telephone Extension:**
Book Review Editor:_____
Business:_____
Lifestyle/Scene:_____
Op-Ed:_____
Writing/Publishing:_____
Sports/Recreation:_____
Health:_____
Religion:_____
Food:_____
Features:_____
Entertainment:_____
Librarian:_____

Name of person submitting information:_____**Phone:**_____
k\misc\other\newsbeat.doc

A few shrewd people arrange to be photographed in the presence of someone important. This is a reverse twist of "guilt by association." The idea is people will perceive them as important because they are in the same photograph with a dignitary or celebrity.

Although most photo requirements are black and white, a stunning color shot might capture a magazine cover position. These are coveted. One editor estimates the cover photo subject typically out pulls the average interior black and white photo subject four to one.

It is wise not to use people in your pictures until they have signed a model release. Your attorney can easily provide one. This even goes for photos that show a customer or client.

Once the photo has fueled the reader's interest, it's the caption's job to leverage that interest into an inquiry or an order. Use an economy of words. Choose colorful, arresting ones. Be sure your company name is included in the caption. Always affix a label to the back of your photo that states what the picture is of, so if it is separated from your other materials they can be reunited.

Holding a Press Conference

Hosting a press conference sounds glamorous and important. In reality, it's a lot of work and could be the *wrong* move. Before talking about how to pull off such a feat, let's talk about why you might not want to. Editors are deluged with invitations to these events. Many of them are dog-and-pony shows: just plain bor-ring! You don't want to get such a reputation with the media. So unless you have something truly newsworthy, stick with a news release or photo release.

Perhaps you should consider an intermediate visual strategy. That's what Pamela Kostmayer, a Washington, DC, PR pro did. She represented a group of California apparel makers and importers who opposed a bill designed to restrict textile imports. Kostmayer dressed a delivery person in a panda suit and delivered teddy bears to every lawmaker on Capital Hill. The bears carried current price tags—and higher ones that would have to go into effect if the proposed legislation went into effect. This was followed up with socks cautioning the bill would "sock it to America." Lastly, neckerchiefs warned the legislation would "choke the American farmer." The visual gimmicks attracted attention and paved the way for lobbyists working against the bill to present their story.

For those who deem their news of significant value to warrant a press conference, here are some clues: Pay particular attention to when you schedule your event. Check out pending local activities to avoid going head-to-head with something—or someone—else of note. (No one will come to your press conference if the Pope is arriving or a well-liked area legislator is announcing his or her intention to run for governor.) Call the Associated Press and United Press International area bureau closest to you and check their "day book" for conflicts. You can get their local numbers in the telephone directory.

Your choice of location will also influence participation. Rather than the usual hotel conference room, consider something different. What about a historical mansion, museum, or yacht setting? Don't book a meeting place sight unseen, however. Mirrored walls will play havoc with TV lighting. Pillars are hard to work around. Also consider noise problems. An air-conditioner that sounds like a jet engine will drown out your carefully prepared remarks. Says Rich Merritt, a former editor at Chilton Company, "Editors feel obligated to do a story to justify the time they have invested in the meeting." What that tells us is your biggest challenge may be getting them there, not what goes on during the conference. Drive the main route to your site yourself to be sure there are no traffic hangups during the time slot you've planned.

Notify the media two to three weeks ahead of time. Include enough detail in your invitation letter so editors can intelligently determine whether your news affects their readers. Also include a SASE for their response.

On the day of the event, have plenty of staff available. While a couple of gracious secretaries can sign people in, company officials are needed to mingle and motivate. Friendships cultivated at such gatherings between editors and executives often result in future expert quotes or feature articles.

Editors will want to ask questions, challenge claims, and clarify points. In addition to a short verbal presentation, followed by a question and answer period, provide them with a media kit. Some sort of a souvenir of the occasion also goes over well if this commemorates a special event.

Creating a Media Kit

A media kit—also called a "press kit"—is to a PR person what the black bag was to the old-time doctor. It is an organized collection of all the materials that may interest a member of the media.

Information is typically inserted into colored folders with two pockets. While some firms have customized folders printed, a label affixed to the front will work to identify your company. Attach your business card to one of the inner pockets.

Flexible in nature, press kit contents vary with the occasion. The backbone is your brochure. There are several other pieces of promotional literature that can complement this. In some industries, a corporate or organization profile is called for. Such background information is useful to editors in fleshing out their stories. This essentially gives a history of how the firm originated and what it's primary focus is. It may also hint at future plans.

A personal biography of the CEO, senior partners, or executive director may also be appropriate. Pertinent photos are appreciated by editors. This is a good place to make use of any previous publicity you've garnered. Include copies of articles by or about you. Such third-party endorsements always carry extra clout.

Good news bears repeating. "Reprints have been a wonderful marketing tool for us," says Kirk Perron, the owner of a San Luis Obispo, California, chain of blended-to-order smoothie shops called the Juice Club.

Newspaper and magazine articles are often missed the first time around. Yet articles make people think your company is important and unique because the publication chose to write about you. Obtaining reprints provides a way for you to make sure existing and potential clients, customers, suppliers, bankers, stockholders, etc. get a look. Most magazines offer a reprinting service for somewhere between 75 cents and $1 apiece for a four-color reprint. Have them add your logo, address, and phone number for added impact. Also consider framing a copy and hanging it in your reception area, restaurant, or shop.

When putting together your media kit, don't overlook pieces authored by others—even if they don't mention you. If they make a good case in support of your cause or service suggestion, they can be useful in winning attention. Of course, a news release highlighting the main reason for the event is a necessity.

But you often don't need a fancy media kit when seeking exposure. Consider providing an entire feature about yourself. This makes the reporters job so easy! Pack it with juicy quotes and include black and white glossies. It's best to center such stories around a timeless topic. This is called an "evergreen" piece.

A simple, one-page Fact Sheet can also be useful. Include a description of your service, information about the primary spokesperson, and how to reach you. This is ideal because it can be faxed to peak a media person's interest.

Another approach we've found that works well is to devise a postcard. Create a colorful photo or illustration for one side, put a brief description on the other, and leave room for a short message. Notice the adjacent one we did for our book, *Country Bound!*™. Good prices can be obtained from Getz & McGrew Lithography, Inc. at (800) 899-0707. We often send the postcard (needing only 19 cents postage) first as a qualifier, then follow up with the full-blown media kit when people respond.

COUNTRY BOUND!™ Postcard

MARILYN and TOM ROSS

COUNTRY BOUND!

Trade Your
Business Suit Blues for Blue Jean Dreams™

POSTCARD

Country Bound!™ by Marilyn and Tom Ross shows how to "trade your business suit blues for blue jean dreams"—how to escape the big city rat race, earn a good living in the country, and experience a better quality of life. Published by Communication Creativity, Box 909-PC, Buena Vista, CO 81211, 1-800-331-8355. $19.95. ISBN 0-918880-30-0, 433-page 6 x 9" trade paperback. Indexed. Quizzes, maps, tables, charts, checklists.

Using Letters to the Editor and "Op-ed" Pages

Writing letters to the editor provides a less demanding method for attracting attention. Rather than being bound to a schedule, you simply submit a short letter in response to timely local issues or events in the news. Done on a fairly regular basis, this helps establish you as a mover and shaker in the community. Be sure not only to end the letters with your name, but also to include your business or organization affiliation. Not all papers will publish this but some may.

Many people think because letters to the editor are short, they are easy. Nothing could be further from the truth. It is much harder to distill your message into 150 words than it is to strew it over three or four pages. Every word serves a purpose in letters to the editor. It's an outstanding training ground for developing a forceful, pithy writing style.

Another editorial showcase possibility is electronic media. We've all heard the general manager of a TV or radio station spout the station's position on a certain issue. Perhaps you've never tuned in to the comment that follows: "This station welcomes opposing views from responsible spokespersons." Does this give you any ideas? If what they said peaks your professional interest—and makes you bristle—this could be a wonderful opportunity to get thousands of dollars worth of free air time. Those with a genuine concern and a desire for higher visibility should write the station and request an airing.

Newspaper op-ed pages are a misunderstood and underused publicity vehicle. This is a page, opposite the editorial page, that appears in most major dailies. If you're seeking instant visibility, it may be your answer.

Newspapers have an immediacy and decide on your contribution in days or weeks rather than the several months it takes to place a magazine article. In some instances you can self-syndicate your piece, offering exclusive rights to different geographic regions. Although some papers have no provision to compensate contributors of these 500-to 700-word pieces, others pay as much as $250 for a column.

Op-ed pieces are perfect for associations or agencies that want to showcase or lobby their cause. As recognized experts in their fields, executive directors and government spokespersons can offer pertinent and insightful commentary on events, issues, surveys, or trends effecting their areas.

Professionals and entrepreneurs can also gain more respect and be seen as having more clout by authoring an op-ed piece. Here again, reprints make impressive additions to proposals aimed at investors, bankers, customers, clients, or the media. To learn how and where to submit contributions, get our *National Directory of Newspaper Op-Ed Pages* by Marilyn Ross. Order it for $19.95 plus $3 shipping from Communication Creativity, Box 909-BI, Buena Vista, CO 81211, or call (800) 331-8355.

Editors of op-ed pages welcome commentaries on a wide array of topics. The *Long Beach Press Telegram,* for instance, is interested in women's issues. (Is your agency involved with abuse? Has your child-care center come up with an innovative idea? Do you speak about female executives penetrating the glass ceiling? If so, this is a perfect place to share your professional views.) While the *New York Times* seeks material on topical issues, the *Dallas Morning News* wants "hard-edged public affairs and issue-oriented columns." The *San Diego Daily Transcript* pursues only legal, real estate, or financial topics. Avoid subjects of national prominence, however, as these are typically covered by regular syndicated columnists.

Contributing Articles and Columns

A large California CPA firm indicated it had received "tangible referrals on new clients from articles in the press." Professional speakers and seminar givers credit published articles as opening new avenues for speaking engagements. Consultants successfully prospect for new clients by contributing articles to targeted publications.

You are an expert in your field. Why not capitalize on your specialized knowledge by publishing articles about this subject you know so well? It will give you visibility, credibility, and profitability.

There are several types of possible articles. How-to's are one of the easiest. You simply provide step-by-step instruction on how to accomplish something. Some people fear if they do this, they will lose business instead of gaining it, because they are revealing their trade secrets. Quite the contrary. Most people recognize there is specialized expertise involved and that you are a bona fide authority. Thus, you position yourself as a leader in the industry—someone they want working for them.

We've found this to be the case time after time. Providing complimentary articles is an important facet of Accelerated Business

Images' publicity program. Never have we been shortcircuited when openly sharing our skills. In fact, our largest client came to us as a result of a how-to article.

Another popular article format is the case history. It explains how your service was used by a client or customer to solve a problem. It traces the path of an actual satisfied user. (Be sure to get their permission to write about them, however.)

Round-up articles are another common approach. This is a collection of several similar situations. It might offer an industry overview featuring input from you and two or three colleagues. Or it could be about several of your clients/customers and their different applications of your service. It may address the same subject, but from far-flung geographical locations. How mental health practices differ in the United States, Canada, and England, for instance.

Still another approach is the personality profile. Many airline magazines, trade journals, and general business publications run stories about colorful CEOs and entrepreneurs. This is a great way to publicize a star in your organization. As that person becomes a symbol, your company gains a special identity. The drive and uniqueness of that individual may be an ideal peg on which to hang your publicity.

A further recommendation is to contact likely magazines and ask for a copy of their annual editorial calendar. This pinpoints the major topics they will be discussing in future editions. When you see a subject that correlates with what you do, think about article slants. Then contact the managing editor about your idea.

Finally, seek ways to align your organization with a "hot" issue already in the news. Then you can piggyback on the attention it incites. A fast-thinking real estate agent did just that when Wall Street took a dive on "Black Monday" in 1987. She told the media how her phone was constantly ringing with people who were bailing out of the stock market and were looking into real estate investments.

Although articles can, of course, be offered for sale, it usually works best to donate them. Before writing a complete piece, you may want to send a *query letter*. This is a one-page sales letter explaining the scope of your proposed article, your credentials for writing it, and citing why it will appeal to the publication's readership.

When a respected publication prints information about a company, it is as if the editor were endorsing the company. This effectively sells prospects on the firm's reputation, quality, reliability, and expertise. It is a proven way to promote intangibles. It sets the company apart from its competitors and creates instant credibility.

Although a story in *Forbes* or *Fortune* is understandably craved by business entities, this is an area where "little things can mean a lot." The client we previously spoke of came to us, not as a result of a powerhouse publication, but from something placed in a carefully targeted newsletter—with a circulation of less than 5,000!

Of course, you're not providing your article without getting something in return. Strike a deal that they will list information about how to reach you at the end of the piece. Some aggressive types ask for more. They bargain for a free display ad to run in the same edition as well.

Sadly, some marketing types feel their job is done when the article appears. This assumption cheats them out of at least half the benefits! Once an article is published, response will (hopefully) be swift and rewarding. However, it shouldn't end there. Reprints are versatile sales aids. Because they carry the editor's implied endorsements, they are inherently more believable than company-produced advertising and promotional items.

Writing a regular newspaper column is another excellent way to focus attention on what you have to offer. This is especially viable for doctors, financial experts, and attorneys who want to expand their practices. It can also apply to owners of service businesses who could provide consumer information—cleaning tips or automobile maintenance, for instance. Do be aware, however, that a column means repetitive work. As opposed to a feature article, column material must be churned out every week and by a strict deadline. Be sure you have enough to say and the time to say it before you commit to 52 columns a year!

If you haven't backed off with that admonition, let's discuss how to go about launching a column. As in any selling situation, you must have a product. Your first task is to decide the slant your column will take and christen it with a name. Now write four or five samples of 500 to 700 words. Think carefully about what you will say. This must be your most excellent work: especially meaty or entertaining. If you're like most neophytes, you'll overwrite. So go back and tighten. Hone your work to a fine edge.

Think locally at first. Put together a package to mail to the managing editor or city editor. Besides your sample columns, it should contain a powerful cover letter explaining these are free test columns and justifying why they will be of interest to readers. Also include tear sheets of any previously published pieces, testimonial letters you've gathered over the years from editors or readers, plus a SASE. If you don't hear anything in two weeks, call and try to set up an appointment.

Once you have established a track record with a local paper, it may be possible to broaden your horizons. Some writers self-syndicate their columns to additional papers; others approach national syndicates to take on their material. Frankly, both are difficult to do. Dr. Morton Walker, a podiatrist, succeeded in syndicating his health column.

Producing a Book Garners Goodwill and New Business

Suppose you've followed the above advice. What's to be gained by taking that a step further and putting your expertise between book covers? Plenty! Books offer unprecedented opportunities. Having one enhances your reputation, gives you a new promotional tool, and provides a fresh profit center.

You can use a book to position yourself and create new opportunities. Print has permanency. Books can lead to fame and fortune. The general public perceives authors as experts. When you've written a book, you are considered *the authority*. This positions you above the competition and gives you more clout in the minds of your prospects. Not only does having a book lay the groundwork for securing more work, it many allow you to command higher fees.

Some consultants and speakers, for instance, use a book as their calling card instead of a brochure. Brochures are tossed. Promotional kits hit the round file. Books, on the other hand, aren't thrown away. Instead they are placed on bookshelves where they may be readily retrieved whenever a need arises. Meanwhile, they serve as impressive reminders of who you are and your area of expertise.

Prestige, however, is only part of the payback. Your book is a wonderful passive income generator. Once it's done and properly promoted, it earns money for you month after month and year after year—while you're out of the office doing your thing. During tough times, this residual income can mean the difference between profit and loss, survival or extinction.

A further advantage to having a book is that it is a time saver. When a client calls to discuss your area of expertise, instead of taking the time on the phone to explain every nuance of what you do, simply promise to send the prospect a complimentary book. This creates a powerful impression as well as provides a wealth of information.

And if you've handled the publishing arrangements astutely, you can sell large quantities of your books to corporate clients or when you speak and make a bundle of money. Organizations who have hired you are already "sold." Convincing them to purchase your book for internal training reinforcement—as gifts to give to their customers—or to use as a prospecting tool to attract new business are all possibilities.

To give your book direction, create a mission statement for it just as you did when starting your business. It needn't be lengthy. The more focused, the better. Twenty to 40 words that target your audience and encapsulate your message is ideal. Here's the one for our previous book: "*Country Bound!*™ will help urban residents realize their vision to escape big city hassles, earn a good livelihood in the country, and experience enhanced quality of life."

Now create an outline or a table of contents. Group likely topics together and put them in the most logical order. If you have two or three main headings with many sub-headings, perhaps a Part I, Part II, Part III format would make it easier for readers to grasp your message.

Don't become preoccupied with trying to start writing from chapter one. Commence with whatever is easiest and most interesting to you. This gets you into the flow and releases your creative juices. Then after you're more comfortable with the written word, come back and create a dynamite beginning to hook readers.

It's a good idea to write the Introduction early since this sets the stage for the whole book. An Introduction tells the scope of the work and shows how people will benefit from reading it. It also keeps you focused. As in visiting the dentist, so in writing—brief is better than lengthy. Lean sentences are the most inviting to read. So are concise paragraphs. Use short, pithy words. This isn't the time to parade your scholarly vocabulary! It's a place to communicate. Easily. Swiftly. Effectively. Spice your pages with case histories, anecdotes, stories, jokes, similes or metaphors, checklists, samples, examples of what works . . . and what doesn't. Such flavoring gives your message zest. For helpful free book writing guidelines, send a SASE with 52 cents postage to: Nine Ways, About Books, Inc., Box 1500-BI, Buena Vista, CO 81211.

One approach some of our clients use is to dictate their thoughts, have the tape transcribed, then partially clean up the manuscript pages before sending it to us for editing. This doesn't require a large time commitment, nor the ability to be an experienced wordcrafter. Weaving a compelling book is no easy task. If you hire someone to write your book, be sure he or she has the skill to leave your mental fingerprints. The book should be written in *your* voice; it must be an extension of your personality and mannerisms.

But perhaps you already have the guts of a book. Have you written several articles or a column? Often these can be linked together and repackaged into an anthology. Collect similar topics under group headings and write transitions to bridge from one piece to the next. If you don't have such a foundation already laid, maybe now's the time to begin.

The company- or association-sponsored book holds much promise. It often takes the form of a corporate history or a biography of the founder or CEO. (It worked so well for Iacocca, people actually went into Chrysler showrooms clutching his book and saying, "I want to buy a car from the guy who wrote this book.")

Some other examples of this type of publicity include *The Safeco Story* (insurance), *The Only Way to Fly, The Story of Western Airlines, America's Senior Air Carrier, Marriott, The Story of Western International Hotels* and *Firstbank: The Story of Seattle-First National Bank.*

Like the genealogy of a family, these stories document the life of a business. Whether for a corporate giant—or a small, family-owned business—such biographies capture forever the people, the frustrations, and the triumphs of commerce.

These corporate profiles are especially appropriate for 25-, 50-, or 100-year anniversaries. Not only are they ideal stockholder gifts, they heighten company pride when given to employees and create customer/client goodwill when presented to constituents. Some also do well in traditional bookstores. Corporate histories have been published by Rand McNally, the Dial Press, Doubleday, even Harper & Row.

Books are also used by some firms as a more aggressive prospecting tool. Usually these are created as how-to booklets or books designed to help/educate prospective clients or customers. This is a tried and true way to separate prospects from suspects.

Media Distribution Services, which performs media and mailing services in the PR field, offers free copies of *The Pocket Media Guide.* Along with it comes a sales letter explaining their various services. *How to Protect Your Business* was produced by the Better Business Bureau.

Chesebrough-Pond's recently commissioned *Great Italian Cooking Starts with Ragu.*

And AT&T advertises free copies of their *The Moving Book,* which is designed as a personal guide to a more organized move. Interlaced among the moving tips are subtle plugs for you know who A smart moving and storage company could produce a similar "Moving Checklist." Those who request it are prime leads as they wouldn't be asking for one unless they anticipated a move. Why not have a salesperson offer to deliver the checklist in person?

Jam-packed with useful information is Quill Corporation's *How to Save Money on Office Supplies.* It arrives in the mailbox of those who request it accompanied by a strong sales letter telling how Quill will save you money, guarantee it's quality, and offer "we care" service. (We've found they live up to all three claims, by the way.)

These company-sponsored premium books are offered as "bait" to encourage prospects to raise their hands and identify themselves. The leads are then followed up by mail, by telephone, or in person. "Books are a wonderful vehicle for a message," says Ray Benjamin of The Benjamin Company. "It is a medium which is so effective that almost any sensible company in America or abroad should consider it."

Of course, writing and producing a company book seems like a herculean task to most people. Our sister company, About Books, Inc., specializes in researching, writing, and publishing such products. For more information, write Box 1500-BI, Buena Vista, CO 81211, or call (719) 395-2459.

A decade ago, we did a book for the owner of a dating service. When *How to Single Out Your Mate: A Guide for Twogetherness in the '80s* came out, the author's business receipts jumped substantially. Yes, "bound messages" are often sound investments.

The two primary ways to get into print are turning to a trade publisher—such as Simon and Schuster, John Wiley & Sons, or William Morrow Company—or doing it yourself (self-publishing). These days, trade publishers accept few newcomers. Many authors are enamored by the idea of affiliating with a well-known trade publisher. While this may give some added credibility, knowledgeable professionals often decide what must be sacrificed isn't worth the trade.

First, we're entrepreneurial souls. We like to be in charge, to control our own destinies. Second, we like to make things happen (not wait for a year and a half while a trade publisher gets our book in print). Third, we're businesspeople; we look at the bottom line. If we can see we'll make more money doing things ourselves, that's the approach we take.

Here's the reality of going with a trade publisher: Unless you're the likes of Stephen Covey, Melody Beattie, or Tom Peters—your book won't get much promotional support. But since you've signed over all rights to the publisher you no longer have the power to influence its destiny. Even if you pour your own money into an author tour to publicize your new baby, there's no guarantee the publisher will even have books in the bookstores!

Now let's talk money. The typical first-time non-fiction author can anticipate an advance of somewhere between $3,000 and $7,000. Understand this is an advance *against* royalties. That means unless your book earns out the advance, this initial advance payment is *all* you will ever see for your work. According to Joni Evans, the former executive vice president and publisher of Random House, "Only 10% of the books published by any house earn out their advances." It is for these reasons many are choosing to publish their own books today.

For them, self-publishing is indeed the "write" way to success. With this method, you invest in your own book and reap all the rewards. You keep control and turn out a product in mere months. For those who don't have the time or inclination to actually do everything personally, turnkey consultants such as ourselves are available to handle all the details. For complete information to clarify and de-mystify the process, get our *Complete Guide to Self-Publishing* (see ordering information in Recommended Reading).

A book equals more jobs, more revenue, more exposure. It gives you a reason to be "news"—to gain exposure not only for your writing, but also for your other accomplishments. By packaging your knowledge between covers, you'll have greater visibility, credibility, and profitability.

Using Radio to Promote Your Service or Practice

The most effective radio programs are interview shows and news features. Early morning and late afternoon drive times, when folks are traveling to and from work, are the first choice. Midday programs are good for some audiences. Of course, a lot depends on the host. Some have vast listening audiences even during bad hours because they are talented, controversial, and dynamic people.

Imagine for a moment what a 30-minute commercial would cost—not 30 seconds, 30 *minutes*. Do you realize if the host likes you and things go well, in essence you get that? It won't cost one red cent! The beauty of publicity demonstrated again.

Radio-programming is not normally scheduled as far in advance as television. Your mailings can go out as little as four weeks in advance of your being in the area. To solicit appearing as a guest, your media kit should be addressed to the producer of an individual show or, if in doubt which show would be best, the station program director. After a couple of weeks, follow up by phone. Once again, be politely persistent.

When an interview is scheduled, ask questions. Find out what they want to cover. Suggest areas you'd like to touch on during the show. You may get insights into the personality of the host or hostess and some hint about the slant needed to put yourself and your cause in the most favorable light. A comprehensive book on the subject is *Getting Your Message Out* by Michael M. Klepper. It tells how to get, use, and survive radio and television air time.

Shows come in several types and hosts come in various degrees of preparedness. Some interviewers will not have bothered to bone up at all. Others pride themselves on being informed on their guest's subjects and will chat at length about specific aspects of your industry. One thing to remember when doing radio is that your voice must do all the work. A smile is important; it *does* carry over a microphone.

By having in mind a clearly defined agenda that you wish to explore, you'll cut through apprehension like a hot knife through butter. Make specific notes of the points you want to cover. Some people even prepare a list of questions to provide interviewers. Anticipate in advance the questions you're likely to get; don't dodge the difficult ones. Then you won't be surprised when you're thrown a "zinger." Train yourself to expect the unexpected. Remember, you're the expert. Know your subject backward and forward. Rehearse your answers and comments to build your self-confidence. The key to successful interviewing is organization; it keeps you focused.

Be sure to speak in human terms; don't get mired in a bunch of statistics. Talk about how your service solves listeners' problems. Brief, clipped, precise answers are better than rambling replies. Mention the name of your company or agency several times; don't just say "we." The whole point of your being on the air is to increase your image and prospect for business. Listeners must know who you represent.

Suppose you get a sticky question—one that requires you to pause and gather your thoughts? Don't panic. Tricks we've used to stall for think time include either repeating the question or saying, "That's a good question . . . "

One other aspect of radio that could be very meaningful is public service announcements, better known as PSAs. If you are a nonprofit organization (by official structure, not happenstance), you are probably eligible for some of this air time. What a boon to churches, associations, and other not-for-profit groups who could benefit from unpaid commercials. This free time goes to those bold enough to seek it. If you qualify, get your share.

While we're talking about radio, there is another option if you don't have time to trot from station to station or you shudder at the thought of a microphone thrust in your face. Many radio programs conduct interviews via phone—from the comfort of your home or office. Syndicated and network shows often go to hundreds of stations. This is a superb way to get national exposure. Financial consultancies, law firms, or others with widespread locations might keep this in mind. Your library has media directories that give details on nationwide radio programming.

Television Interviewing

If the thought of being grilled by a television interviewer scares your socks off, don't be dismayed. This is common with many people we've worked with in the past. The world of television—studios behind closed doors, green rooms, cameras, bright lights, people rushing everywhere—is foreign to most people. (One way to become more at ease is to muster your bravado and join Toastmasters.)

Always contact TV stations in main metropolitan areas at least eight weeks before your availability date. Major network shows will require even longer lead times. Main libraries have directories in which you can prospect for appropriate shows. Call the producer's office to find out how far ahead their guests are booked, and ask the name of the producer or guest coordinator. Again your media kit will serve nicely as a door opener. Follow up if you haven't heard anything in a couple of weeks. As with all publicity, tenacity and repetition often turn the key.

Watching the shows you'll be on gives you a higher comfort level, as you'll know more what to expect. Role-playing with friends or family is also excellent training. Do you want to know exactly how you'll look and sound? Use a VCR or a mirror and tape recorder.

Think about your business and how it can be made interesting to television audiences. Offer suggestions to vary the normal interview format. A nutritionist might do a food demonstration on the air. An outfitter could give a demo on how to pack a backpack, whereas a florist has a natural visual opportunity to prepare a flower arrangement. Show and tell goes on in broadcasting as well as in kindergarten.

When dressing for television, avoid distracting plaids and busy stripes. Keep it simple. Women shouldn't wear glittering or jangly jewelry. Take your notes, visuals that you plan to use, a copy of any book you've authored, and a duplicate media kit along. Plan to arrive about a half-hour early. You'll be escorted to the "green room," where media guests wait. Ask someone for a glass of water if you feel tense. Take several deep breaths. Before air time, study your notes, psyche out probable questions, and rehearse your answers.

With this kind of preparation you're bound to have a good interviewing "presence." This is the quality every television producer seeks: someone who is relaxed but not sloppy, informed but not overbearing, vivacious but not silly. During the actual interview, ignore the camera and crew. Rivet your full attention on the person interviewing you. Resist the urge to fiddle with the mike, a handkerchief, or any other object. Keep your voice lively and assured. Smile—be friendly, articulate, enthusiastic.

Don't expect to start your television-interviewing career on "Oprah" or "Donahue' You must prove yourself first. Get several local interviews under your belt before tackling a major network show.

Television guest coordinators and producers of large national shows are understandably particular about the interviewees scheduled. They are responsible for the show's ratings and will only book people they are convinced will be interesting to viewers. Not willing to take as big a gamble as the smaller shows, they want to know about past appearances on radio and television. Sharing your track record with them will be necessary if you hope to be booked. One way to do this is to buy a videotape of previous good performances. This can be arranged with the production staff at the close of an interview.

Getting on the News

Something not to be underestimated is the power of a short news spot. Today there are more outlets for broadcast news than ever before. News falls into two types: "hard," which covers matters of local, national, and international consequence; and "soft," which is the kind of human-interest feature people find fascinating.

You are more likely to capture the latter. As we discussed earlier, you can also piggyback and "use news to make news" by packaging your subject matter with a current issue. Perhaps you can create news. Did you do a survey or study on a topic of timely interest? Are you a featured speaker at a convention or trade show? Have you received, or given, an award? All of these things can be catapulted into soft stories for the media.

News time is precious time. Learn to zero quickly in on the essence of your story. You may only have 75 to 90 seconds in which to pack your punch. Think of all the 30- and 60-second commercials that sell millions of dollars' worth of products and services each year. (The sponsors have to pay for those.)

Soft news stories can actually be quite effective. A few years ago Marilyn was taped by a popular station in Phoenix. The interview centered around a book she had just written. Imagine our surprise when we walked into our hotel room, flipped on the 6 o'clock news, and heard the anchorman say they would be talking about *Creative Loafing* later. Then a full-screen shot of the book appeared. We were glued to the set, afraid to blink for fear we would miss the anticipated few-seconds spot.

What transpired left us a little breathless. A 30-second clip from the prerecorded 15-minute interview had her introduce the subject and the book. Then for five minutes we were entranced by film clips from the station's news file showing people participating in many of the activities suggested as pastimes in the book. These were interspersed with narrated closeups of the front cover. Another 30 seconds of Marilyn's prerecorded interview closed the segment.

Six minutes of prime TV time, including a long plug by a local news celebrity. Who could have guessed such a gem would be aired on the news program of the most popular network TV station in town. The great equalizer struck! It can strike for you, too.

Our point, of course, is that a minute or two of prime-time news coverage can have greater impact than a half-hour midmorning talk show. Because TV is so prestigious, competition for available time is fierce—especially with all the celebrities out stumping. With imagination, a creative approach, and tenacity, however, you can probably land some shows.

As you work with prime media in the large markets, another dimension could be added. You may be asked for an exclusive. That means you will appear on that television show, that radio station, or in that paper *only* (or at least first). Don't take exclusivity lightly. Be sure what you're getting is worth the concession. Look at such things as audience size or circulation, prime-time exposure, the prestige of the program or paper, and the enthusiasm of the people involved. Then be grateful they feel you are important enough to warrant such a request.

Networking to Create Synergy and Momentum

Do you want to succeed in business? Expose yourself! Well, ahem, not literally, of course. What we're suggesting is to take off the wraps and pursue new alliances. Developing new relationships—and rekindling old ones—is not only enjoyable, but profitable.

How do you begin? First collect current contact's names, addresses, and phone numbers from various Rolodex files, address books, Christmas lists, business card holders, etc. Compile them into one master list. A computer database is ideal for this purpose. (Also include available FAX numbers. You never know when you'll want to quickly send something to a colleague.) Now prioritize these names as "A," "B," or "C."

Initially work only the A's. Build a file on each of these people. Include such things as spouse name, number of children, hobbies, pet peeves, food/drink preferences, community involvement, causes they support, birthday, etc. As you have future meetings with these folks, embellish their file.

Of course, many people you'd like to network with are not yet in your sphere of influence. Start watching for information about specific people (or individuals in key fields) you've been wanting to meet. Assemble individual files on them from newspaper and magazine feature stories, ads, radio shows, TV programs, even conversations with mutual acquaintances.

Have your assistant look up potential key contacts in who's who directories. (Perhaps you can meet them by joining a club, group, or cause with which they are affiliated or by attending a charity affair where they will be present.) Also check membership rosters of organizations to which you both belong. Additionally, collect data on new people you hear of who impress you.

One way to draw these people into your personal circle is to acknowledge them. (Don't limit this to strangers, however. It is seldom done and will be much appreciated by those you already know.) When people are elected to an office or selected to serve on a board of directors, send a note of congratulations. If they volunteer their time to a worthy cause, earn an award, or write a provocative letter to the editor, seize these opportunities to get in touch.

Just a few words to introduce yourself and send your personal congratulations is all that's needed. This is a prime example of "it's the thought that counts." Of course, use your letterhead and slip in a business card. You may get no immediate results, but the long-term benefits can be impressive. Also watch your mail for items that could prove useful to your colleagues. Just this week we received a sample copy of a printing trade journal we are passing on to the editor of our local paper.

As a matter of course, we duplicate and mail copies of articles that will appeal to friends, clients, or business associates. Many other professionals do likewise. William H. Roth of Kelly, Roth & Hazen, a New York general practice law firm, is always on the lookout for American articles to clip and send to his foreign corporate clients. "I think it's important to communicate with clients," says Roth. "It makes them realize that I'm conscientious and that, even during my hours of relaxation, I'm thinking about them." Such attention is sure to be reflected in client retention and new business development.

We'd love to start a trend where business and professional people regularly remember each other with appropriate articles and information. That way you have the eyes of all you know watching out for your best interest. Such a practice, however, necessitates action in return. Be sure to always thank people who do kind things for you. This can take the form of a brief note or a phone call.

Speaking of thank yous, have you ever thought of printing a public thank you in the daily paper? Although you will have to pay for it, it isn't perceived as an advertisement, but rather as a show of appreciation. This allows you to keep a low-key professional image. You would state something like "(name of firm, address, and phone) wishes to thank its 235 clients for allowing us to serve your needs over the last year. May this coming year be even more profitable for you than the one just passed." Having the partners, owner, key executives, or people involved in public contact personally sign their names is a nice touch. An appropriate time to run such an ad would be at Thanksgiving.

Holidays and other special dates could play another kind of role in your publicity endeavors. Allen Klein, a humorous professional speaker dubbed the "Jollytologist," sends his clients April Fool's Day cards. George Walther, who speaks on telephone marketing and effective phone power, picks March 3—or the nearest Friday—to celebrate the anniversary of Alexander Graham Bell's birth. Around this date invitations go out to clients, prospects, local press, family, and friends encouraging them to attend his annual office party.

Becoming a "joiner" is another way to meet new people. In fact, a service called Lunch Impressions, Inc. sprang up in New York to facilitate just that. Says creator David G. Becker, "You give us a profile of the type of professionals you're interested in meeting. We find the people you seek and arrange a meeting over lunch." In his first two months Becker attracted over 500 members at $75 per head and plans to open branches throughout the country.

On a more traditional plane, chambers of commerce often provide fertile meeting grounds. Bigger metropolitan areas have city, county, and state chambers—even ethnic chambers for blacks, Hispanics and Jews. Jaycees are sometimes the most dynamic bunch around town. Comprised of young business owners, professionals, and executives on the way up, this organization typically attracts accomplished, high-energy people. You'll get the most out of chamber membership by attending meetings and committing your time, not just your dues. Volunteering to chair a committee with high visibility will help the chamber and is good professional strategy.

Of course, every town has civic organizations like Kiwanis, Optimists, Rotary, and Lions. Most cities have groups comprised of high-powered women executives. Many have "leads" clubs where only one representative per industry is admitted to membership. The sole thrust of these groups is referring business leads back and forth. Another networking front is charity groups. Seminars, workshops, and classes also provide an arena in which to become acquainted with like-minded people.

Political involvement certainly nets some useful contacts. Participating as a volunteer in local and regional campaigns can get you on the inside track and lead to running for office if that is appealing. It makes sense to cultivate your legislators and other appointed officials. It's only human nature to go more out of our way for someone we know. If you need a zoning variance, want guidance through a maze of bureaucratic red tape, or seek to get a statement into the Congressional Record, these contacts pay off.

Networking can also come to the rescue during especially slow periods. One entrepreneur doubles up on her social contacts during tough times. She hits with gusto every meeting and cocktail party she can find. And when asked "How's business?," her reply is always "Great!" even if things are shaky. "I want to program my subconscious to expect wonderful results, not feed it negative tripe," is her wise rationale.

An unlikely place some businesspeople are making good connections is in the Bed & Breakfasts where they stay. Says Bernice Chesler, who has written about B&Bs for 12 years, "I can't count the number of times I've seen salesmen having breakfast with other travelers and they walk away with fresh leads."

In our Information Age, the computer can also serve as a masterful networking partner. Nationwide on-line services such as CompuServe, America Online, and DELPHI can connect you with thousands who could spend millions. And you don't even need to leave home if you've got a PC, telephone, modem, and the right software.

Electronic bulletin boards, or forums, are targeted to any number of special interests. Most services have Working From Home or Entrepreneurs bulletin boards—not to mention dozens geared to specific pursuits. They let you communicate with other subscribers by posting messages or sending electronic mail. DELPHI even lets members start their own custom forums. And some cities also offer great opportunities. In Sausalito, California, for instance, there is The Whole Earth 'Lectronic Link (The WELL).

Connecting: that's the bottom line of what this whole book is about. Now let's move on to more ways to promote yourself and your business.

THE ROSS MARKETING IDEA GENERATOR: 26 WINNING STRATEGIES

- Find an angle that makes you controversial
- Do radio phone interviews originating from your home or office
- Go after *all* TV (not everyone can crack Oprah or Donahue)
- Pursue newspaper features about your service
- Write op-ed pieces addressing the subject
- Submit letters to the editor piggybacking on related articles
- Plant news items with local newspaper/magazine columnists
- Provide gratis articles to national magazines
- Solicit plugs in newsletters
- Go after mentions in nationally syndicated columns
- Develop alliances with complementary associations
- Request testimonials from leaders in the industry
- Create a sales flyer and customer order form
- Prepare a "Here's What People Are Saying" flyer of favorable comments
- Generate a mailing list of interested professionals
- Create an "event" centered around your service
- Establish an award that correlates with your subject
- Tie in with a special national or day/week/month activity
- Establish "P.I." (Per Inquiry) advertising arrangements
- Speak about your topic
- Do co-op mailings with others who have complementary services
- Be alert to news events and hot issues you can piggyback on
- Enter any contests for which you qualify
- Take out inexpensive classified ads in targeted magazines
- Always make it *easy* for people to do what you want
- Follow up follow up, follow up

7

Promotion: Creative Ideas for Getting Known and Getting Ahead

Those who understand the power of promotional activities don't wait for their ships to come in—they swim out to meet them. There are dozens of things you can do to promote your business to greater profits. However, making money may not be your motive. Maybe you're involved with a nonprofit association or group that desires a more distinguished presence in the community. In either case, promotion is an answer.

In this chapter we'll give you the keys to unlock dozens of promotional doors. Some of them lead to elaborate activities, others are simple. In either case, we'll leave the porch light on for you. Together we will explore the topics of consumer education, community involvement, and creating an event. We will also look at the whys and wherefores of publishing a newsletter. In addition to discovering how valuable directory listings can be, you'll be treated to an array of miscellaneous promotional tactics.

Consumer Education

Canny leaders all across America are finding ways to inform, entertain, or assist the public while maximizing their own exposure. They lead seminars, symposiums, and workshops; give talks; sponsor clinics; provide in-store or in-office demonstrations; even hold open houses or receptions. All of these functions are designed to bring prospective clients or customers together and to build goodwill.

Sheehy Ford sponsors a learning situation far afield from a Harvard University class. Rather than wearing tweed and having tenure, the instructor dons a shop coat and speaks from practical experience. His students are all female. Although most of them realize a distributor cap is not the latest in fashionable headgear, their knowledge about their cars is limited. The aim of this Philadelphia dealership's Auto Clinic for Women Only is to educate the area female population about their vehicles. Naturally the dealership anticipates picking up new service customers in the process, not to mention future new car purchasers.

The AMI Denver Broncos Sports Medical Center offers a free sports injury evaluation. They implore athletes to "Give us your tired ankles, your poor knees, your tennis elbows . . . " One health professional who had spent $150,000 on an ad campaign that netted no known results switched to seminars. Eighty new patients were tracked to this activity!

Based in Massachusetts, the InVision Institute—a nonprofit organization—sponsors "Eyes on the Road," a 45-foot traveling van. It houses an educational facility that promotes eye care and vision correction with interactive displays. With a tour agenda that includes 80 U.S. cities, the van appears at high-traffic locations like science museums, trade shows, and outdoor events. The institute was formed by Bausch & Lomb to heighten the public's knowledge of eye care.

The other day an invitation came in the mail from AT&T to attend a complimentary seminar on "Telemarketing for Small Businesses." The content covers how to creatively improve sales support, order processing, account management, and customer service. Of course, it is also aimed at improving AT&T's bottom line. The more small businesses understand the power of telemarketing, the larger their phone bills will be!

These are just a few examples of consumer education projects. You can do similar things. Many service specialties lend themselves to in-office or in-store clinics. A travel agent could give a demonstration on how to pack a suitcase. A landscape architect would find an eager audience for a workshop on easy-care plantings—especially if it were offered to recent home buyers in a new subdivision. A financial planner or accounting firm might sponsor a Personal Finance Fair—a consumer show providing pertinent seminars, speakers, and attractions.

A nutritionist, ad agency, plant watching service employment counselor, tax consultant, modeling agency, or caterer might sponsor a free public seminar to generate exposure and patronage. Chiropractors could put together a miniprogram about the spine; veterinarians a short presentation on how to keep your dog or cat healthy. A child-care facility might sponsor a nursery school art show. The possibilities abound for individuals using imagination to discover topics of general interest that also correlate with their business.

Such activities can often be held right in your place of business. If this isn't practical, consider renting a local hotel banquet room or a private dining room in your favorite restaurant. Other possible options are schools, community centers, banks/savings and loan companies, perhaps even the conference room of a business associate. To let people know about your activity, use the techniques you learned in the previous chapter.

Hospitality Happenings Mix Business with Pleasure

Conventional wisdom says business and pleasure don't mix. They're as contradictory as silk and burlap. A more unorthodox view blends them to increase a company's visibility and build sales. Let's explore the latter attitude.

Corporate entertaining can help differentiate your firm from its competitors. Parties give you a chance to talk with prospective clients as well as thank current customers. Many executives and salespeople recognize this form of hospitality saves them countless hours of individual breakfasts, lunches, and dinners. Mass corporate entertaining allows you to reach many people at once. It's cheaper than one-on-one entertaining and much more effective time-wise. When employees are included, business socializing often enhances the company in associate's eyes, forging a deeper bond of loyalty.

Whatever kind of gala function you have in mind, planning is fundamental to having a successful get-together. First, consider timing. Don't conflict with important trade conventions for your industry. Also avoid both secular and religious holidays. People prefer these events be tacked on to the normal business day rather than scheduled on a weekend.

Compile the guest list with input from key staff members. Invitations will, of course, go to prime prospects and current clients. What about including major suppliers, such as your attorney, accountant, banker, and landlord? Perhaps local government officials or area association executives should be on the guest list. Invite more than you hope will attend; not everyone can or will come. It is more personal if invitations are hand-addressed and carry regular stamps.

A flower arrangement or two is nice for such occasions. Have you ever thought of turning your office into an art gallery? Many local artists and artists' societies will welcome a chance to hang their work on consignment. You can then have a "showing" complete with refreshments and a small printed catalog. Always assign one person responsibility for coordinating corporate entertainment functions. He or she makes sure executives review the guest list the day of the event, mingles with the attendees, monitors how things are going, and troubleshoots.

Some firms find this such a good policy that they schedule event-driven marketing activities about every three months. In the summer it might be attending a sports activity or a picnic. Because selling has to do with relationships, many find it makes sense to socialize with prospects.

Creating a Special Event

For those who shun outright business/personal hobnobbing, many other kinds of events can be staged. Although breweries and tobacco companies lead the way in sponsoring big-league wingdings, special grass roots activities and offbeat events are thriving.

The Grain Mill is a Yuba City, California, natural foods store. They recently staged a "Half-Ton Bake-Off" with proceeds going to the American Heart Association. Using a Bosch bread maker, on one Sunday between 6:00 A.M. and 2:00 P.M., they, along with many volunteers, baked half a ton of bread—approximately 1,025 loaves! They enlisted the Veterans Memorial Community Building kitchen and were allowed to sell the baked loaves of bread outside local markets and other establishments. Newspaper ads told people, "We "Knead" You!" and "Help us make a mountain of "dough" for the American Heart Association." (A well-bread effort, wouldn't you say?) It was ingenious and done on a very low budget.

Teaming up with a nonprofit organization helps both entities. Instead of sponsoring existing events, why not pioneer something new? Work with the nonprofit to mold a newsworthy event, a solid fund-raiser for the charity, and an investment that yields you measurable mileage. Negotiate for visible recognition, such as banners posted around arenas, public address system announcements, mention in event advertisements, and an ad in the souvenir program.

A mother/daughter or father/son function sometimes works well. You might get likely candidate names by working with Job's Daughters, Rainbow Girls, DeMolay, YMCA, YWCA, Boys Club, or Scouts. When sponsoring similar events, have flyers printed and distribute them to key points in the community. You might leave some with bookstores, restaurants, laundromats, beauty and barber shops, libraries, and other public places.

Sports-marketing is becoming as popular as FAX machines. Such sponsorships allow corporations to reach a finely targeted market in a nonintrusive way. Joe Barrow, president of Louis Barrow Limited in Denver, produces and manages a series of walking events called the Grand Walk Series. Barrow feels that special events should do more than just be a public affairs tool. He works to convert participants into prospects, then into customers.

It is important to find a sport that matches the sponsor's service or company image. Each sport and its participants have their own cultures. Possibilities range from fly-fishing to bowl games, tractor pulls to marathons.

Lutheran Medical Center was one of the underwriters of the city of Lakewood's (Colorado) Summer Series. They invested $10,000 and untold hours of service for the event. Says director of marketing, Beth Christie, "It afforded us the opportunity to reach out and touch the community." They had their name in front of people for eight to 10 weeks during the summer.

United Bank of Denver used to sponsor the Tennis Classic. When they had a major portfolio with agriculture and farming groups, United worked with various rodeo associations. (Talk about aligning your events with the markets you aim to serve.) More recently they affiliated with the International Film Festival and the Denver Botanic Gardens outdoor concert series.

When embarking on a major event, try to locate the promotion manager in a nonrelated industry who will candidly share his or her experience with you. Ask things like how much did you spend? How did you plan for the occasion? Did it work as well as you anticipated? See if you can entice a radio station to do a "remote." This is a live radio broadcast emanating from the actual location of the event. The first year is a learning process. It takes a minimum of three years to establish an event and reap maximum benefits. Immediate payoffs may not be overwhelming, but downstream the impact of a good event is solidly felt.

Community Involvement

There are many socially conscious steps your business can take to help individuals or groups in your community. Initiating such actions not only aids others, but assists in promoting you.

During a major recession, a commercial printer offered 25 copies of a resume free to unemployed people, plus a booklet on successful interviewing tips. A paper supplier even donated a case of paper. Four newspapers and two radio stations picked up the news item. This gave the printer a couple of thousand dollars worth of free advertising and helped countless out-of-work individuals.

There are also other creative ways to contribute. Could some worthy cause use your support? A word processor or secretarial service might, for instance, advertise that 1% of their total receipts will go to buy typewriters or computers for a local school or library. Add a company nameplate to the gift and get a photographer and reporter from the paper to cover the donation ceremony.

Could you sponsor a scholarship? This is especially appropriate for professional firms, such as attorneys, certified public accountants, or engineers. You might also talk with suppliers to see if they would cooperate with you in such a program.

In what other ways might you serve your community? Do you have a conference room or meeting space going to waste? By offering a free meeting room to charities or civic organizations you build your image and help them. These groups often only need a room for a couple of hours a month, but are extremely thankful when one is provided.

Perhaps you can sponsor a team. In our town, softball is very big. Another possibility is bowling or more unusual sports like over-the-line tournaments or bathtub races.

One chiropractor we know held a Community Appreciation Day. He offered his services at a greatly reduced fee and all the proceeds from the event were given to the local volunteer fire department. This was a clever way to supplement his normal advertising program and create goodwill.

Donating and Volunteering

Doing good is indeed good for business. Volunteering your time to a worthy cause can pay big dividends. An attorney might do pro bono work one day a month. If you're an artist, have you thought of creating an eye-catching poster to help publicize a nonprofit organization's special event? A graphic designer we know of provides reproductions of drawings he has done of sports figures. Auctioned at fund-raising events, they bring in tidy sums—especially when signed by the celebrity. And those of you who are trained promotional writers might offer to do the copywriting for a brochure or fund-raising letter.

Linda Dial, the founder of World Hope Creations, makes Special Angel Dolls. The company's mission is to "give hope" to disadvantaged, sick, or abused children. In addition to selling the dolls, she donates them to hospitals and law enforcement agencies, which give them to abused children to hold during the terrifying interview process. She also gives them to seriously or terminally ill children. Although she only began her business in August of 1992, Dial expects to sell $5 million worth of dolls by the end of 1993. Obviously, presenting free dolls to worthy recipients has brought her heaven-sent success.

Many smart businesspeople believe in making their donations count double: once for the worthy cause and once for themselves. Laura Wyraz, co-owner of Barry Bagels, has a no-cash donation policy. "Yet people are amazed at how much we return to the community," says Wyraz. Her company recently gave 250 *dozen* bagels to runners and workers at a big local fund-raising race. In exchange, the race organizers distributed money-off coupons she devised and had a big sign thanking them. Thus Barry Bagels not only received lots of local recognition, but also used this as an opportunity to expand their customer base.

Mary Nack Childs, president of the Relocation Counseling Center headquartered in McLean, Virginia, donates hundreds of hours each year to her community. "Truly believe in the organizations you choose to affiliate with," is her advice. Because she feels society needs to support the arts, she joined the Fairfax Symphony. At cocktail parties before the concerts, she socializes with many trend-setters and high level corporate executives. However, Childs cautions, "Don't talk business there, simply make contacts. If you care about your community and develop a level of personal trust, people will automatically want to do business with you." She builds coalitions with constituents while serving the needs of the community.

Before long she was involved with the symphony's fund-raising. This not only tapped into her own contacts to benefit the nonprofit organization, but allowed her to access important area CEOs as she prospected for symphony support. Consequently Childs developed a unique entre to top management in many local companies. She can now either call the president directly and ask who in the organization to talk with regarding her business-to-business services, or talk with decision makers farther down the corporate ladder and tell them she has spoken with their president.

What about donating your services? This can be done individually or in tandem with others. For instance, chambers of commerce, TV stations, and other entities hold annual fund-raising auctions. Those who contribute receive a plug. Not to mention that helping others can "plug" dwindling cash flow holes and infuse your business with new vitality.

A B&B owner in Madison, Wisconsin, offered fellow innkeepers a free night's stay in her Canterbury Inn. Her hope is they will refer customers to her when there's no room at their inns.

Contests, Awards, and Surveys

A Dallas, Texas, exterminator got a promotional bug (yes you read right) a while back that netted him nationwide exposure. Bizzy Bees Pest Control sponsored the Largest American Cockroach Contest, offering a $1,000 prize for the biggest culprit—dead or alive. The winner was 1.92 inches long and bested over 200 other entries. Michael Bohadan, company owner, appeared on numerous radio and TV shows—including Johnny Carson. He made his $1,000 pay many times over.

Texas is the birthplace of a lot of big ideas. The first Living Legends Classic, an annual bodybuilding competition, was held in Warton, Texas. What an ideal contest for a gym to sponsor. And you might know a Texas bank, TransFirst, came up with a sweepstakes idea to encourage customers to use its Moneymaker automatic teller machines (ATM). A joint promotion with a local radio station and 7-Eleven stores, where the machines were placed, made the costs affordable. Sweepstake numbers appeared on each Moneymaker ATM transaction slip. A whopping 2½ million entries resulted.

One Halloween, a market placed a giant pumpkin in its window and offered cash prizes to the person who guessed closest to the number of seeds inside the pumpkin. The contest drew thousands of entries—and sold an unprecedented number of pumpkins. Experimenters counted the seeds, seeking clues to aid in the guesstimating. Could you mold this concept to fit your operation in some way?

Do be aware contests could dump you into legal hot water. Most states have laws regulating contests and declaring lotteries illegal unless they are sponsored by the government or a charity. The Federal Trade Commission also monitors some contests, as does the Federal Communications Commission and the U. S. Postal Service. You may want to check with an attorney before embarking on a journey into this highly regulated jungle.

Contests are limited primarily by our imagination. What can you do to delight someone else and get free promotion for yourself? Just be sure your contest is relevant to your service. A beauty shop might give a free shampoo and set to the woman with the longest hair, a church could award their longest-standing member a token gift. An insurance agent could honor the driver with the longest safe-driving/no-ticket record. How about a travel agent giving the customer who has logged the most miles in a year a free trip to somewhere or a catered breakfast in bed *at home.* A weight control center might make the woman who lost the most pounds Queen for a Day.

Awards are another intriguing promotional tactic. If no one in your area is doing so, why not institute a Good Citizen award? Have your secretary scan papers watching for stories of people who have performed a kind deed or helped significantly in the community. Each month select a winner, then send him or her a certificate and a letter explaining the program. Also, be sure the media gets a copy of the letter and the name of that month's award recipient. Cap it with an annual award drawn from the monthly winners—and a big media splash.

A New York-based consultancy, The Communication Workshop, annually presents the Percy Awards. They are presented for the business world's most fuzzy, laughable, and misworded communications. Although copies of the winners are available, company names are not released "to protect the guilty."

Award programs work both ways. Perhaps there is a local, state, or national award opportunity you could be entering. Architectural firms, for instance, should be aware of designoriented programs on every level. Just because a project doesn't win one time doesn't mean it won't another. Juries change. Resubmit eligible projects even if they were previously rejected.

Besides a huge jump in the number of politically oriented commercials, what else accompanies a national election? Yep, political polls abound. However, you don't have to wait for an election to focus attention on industry issues. You can conduct a poll—complete with percentages and statistics—any time. Surveys display your knowledge and specialty. They establish you as the expert and inevitably lead to new business.

If you have the bucks, you can hire survey help. A public relations firm typically spends anywhere from $18,000 to $45,000 to complete a survey. For most, that's out of the question. But some research firms do what are called "omnibus polls." These polls are organized by the research firms to cover a broad range of topics. You can buy in for around $1,000 a question. For those on more restricted budgets, smaller polling samples and less sophisticated methods are the order of the day. Word survey questionnaires objectively, get as large a sample as possible, and double-check all mathematical calculations.

Your survey can be an informal analysis done among your customers/clients. A health spa, for instance, might shape questions to explore attitudes about exercise, weight loss, and the importance of a careful diet. Another approach is to explore your company files. You may be sitting on proprietary information that could be molded into a fascinating survey. Be sensitive to gathering information that will involve your prospects. Human interest stuff is always appreciated. For instance, the public "gobbled up" Nabisco Brands, Inc.'s study on how people eat its Oreo cookies.

Once the poll is complete, write up your conclusions and offer them both locally and to the wire services. Recycle this information in other ways. How about a direct-mail piece, slated for prospects, summarizing your findings? Conducting a research study, then circulating the results, is a low-budget, high-impact way to promote yourself.

Speak Your Way to Success

Public speaking certainly isn't for everyone. If the mere thought pushes your panic button, skip this section. For those still with us, realize you don't have to be a great orator to successfully use this method of prospecting. Speaking is simply being your own cheerleader. Sharing your specialized knowledge. Helping people on a grander scale.

Whether you're talking about financial planning, nutrition, garden care, interior decorating, or child care—the same guidelines apply. Please be prepared. That doesn't mean memorize your speech. Don't!

You are an expert in your subject area. And you're simply going to be talking to several people at once instead of only one.

A proven formula is to tell them what you're going to tell them. Tell them. Tell them what you've told them. Jot down three or four main points you want to make, and include reminders of examples to support each. People enjoy anecdotes. These little stories make your presentation come alive. You don't have to dazzle the audience. Take a deep breath—relax—be brief—look at different parts of the audience so people don't feel left out—and share your special knowledge.

Self-employment expert Sarah Edwards recommends taking a presentation-skills class through an adult-education class. "Not only will you learn how to sell yourself better, you'll come out realizing that you're not as inept as you thought," she explains. Another excellent training ground is joining a Toastmasters club. Once you've become comfortable in front of an audience, you'll truly appreciate what a wonderful way this is to publicize what you do and meet prospective customers or clients.

Producing a Newsletter

An external company newsletter has two purposes: to stay in touch with current prospects and to generate new leads in a cost-effective way. Although many people toss direct-mail packages in the wastebasket without so much as a guilty twinge, they hesitate to do so with a newsletter. Therein lies your power!

There are numerous decisions once you've made the commitment to produce an external newsletter. How often will you publish? It is a good idea to begin conservatively; you can always increase the frequency later. Quarterly is a good starting point. Regularity spurs your momentum, so avoid the temptation to discontinue mailings in the summer or winter. Will you send this communication via bulk mail or first class?

Think about the format. What size will it be? Many begin with a normal two-sided 8½-by 11-inch piece of paper, folded into thirds. Are two or three columns preferable? Should it be a self-mailer? Design a sharp-looking masthead. For an extra attractive appearance, have a year's supply of the masthead printed in a bright color. Then for each edition, print the news in black or brown.

What will you call your newsletter? Don't be so cute you'll be embarrassed to claim the publication a year from now. (Reread the section called "What's in a Name" in Chapter 2.) Get a copy of Mark Beach's *Editing Your Newsletter.*

A newsletter provides news—something useful to the recipient. Although commercial clients are interested in business improvement ideas, residential customers appreciate household tips. Decide which is your market. You can provide either by subscribing to periodicals in your readers' area of interest, then culling interesting items and rewriting them. News releases from suppliers also provide story material. Will you want regular features, such as a profile of an outstanding customer or client?

Some professions, such as medicine, dentistry, and banking, are the target of national companies that produce "canned" generic newsletters for various industries. These are designed so the individual firm is mentioned on the front, but the information inside is all uniform. Whether you create your newsletter "from scratch" or use a generic version, having such a communication tool establishes customer confidence and loyalty. Because it puts you in a position of authority, it can also lead to added profits.

Becoming an Industry Leader

Why should a prospective client choose your firm over the competition? One reason might be because you've established yourself as a leader in your industry, someone they can trust and respect.

There's an adage that says you have to give to get. Nowhere is this more true than for the professional or service-based entrepreneur. If you aspire to more publicity, elevated success, and greater affluence—it's time to get involved.

One way is by becoming a nationally recognized leader in your industry. This doesn't happen overnight; such prominence takes years to cultivate. You'll have to join the right groups, spend time serving on panels and committees, maintain contact with the media, and "know your stuff." But it pays big dividends.

When you become a source the media can depend on—and they need the big picture about trends and issues that impact your industry—*you* are the person they will turn to. Most small firms couldn't possibly afford to buy such coverage. It gives you a significant competitive edge. Such credibility pays an enormous return on your investment of time and energy. You'll be a resource. Resources are people with a *presence* in their field. They are the experts. Reporters for both print and electronic sources seek them out.

Dr. Robert R. Butterworth of Contemporary Psychology Associates, Inc., in Los Angeles is a master media player. "To make comments, you have to know what s going on. Do your homework," he counsels. "I read three newspapers and use my computer to access the wire services on CompuServe."

This psychologist is an authority on teens and youngsters. Butterworth has been noted and quoted about teen drug abuse, letting kids view the disastrous shuttle Discovery launch, the ramifications of punk rock, how teens worry about nuclear war, etc. He began by sending out two- or three-page evergreen features—stories that are timeless.

While he started small with local newspapers and radio stations, he soon graduated to larger media, such as the *Los Angeles Times* and TV. Dr. Butterworth's comments and observations have appeared in most of the major newspapers in the U.S. and Europe. Additionally, he's been interviewed on the news by all three networks and frequently appears on CNN and various other talk shows.

"Identify your expertise and let people know about it," Butterworth advises. "This makes reporters' jobs easier." Once they recognize you have knowledge in a specialized field, they'll contact you when an appropriate news story breaks.

When the San Francisco earthquake hit, Dr. Butterworth's phone didn't stop ringing for three days. Understanding—and coping with—the quake's lingering effects on children was a hot topic. In a nonintrusive way, he offered help. Of course, this resulted in more people learning about this clinical psychologist who specializes in children at his offices in Downey, West Los Angeles, and Sherman Oaks.

Every industry has one or more trade associations that cater to the needs and interests of their specific profession. Join. Get active. Affiliating has many benefits. In addition to magazines or newsletters chock-full of useful information, most associations sponsor educational workshops and conventions.

"Association membership affords an ideal opportunity to rub shoulders with the giants in the industry," believes motivational speaker and management consultant James F. (Jim) Hennig, Ph.D. "I feel it's important to study successful people—people who are making it happen in your area. Learn from them; digest what they do well. But don't copy them. Adapt, don't adopt." That was his goal the first few years he belonged to the National Speakers Association (NSA).

Besides getting, Hennig has done a lot of giving. He began by participating at the state chapter level in NSA—serving as program chair, vice president, then president. Hennig is prompted by a genuine desire to serve, to do anything he can do well to forward the organization. That attitude gained him a seat on the national board of directors and chairmanship of their prestigious annual convention. This volunteer work guarantees Hennig, whose speaking practice is located in Green Bay, Wisconsin, excellent visibility.

"I've made wonderful contacts in the industry," he says. "A lot of my speaking business comes from the people I've met in NSA." At their '93 convention, he was singled out for a special award and tapped for the future presidency.

The way to make such contacts is to leave the fringes for the inner circle. This is where the movers and shakers of any industry congregate. When you're planning strategy at committee sessions or hammering out decisions at board meetings, people really get to know one another. And the typical opportunities for breaking bread or sharing a drink that accompany such work sessions further set the stage for fruitful professional and personal relationships.

Another way to solidify your industry leadership position is to offer your services on a complimentary basis. Provide free information. Perhaps you've seen the effective institutional ad campaign New York Life has launched in support of the Boston Ballet Company. The print ad shows a man in a business suit surrounded by beautiful ballerinas. The message? That the Boston Ballet Company has grown from a fledgling New England company to one of national stature. It has done so with the help of this man—a New York Life agent who provides them regular free business consulting.

Naturally small businesses can't afford such flamboyant advertising. But you can lend your professional expertise to nonprofit groups. And you can capitalize on this goodwill by making the media aware of it.

One corporate business development firm we know works with local economic development groups, supplying them with valuable free statistical information. In turn, the firm either receives verbal credit, their corporate name appears on the data, or the group gives them direct referrals.

Miscellaneous Promotional Strategies

We've been collecting ideas for this book for several years. Many of them are, in our opinion, priceless gems. But they don't fit into any overall section. So we've gathered them under the umbrella of "miscellaneous" with the hope one will spark your imagination.

Sponsoring a telephone hotline can lead to increased revenue. A Littleton, Colorado, law firm provides a recording of basic information on bankruptcies. A dozen potential clients leave messages at the end of the recording each week

A free-lance copywriter who specializes in direct-response advertising has an advertising hotline. Callers are treated to three- to five-minute taped messages on such subjects as "10 Ways to Stretch Your Advertising Budget" or "13 Questions to Ask before You Create Your Next Ad Campaign." His minimessages are changed every week. This gimmick could be used successfully by travel agents, gardeners, animal boarding kennels, insurance agents, nutritionists, printers, and a host of other service providers.

Can you use greeting cards to hitch your service to a special event or time? An accountant or tax planner might devise a humorous greeting card to send out April 15th. A dating service or therapist who specializes in relationships could capitalize on Valentine's Day.

Speaking of greeting cards, always keep a supply at your desk. You will be perceived as a thoughtful person when you remember a key prospect's or client's birthday or anniversary. Sending congratulatory cards for a new job, baby, or home is also an appreciated touch. So is a get well or thinking of you card when illness or tragedy has struck. Have you ever thought of sending a thank you card after someone retains your services?

Do you realize each year just after Easter a dramatic promotional opportunity occurs? Daylight savings time is welcomed by all. Have you ever thought about how you could use this annual occurrence to your advantage? Anyone who deals with growing things can play on it. Because people will be outdoors more, many recreational and sporting facilities will also find it a natural. Can you think of other ways to tie in your business?

Have you ever noticed the fishbowls or large brandy snifters full of business cards in some restaurants? Using this concept, you can team up with another business to get yourself before the public and develop more leads. Offer something for free—such as an hour of consulting, a lube and oil change, a lesson, or free admittance for two. Print a little sign to explain the prize and attach it to a transparent container in which people can deposit their business cards for the drawing.

All that remains is to make arrangements with a receptive merchant. This is a win/win proposition. The proprietor gets the benefit of providing a free bonus to his or her customers, you gain exposure before hundreds of prospects. Alliances can be set up with beauty shops, drug stores, boutiques, music stores, even restaurants.

There is another way businesses in a small town, or those located in a neighborhood of a larger city, can band together for mutual gain. How about printing a discount coupon book? This has proven to be a wonderful sales stimulator in several places.

When we gave a seminar in Steamboat Springs, Colorado, a few years ago, we picked up such a book at the chamber of commerce office. It contained coupons for reduced rates or special bonuses from hotels, motels, and resort accommodations—plus recreational activities like balloon trips, river-rafting, hydrotubing, bicycle rentals, golfing, and kayak school. Other participating services included a picture framing shop, service stations, a landscaping firm, and a video camera rental shop.

When doing such a promotion, be sure to protect yourself. Print an expiration date on the coupon, limit one coupon to customer, and don't honor it in conjunction with any other discount. One of the advantages of this type of program is, simply by keeping the coupons, you can clearly track the results. Discount booklets can be mailed to area residents, made available on the counters of participating businesses, and dispensed at the chamber of commerce, town hall, library, etc.

Here is an idea for nonprofit organizations that need to produce more revenue. Why not create a special Committee of One Hundred? To be part of this committee, 100 people (or businesses) have to donate $100 dollars apiece. (Large associations or groups could expand this to a Committee of One Thousand, thus potentially raising $100,000 instead of $10,000!)

Speaking of nonprofits reminds us of the story of Grace Memorial House of Prayer in Fort Lauderdale, Florida. To support their ministry, every Friday and Saturday afternoons they sell take-out barbecue alongside a busy thoroughfare. Pork ribs and chicken wings smothered in the Reverend Noble Harris' barbecue sauce have been sustaining the church for more than a decade. No rummage sales, bingo games, or bake sales here.

While we're talking about doing gutsy things, how about seeking governmental recognition? For the lion-hearted, it may be available in several forms. There are resolutions from the city council or the county board of supervisors. You might approach the mayor or governor to make a proclamation. Legislators have also been known to get statements entered into the Congressional Record. These, by the way, make impressive reprints.

One final promotional idea. Although it won't work for most service businesses, it could succeed royally for a few. How about starting a national association? Such action would definitely put you in the limelight. Associations typically offer educational services (workshops, seminars, conferences), publish a regular newsletter, and provide networking opportunities. Often they also serve as an information clearinghouse on the topic around which they are formed. What a way to position yourself as the official expert!

Be aware that launching such an organization requires a huge commitment—both in time and money. You would need an advisory board representing both a geographic and size mix in the industry. You must decide on a carefully honed mission statement encapsulating your purpose. Membership categories, such as charter members, regular, professional, and associate members, must be determined. Most important, you'll need a strong marketing plan to sell people on your idea.

Seeking Professional Listings

Publicizing your firm via professional directories is a tangible way to market an intangible There are thousands of such directories, some admittedly more powerful than others. At About Books, Inc., our sister company, we find it revealing that about a third of all inquiries are generated from free listings in *Literary Market Place*. After several years of fine-tuning this source, we appear under so many different headings, we've coded the addresses to track which sections are working best!

One of the especially appealing aspects of directory listings is that many of them are free of charge. Every industry has such directories. Yet few people know about them or bother to do the paperwork necessary to be included even when they're aware of such publications.

This is one of the first things we do for a new client. When a Houston management consulting and training firm hired our agency to come on-site for an individualized 3-day PR conference, we tracked down the following potential listing sources: the *Consultants Directory, Business Consultants Directory, Management Consultants,* and the *Consultants and Consulting Organizations Directory.* To promote the CEO, we requested listing forms from *Who's Who in America, Who's*

Who in the World, and *WHO Houston, Inc.*, where the company is based. Additional personal listings were solicited in *Dictionary of International Biography, International Businessmen's Who's Who, Biographical Dictionary of American Business Leaders, Directory of Distinguished Americans*, and *Men of Achievement.* Because he is the author of three management books, we also went after *The International Authors and Writers Who's Who, Contemporary Authors, and Who's Who in the U.S. Writers, Editors, and Poets.* Whew!

It will take up to three years for these listings to get into print. Some directories are only published every other year, and we will have just missed a few deadlines. However, this shouldn't bother any forward-thinking company. The above firm has been in business for 25 years; it's no passing fancy. When the listings take hold, not only will the CEO experience wider visibility and credibility, but we can almost guarantee the company will enjoy increased sales.

If you want to guarantee increased sales for your organization, spend quality time reading the next chapter. Surprisingly it isn't about selling. It is about service and satisfaction—keeping your existing customers or clients happy. They after all, represent your most viable source for future growth.

Part II

More Methods to Maximize Your Strengths

Part II

More Methods to Maximize Your Strengths

8

Providing Outstanding Service and Customer/ Client Satisfaction

Simply attracting clients and customers isn't enough. The trick is to turn that first timer into a loyal repeater. Happy, satisfied patrons are the best publicity a small service business can have. You want them "Blinded by Delight." Faithful customers singing your praises are better than all the advertising space money can buy. Benefits mushroom with each person who spreads the good word.

What makes some businesses stand out above the crowd? Why do the Joneses rave about the Acme Lawn Service when there are hundreds of others listed in the yellow pages? Why do the Smiths drive miles out of their way to take Rover to Arnold's Animal Clinic when there are other vets located much closer to home? What is it about Dr. Reed that makes patients actually *look forward* to seeing him? The answer is a simple yet often overlooked key. The stars of the industry know the main difference between them and their competitors is their level of service. That difference keeps clientele and patients coming back.

This chapter looks at some creative ways to furnish a quality standard of customer service and maintain a high level of satisfaction.

We'll explore vital keys that unlock the doors to superior service. Discover how to defuse customer complaints and transform the "problem" into a valuable promotional tool. We include a sample of a client survey, plus you'll also learn how client perceptions and expectations can be employed to your advantage.

A recent study by the International Customer Service Association found it costs five times as much to win a new customer as it does to keep an old one. We'll show you how to save precious time and make more money by keeping those clients coming back again and again. Finally, we'll look at some unique tactics for going beyond the call of duty in customer satisfaction.

Keys to Ensuring Satisfaction

Superior service has always been a bestseller. Walt Disney, Ritz Carlton Hotels, Nordstrom's specialty retailer, and L. L. Bean achieved legendary status for placing the customer first. However, this commitment to quality service was the exception rather than the rule. Few utilized this tool to its full potential. Other marketing strategies claimed top priority; the customer's satisfaction took a back seat. Yet the general public has not been fooled.

Unfortunately, the biggest black eye has been dealt to the service industry. According to a study by the National Family Opinion for the Consumer Research Center of the Conference Board, service businesses have a serious image problem. In a survey of 6,000 households, they found the "vast majority of consumers believe that they receive good value for their dollar" when purchasing products. However, there is a "rather pervasive discontent with what they get for the money" when they buy services. The biggest offenders include health care givers, all categories of repair work, lawyers, dentists, banks, and credit card companies.

The landscape is changing on the customer service scene. Americans are demanding high-quality service as never before. Two-career couples find themselves with more available money—at the expense of time. Don Shapiro of California-based First Concepts Development Corporation, a specialist in the fields of customer satisfaction and employee motivation, believes people now have less free time and they don't want to waste it trying to solve problems with the places where they spend their money. "Their expectations for quality and service have risen dramatically," says Shapiro.

Companies who ignore these national trends jeopardize their future. Survival in today's crowded marketplace depends on the ability to take the pulse of the consumer and then supply the needed prescription. In an economy based on businesses that perform rather than produce, that Rx is outstanding service. The reward for suppliers is simple—bigger profits.

So what's the first step in gaining a competitive service edge and ensuring customer satisfaction? Start by defining exactly who your clients are. Where do they live? What is their median income? Then listen to them. Ask questions. What do they want? What do they need? Then listen some more.

Next, develop a strategy that will meet the expectations of those clients. Be sure you're offering top-quality service with no corners cut. Brainstorm creative methods of delivering more for the money than competitors. Enlist employee input in the creative process. Your associates may surprise you with their innovative responses on going that extra mile.

Brittany's Ltd., a Philadelphia dry-cleaning company, found these "extras" the key to whopping success in an often ho-hum field. This progressive firm targeted the needs of the up-scale suburbanites in their area. Brittany's rolls out the red carpet in a world where normal service is usually limited to a hanger, plastic bag, and maybe 24-hour cleaning. Included in their perks are pickup and delivery, drive-in windows, and free minor mending. They charge a little more, but customers are lined up to pay the prices.

"Providing top-notch service is the only inexpensive way small companies have to really distinguish themselves from their competitors and lift themselves above the pack," states John Tschohl, customer-service expert and president of Minnesota-based Better Than Money Corporation. "Customers expect small firms to be closer to them and to deliver better service."

Now take a good look in the mirror. First impressions are vital and can make all the difference in influencing the first-time client. Few take seriously the salesperson with unkempt hair and food spots on her shirt. Businesses also need to consider what their "looks" are telling patrons. Walk your premises and observe what your patrons see.

Consider the corner automobile repair shop. The mechanics may be first class, but what do the customers actually see? Is it a grubby waiting area, greasy chairs, and a filthy water cooler? Spruce up the room, add a few plants and paintings, provide complimentary coffee, tea, cocoa, or cider, and set out some diversified reading material. Customers will find waiting for repairs easier, and their impression of the entire operation will jump dramatically.

Some chimney sweeps latched on to the image connection several years ago. During the energy crunch, woodburning stoves and fireplaces made a comeback. So did the old-fashioned sweep, complete in top hat and tails. Customers are charmed by the spectacle of what would otherwise be considered just another dirty job to be hired out. The approach provides a free publicity bonus, because newspaper photographers can't seem to resist the snazzily dressed chimney sweep in action.

Once the service strategy is in place, train the front-line troops in the battle plan. Let employees know the policies and how they will be implemented. Give them the ammunition to do their job effectively. Send them to seminars, provide books or cassette tapes, and (most importantly) set a positive example.

John and Maryanne McCormack own the Houston-based Visible Changes hair salons. They hold motivational classes designed to enhance employees' service-oriented attitudes and build confidence. Periodic refresher training keeps the stylists up-to-date and on top of current trends. John believes if you take care of your employees, they will take care of customers.

"The first step is setting the standards," he explains. "Then make sure everybody in the company understands those standards. Finally, reward people for achieving your standards and goals. If you reward your associates for superior performance, then your customers are going to get the service you ultimately wish to deliver."

Firms with only one, two, or three employees may think this aspect is not as important for them. Wrong. Very wrong. In fact, it may be of even greater importance. Those few employees are the only contacts (besides you) the clients have with your firm. The first face a patient sees at a dentist's office is the receptionist. A rude or indifferent attitude sets the tone for the entire visit. The dentist might be top-notch in the field, but the patient only remembers an uncaring experience. The next time dental care is needed the person goes to Dr. Smith down the street. After all, Aunt Betty thinks he's great.

Reward associates who display a strong customer orientation. Positive recognition reinforces their behavior, guaranteeing a happy employee and a satisfied patron. The reward needn't be financial either. A word of praise in front of coworkers, a complimentary handwritten note, or a special lunch after successfully handling a difficult client—these small efforts build team spirit and show you are serious about the customer strategy.

Outstanding customer service delivered by *others* could result in an unusual solution for *you*. Blayne Blowers of the laundry chain, Clean Duds, uses it as a clever hiring tool. Blowers watches for people who are sincere, responsive, have a friendly smile, and enjoy servicing. When he finds such an individual, he hands that person a card that reads, "I was impressed by your service. If you're ever looking for a job, please call me." This has proven to be a wonderful way to prospect for those who already appreciate the value of good customer service.

Handling Objections with Finesse

No, the customer isn't *always* right. But it's easier, and more cost-effective, to please a current customer than to develop a new one. Clients with problems left unresolved will beat a path straight to the competition, bad-mouthing you all the way.

A recent study by the Technical Assistance Research Programs Institute (TARP) found 91% of unhappy customers will never again purchase the services of the offending firm and will tell their tale of woe to at least nine other people! The upside of that study shows 54 to 70% of customers who complain will do business with the firm again if the complaint is resolved satisfactorily. If the client feels the problem is speedily handled, the figure jumps to a whopping 95%.

No matter what type of service you supply and how well you do it, there will be times when people are dissatisfied. Perhaps a box is missing when the moving van is unloaded. Or a person is unhappy with the condition of a motel room. Maybe a print job is done on the wrong color of paper; or a service representative is tactless. These are just a few of the problems that plague every business from time to time. Each seems insignificant by itself. Yet they can form an extremely damaging pattern that can erode the profits of your business. If not resolved in a favorable way, not only do you lose the dissatisfied customer, your business will suffer as he or she relates the story of your unfair practices. It's important to fix the problem—not the blame.

So how do you handle customer objections? If the complaint is in person or over the telephone, the first rule is to let the person have their say without interrupting. If the incident takes place in a public area, you may want to invite the individual into your office or a secluded area so other customers don't overhear any tirades. Keep the person talking by asking open-ended questions. Use such words as *which, why, what, when, and where.* Resist the natural urge to become defensive. Instead, try to really *listen* and understand what the person is saying. Don't offer a solution until the individual has had time to vocalize all his or her feelings.

Employing good communication skills helps assure the customer you are listening attentively. Make direct eye contact, nod occasionally in response to their story, and, if seated, lean forward slightly in the chair. This effective use of body language conveys the message "I care about you and your problem." Be sympathetic in your initial reply: "I can certainly understand why you're unhappy, Mrs. Jones. I'd feel the same way in your place." This kind of response will take the angry wind out of most people's sails and make them much more reasonable.

Now continue by asking, "What can I do to make things right with you?" This is a very important question. If you don't find out what they want, you're playing a guessing game on solving the problem. You might volunteer more than you need to! Mrs. Jones may only expect you to repair a ripped carpet seam, so why offer to give her a big discount if that isn't her expectation?

On the other hand, going beyond customer expectations can be a powerful tool. Stew Leonard encourages his employees to go beyond the call of duty when dealing with problems. The spirit of customer service reigns supreme in both his 100,000 square-foot dairy store in Norwalk, Connecticut, and a farmer's market in Danbury. One evening the manager of the market found a note that had been stuffed in a counter suggestion box only a half-hour earlier: "I'm upset. I made a special stop on my way home from work to buy chicken breasts for dinner, but you're sold out and now I'll have to eat a TV dinner instead." As he read the note, up rolled the poultry delivery truck. Five minutes later a complimentary two-pound package of fresh chicken breasts was on its way to the customer's door in an employee's car. This example of going the extra mile did more than soothe an angry customer. It transformed him into a loyal, repeat patron who tells his friends and neighbors what a wonderful place the market is to shop.

As the TARP study showed, the key to customer retention is a *speedy* solution. The moving company that requires weeks or even months, plus tons of paperwork, to settle an insurance claim on a missing box will not win any points. Although the customer will eventually be reimbursed, it is unlikely he will dial their number again. Neither will his friends.

Offering the irate customer a choice of possible solutions often solves the problem on the spot. If Mrs. Smith doesn't like her motel room, let her take her pick of two or three other available rooms. If the flyers have been printed on the wrong colored paper, ask if they would like you to quickly reprint the job correctly or would they rather take the order at a reduced rate?

If you discover an employee was rude, an apology to the customer (preferably by the offender) will create a lot of goodwill. Although everyone can have an off day occasionally, rudeness cannot be tolerated in a firm committed to customer satisfaction. Make sure the employee understands your policies in dealing with the public. If the offense reoccurs, it's time to replace the offender with someone who enjoys interacting with the public.

Complaints may also arrive via the mail. Again, the emphasis is placed on speed. Paul Mescher, director of fulfillment for Meredith Corporation of Des Moines, Iowa, believes customers demand a swift response. "It used to be acceptable to turn correspondence around in seven or eight days," he says. "Now four or five days is the most you can get away with."

Consider calling the person immediately rather than responding by writing a letter. It's a sound investment in client satisfaction. Almost everyone has a horror story of a computer billing error and the nightmare of correcting the problem. Calling the customer with a billing complaint assures him or her that a *real person* is indeed working on the problem versus an endless trip on a computer merry-go-round.

Most people don't expect more than what is fair. They just want "what they paid for" in the shortest possible amount of time. A caring attitude combined with a dash of respect goes a long way in soothing angry feelings. However, there is a small percentage of complainers who are grasping, unreasonable people. You must make a decision with them: either give in to their demands and pass it off as the price of doing business, or be willing to suffer their ill will and the resulting abuse to your reputation. Weigh the costs before you decide. You may have your fill of dealing with Mr. Brown, but are you ready to risk the unknown number of potential clients he might influence?

The vast majority of customer objections are justified. In fact, complaints should be considered a valuable resource. Handled well, they offer an opportunity to not only make amends, but develop a renewed and intensified customer loyalty.

Managing Constituent Expectations

There are times when the old adage "what you see is what you get" isn't worth the paper its written on. When dealing with the buying public, the truth reads "what I feel is what I've got." The client/customer's perception is the final factor in how he or she views the quality of service received. Unfortunately, many small businesses and professional firms fail to understand that customer expectations and perceptions play a pivotal role in their success. This vital facet of quality service is a basic prerequisite in any well-rounded strategy.

Mrs. Smith drops her shoes off at the ABC Repair Shop. The clerk promises they will be ready in two days. When Mrs. Smith arrives to pick them up, she discovers they won't be ready for another day.

Mr. Doe leaves his shoes at the XYZ Repair Shop. The clerk promises they will be ready in five days. But on the third day the clerk calls and says: "Mr. Doe, you're shoes are ready, you can pick them up anytime!"

Both pairs of shoes were repaired with the same level of care and expertise. Both were ready in three days. However, Mrs. Smith is not pleased with ABC. She feels misused and cheated. Mr. Doe, on the other hand, believes XYZ is wonderful. He thinks he's been given special treatment. By managing expectations, the second shop appears more professional, more capable, more caring.

If customers expect too much from your firm, satisfaction will suffer when you can't deliver. If your service is promoted as top of the line, but turns out to be mediocre, your clients will feel cheated.

The U.S. auto industry has fallen into this trap. Print and television advertisements tout the incredible quality of certain American-made cars. Contained within the message is the implication that ownership will bestow freedom, happiness, and friends. By raising customer expectations to unrealistic levels, buyers are sure to be disappointed with reality. The new car in the garage won't start, the world is not full of bliss, and new friends aren't waiting at the door. No wonder Detroit's image lags.

Savvy businesspeople use customer perceptions to their advantage. The key is to be realistic. Don't overpromise. Don't sell what you can't deliver. A writer who tells an editor a story will be finished in three days when a week is really needed is gambling with future assignments.

It's far better to be honest from the start than deal with an angry editor whose expectations (and deadline) weren't met.

The bottom line is respect—respect yourself and the customer. Clients don't like delays or problems, but will deal with them far better if treated honestly. Be up front and as specific as possible. Make sure your actions match your words. Treat your customers the way you would like to be treated in the same circumstance.

Warren Blanding of the Customer Service Institute, a Maryland-based educational and training organization, points out the missing link in service is usually the customer point of view. "The secret of good service is to do things for a customer the way that customer would do them if given the opportunity," he adds.

When communicating with the public, keep messages precise and easy to understand. Federal Express Corporation promises to deliver "absolutely, positively" overnight by 10:30 A.M., pick up packages, and respond to questions within 30 minutes. When customers know exactly what to expect, the risk of a "perception error" plummets.

Keep those lines of communication to the customer open and effective. If dealing with a problem, alert clients in plenty of time. If there is a possibility the secretarial service can't come up with a temporary for Friday, advising the client late Thursday afternoon is a poor idea. The customer may still be short one secretary on Friday, but will deal with it far better with more advance notice.

How is your firm's "body language" molding client expectations? The environment surrounding your service correlates directly with customer perceptions. A badly designed office makes one wonder about the capabilities of an architect. An unknowledgeable attendant speaks poorly of the art gallery in which she's employed. What person wants to sit in the chair of a beautician with a bad cut?

Physical criteria can signal either a red or green light to clients. Inconvenient locations, faulty telephone systems, and poor lighting practically scream "poor service!" Well-groomed employees, an upscale office, and professional attitudes bespeak quality. Customers may not consciously notice the subtle environmental factors, but the unconscious mind reads them loud and clear.

In order to manage expectations you must first discover how your clients feel about your service in the here and now. The only way to do that accurately is through research. Unfortunately, many service firms assume they already know what their customers think. This is a "fatal flaw," according to Karen Gershowitz, senior vice president of BAI, a

Tarrytown, New York, marketing consulting and research firm. "Often an outsider will see something that the company takes for granted."

Resistance to research is greatest among professional service providers. The tradition of protecting client relationships among lawyers, accountants, and others often interferes with the measurement of client satisfaction. The answer is to conduct research in-house.

There are methods of discovering the truth. Focus groups and in-depth personal and telephone interviews are particularly revealing. "You bump into problems you didn't know you had," says Eugene Fram, professor of marketing and management at the Rochester Institute of Technology, Rochester, New York. "It never hurts to ask the customer, 'How do you feel about me? How have I failed you?'"

We recently used a written survey to scrutinize the performance of our sister corporation, About Books, Inc. and provide our clients with continuous improvement. We had over a 25% return. It not only made us aware of our strengths and areas for improvement, but helped our clients feel as if they're part of the team. You might want to use the adjacent survey as a model for creating one of your own.

The Savings and Loan Network, a small Chicago-based company that markets financial services to savings and loans, recently surveyed about 25 customers by telephone. The hopedfor result was to discover why they weren't getting as many deals as they'd predicted. Those 25 calls were all it took. A few policy changes later, they were back on target.

American Express mails a survey to customers who have complained. Included are questions concerning courtesy, competence, and whether the problem was handled correctly. Overall service is also measured. Hotels commonly employ the in-room survey, that familiar little card asking questions about the stay. Virtually any firm can tuck a questionnaire in with the monthly billing. (A little tip: For a bigger response, offer a small percentage off the bill if the survey is completed and returned with the payment.)

Client Survey Sample

p.o. box 1500, 425 cedar street, buena vista, co 81211-1500 • (719) 395-2459, FAX (719) 395-8374

Client Survey

How are we doing? In an effort to provide our clients with continuous quality improvement, we'd greatly appreciate your feedback on how you feel about our performance on your book project. Won't you take 10 minutes to complete this brief questionnaire? As a token of our appreciation, we'll send you a complimentary gift book that will be fun to use yourself—or pass on to someone else. For your convenience, a self-addressed envelope is enclosed. Please rank items 1-10 (10 being the highest) or n/a for not applicable. Thanks so much for your help!

Value of project evaluation/manuscript critique

Handling of pre-publication functions

Effectiveness of editing

Caliber of cover design

Quality of interior design and typesetting

Quality of printing

Satisfaction with written promotional materials

Effectiveness of national marketing plan

Value received for dollars invested

Timeliness of turn-around

Availability of key personnel to answer your questions

Prompt response to your needs

Attitude of caring by About Books, Inc. staff

Overall satisfaction

more over . . .

What you liked best in dealing with ABI:

What you liked least:

Are there other ways we could be of service to you?

Suggestions on how we can improve and serve you better:

Name and address (optional):

1/F1/2/c-survey.doc 3/93 (enclosure: self-addressed envelope)

What are the most important characteristics to measure? Researchers with the Marketing Science Institute quizzed customers from a wide range of service business. They found clients of everyone from lawyers to repair firms look for five items to assure satisfaction:

1. *Reliability.* The number one concern of customers is the ability to perform dependably, accurately, and consistently. Always, always keep promises!

2. *Responsiveness.* Prompt service and a helpful attitude.

3. *Assurance.* Knowledgeable and courteous employees who convey confidence.

4. *Empathy.* Individualized attention and a sympathetic ear.

5. *Tangibles.* Physical facilities and equipment and well-groomed employees.

Once customer feedback is tabulated, evaluate the results. Is the information about something you can change? Explore creative options. Share the results with the right people. The repair crew can only alter factors under their control. Correct any highlighted weaknesses. Remember, research is conducted to understand customer satisfaction, not to place blame after you have received the results. When you point your finger at someone else, three fingers point back at you!

The Value of Customer/Client Retention

We've spent a lot of time in this book showing you how to acquire customers. The other side of the coin is knowing how to keep them. The "once you've got 'em, forget 'em" attitude is financial suicide for the small service business or professional practice. Clients and customers are not disposable commodities. Unlike paper plates or napkins, you can't use them once, then toss them aside. That may seem like ordinary common sense, but it's a fact many tend to forget.

The emphasis in many marketing plans is on attracting new clients rather than on retaining the current ones. However, the brightest prospects for future business are present customers. The American Management Association says that 65% of the average company's business comes from its existing, satisfied patrons.

It's clearly a smart move to invest company energy into a comprehensive internal marketing program. Keeping the current customer happy and satisfied is not always easy but it's certainly profitable.

Hotels offer a prime example. Bob spends a relaxing weekend at the City Hotel. The service was excellent, the room a delight, and he couldn't have asked for a friendlier staff. Guess where Bob now stays every time he comes to the city? He sings their praises to Uncle Joe and his business partner and they, too, stay at City Hotel when in town. What did it cost the hotel? Merely the investment to attract Bob to register that first time.

On the other hand, Pete stays a few days at Town Hotel and is miserable the entire time. The room was too hot, the restaurant was below par, and he couldn't find help when he needed it. Pete will not return. It's back to square one for Town Hotel. They not only lost the chance for a repeat customer, they forfeited any referrals he might have sent their way.

Because service is such an intangible commodity, it is even more important for those within this universe to maintain a close alliance with their customers. Performance ratings are often elusive—unlike the product that either works or it doesn't. How does a client judge the quality of his or her lawyer amidst a bewildering jumble of papers and briefs? That call is influenced largely by the relationship between the two. Does the attorney seem to care about me and my problem? Are telephone messages and correspondence answered promptly? Is the lawyer there when I need help? Often, the only difference between lawyer A and lawyer B is common courtesy and service.

By holding the hand of today's customer, you're ensuring future success. If you've already installed a top-notch service strategy to keep clients happy, you've taken a giant step in the right direction. Developing a strong service culture in itself draws customers back. Regard it as an investment in future profits. Hyundai does. Before they sold a single car on American soil, they implemented an advance customer communication program.

People buy relationships. That's what service is all about: a caring, loving, serving attitude. Keeping customers content involves maintaining a continual positive association. Loyalty to a brand or vendor isn't the motivating factor it was 30 years ago. Cultivating the allegiance of customers is a high-priority marketing move. The client should feel a close association with your firm even when he or she does not immediately need your services.

Often it's the little things that make the difference. As we've said before, let customers know they're appreciated. Call or write and say thanks for their business. Acknowledge any large or out-of-the-ordinary orders. Professionals should personally welcome each new client to the practice. Create a list of birthdays, anniversaries, and other important dates and congratulate clients on those special days. Forward newspaper or magazine articles that might be of interest. Use any means to *stay in contact* and in the customer's mind.

"Servicing your accounts" is sales terminology, but the technique is viable for everyone in your organization. Call and suggest further service. Is it time for little Johnnie to have his teeth cleaned? Would the new mother be interested in an exercise class held evenings at the hospital? Now that summer's here, does Jane need a pair of prescription sunglasses? Does Ralph's will need to be updated now that he's remarried?

Encourage feedback. Elicit comments concerning existing services and ways they could be improved. Invite ideas about how your approach might be improved. Thoughts on any additional services could boost your business, because suggestions are truly from the customer's point of view. Tips on what they want or need can open up new profit centers for your business.

So you've sent the thank you's and clipped and mailed interesting articles. But the client hasn't darkened the door of your establishment in ages. It's time to take the direct, straight-as-an-arrow approach. Call. Say: "Mr. Smith, we miss you. Is there a reason we haven't seen you lately?" He may have a very good reason—one you somehow overlooked. On the other hand, the factors involved might be completely out of your control. Whatever the cause, don't lose a customer or client without a good Fight.

Going Beyond the Call of Duty

What are you selling? Is it information, insurance, or child care? Maybe you operate a radio station, a photo lab, or a weight control center. Whatever arena you operate within, you're still packaging and marketing a "service product" to consumers. Your small service business or professional practice may not be rolling widgets off an assembly line, but quality should still be top priority.

Quality means offering the best service you can possibly render. As the U.S. Army says, "Be the best that you can be." Half-hearted efforts won't stand a chance with today's smart, sophisticated consumers.

Quality, combined with reliability, is the answer. Harley-Davidson discovered this in the early 1980s. A variety of problems plagued its motorcycles. At the same time, a wave of reliable machines rolled in from Japan. The company came very close to disaster.

"We learned a painful, but vital lesson: Your product is the most vital relationship you have with a customer," explains Vaughn Beals, CEO of Harley Davidson. "If you let anything disturb that relationship, trouble will follow." The company rallied, thanks to customer input and an internal commitment to quality. "But we don't take our comeback for granted," Beals adds. "If we ever fail to deliver what the customer wants, we'll be right back where we started."

Service businesses take heed. Deliver the best health care, furnish superb catering, or give completely honest car repair. For you, providing a top-notch "product" means providing top-notch service.

Another side to the service coin is follow-up. The shining stars of the industry emphasize its importance. Mini Maid Services contacts every single customer the day after they receive services. All comments are recorded, evaluated, and placed in the hands of the employees who performed the service. Customers are pleased, and employees have a yardstick to measure customer perception of their work.

Going above and beyond means taking a critical look at the hiring process. Daniel Krumm, chairman and CEO of Maytag Corporation, points to *people* as the key ingredient in producing quality. "We preach quality throughout the organization, and hire the best people we can." he says. "They understand the importance of quality to our success and to their own job security."

Stew Leonard, owner of "the world's largest dairy store" in Norwalk, Connecticut, interviews 15 to 25 applicants to find the right person for each position. What makes an individual special? According to Leonard, it's attitude. "The main thing . . . our director of personnel looks for is a good attitude—above experience, skills, training, education, or appearance," he explains. "If applicants have a good attitude, we can give them the rest."

Just what does this service cheerleader give his employees? The answer is training. By sending them to seminars, providing tapes and books, and giving in-house training, Leonard molds employees into service-conscious helpers. "But if they have a bad attitude to start with, everything we try to do seems to fail," he adds. What employee traits complement your business or profession? Do you need enthusiasm, empathy, or simply that "right attitude?" Before you read a single resume, make a list of what you (and your customers) need in that new employee.

Take a look at company policies. In fact, take a good look at the word *policy* itself. It's from the same root word as police. Are you servicing your customers or "police-ing" them? Are you punishing the 99% of your clients who are good, honest people simply because of a dishonest 1%? Stop and consider each customer on an individual level. If you need a policy, keep it short and simple. Customers don't want a policy, they want a person who listens, cares, and can *do something* about their concern.

Providing outstanding service also means offering it to all segments of society. Can someone in a wheelchair reach your office or business? Can the elderly master any stairs in the process? The handicapped and senior citizens are powerful economic forces who are no longer sitting quietly on the sidelines. Do you want their patronage? Then remember their special needs.

The Greyhound Bus Company targets those requirements in its Helping Hand program. If a handicapped person needs assistance in traveling, a companion may ride free. Wheelchairs, crutches, and walkers are carried in the baggage compartment without extra charge.

Modern technology has boosted expectations when it comes to communications. Customers demand an immediate response to their inquiries, or they'll let their fingers do the walking. From necessity, doctors were among the first to utilize paging devices. Obstetricians are keenly aware that babies seldom wait until halftime to enter the world. Nowadays, everyone from real estate appraisers to interior decorators use this tool to keep in close contact with the office and customers.

Maybe there's no one back at the office to answer the telephone in the first place. If you haven't purchased an answering machine or hired an answering service, do it now. What would your impression be of a company that didn't answer its telephone? The majority of customers immediately envision a fly-by-night establishment. Is this the image you're portraying?

Another communication option is a pager. These electronic leashes extend your reach and allow you to do business more efficiently. In 1993 almost 19 million Americans carry pagers. These pocket-sized electronic devices beep (the old models), play a tune, or vibrate when someone needs to reach you. You can even find out who's calling and why if you have the newer alphanumeric technology that has a liquid-crystal display screen allowing for 80 characters of text or numbers.

Prices are dropping fast, so reinvestigate this if you decided against this communication tool because of excess cost a few years ago.

A repairperson needn't stop by the office or even be near a telephone to receive instantaneous messages. Have the water pipes burst at Mrs. Smith's? Is the basement rapidly filling with water? Getting your worker to her emergency in record time will ensure a loyal patron. And couriers can receive last minute instructions whether they're walking down the street or picking up a package in a building. Pagers have a multitude of uses. Some restaurants lend them to waiting customers, freeing them from waiting for a call in a smoky lounge.

Cellular telephones are revolutionizing our ability to communicate. Users can drive from New York to Los Angeles with very little disruption in service. According to the Cellular Telecommunications Industry Association, the average charge for the ability to maintain direct customer contact is $97 per month. For those traveling in distant cities, Hertz, National, Budget, and Dollar car rentals offer this option in their autos.

How often do you pick up the phone and dial a toll-free 800 number? AT&T's toll-free directory is now larger than the telephone books in some major cities. Customers have come to expect this method of contacting businesses. They reason that the company should pick up the tab for inquiries or orders, not the customer. Have they got a point? If you deal with out-of-town clients, this option may be for you. Many companies are realizing that providing a toll-free number for repair and service inquiries also makes sense.

A competitive edge guaranteed to increase customer satisfaction is the fulfillment of rush or special orders. When a frantic client calls asking for air-conditioning repair by 5:00 P.M. because they are having an anniversary party, opportunity is knocking at the door. Make that repair and appreciation soars. Consider what other arrangements are feasible and how much they will cost. Then inform the client of the charge for this extraordinary service. Whether it's a repair, the advice of a consultant, or a vital part, most customers will gladly pay more to get what they need. And the company comes out looking like a winner.

Whatever your business or profession, take the initiative and go that extra mile. You don't need to be the size of IBM or Maytag to share in their shining reputation for service. Catering to customers and clients fulfills their needs and launches your firm on a steady road to success. Believe in customer satisfaction. Become a dedicated fanatic. When you let your enthusiasm for the cause grow, so will your company and your bank account.

Now let's delve into the subject of employee motivation. Your enthusiasm must be transmitted to others in the organization if the greatest potential is to be realized.

9

Employee Motivation: Critical to Your Success

No matter what service you provide, you're primarily in the people business. To grow and prosper, every enterprise must stretch beyond it's founder. That means adding associates—and developing a sensitivity to their needs.

Do you want your employees (or volunteers in the case of nonprofits) to be outstanding? Hardworking? Extra conscientious? Your personal actions and organizational policies go a long way toward achieving that result! "But I can't change people," you say. You're only partly right. You can influence people's attitudes. By making them feel personally valued or by coming up with imaginative "extras" that don't cost much but offer genuine benefits for your workers, you motivate others to be more and do more. If that's not enough, replace them. You have too much to lose to keep bad apples!

Today's workers seek challenge and personal meaning from their jobs, even above a fatter paycheck and security. They want to know you are genuinely interested in what they are doing. They want a part in shaping the future of the company. Associates need to feel they are partners in making the business work and that they really contribute. Additionally, they want the personal respect you afford any self-directed adult.

Most small service businesses and nonprofit organizations must retain employees without the funds available in large corporate coffers. Is there a way to motivate these people besides hefty pay raises? You bet! That's the message of this chapter.

The first step is to lay the right foundation. Listen to your workers. Involve them in your business. Even Attila the Hun realized the importance of seeking recommendations from others. "A king with chieftains who always agree with him reaps the counsel of mediocrity," he said.

Give people recognition. Offer versatile, as opposed to traditional, company benefits. This may not cost you any more, but it could provide a welcome alternative for employees. Within this chapter we also delve into options you may want to consider outside the typical work force.

Laying the Right Foundation

Do you realize you're already putting employee/employer building blocks in place before you ever hire a person? The tone of your ad, the atmosphere in your office or shop, how people are treated when they apply for a job—these are the bricks and mortar of a first impression. If things are impersonal and hurried during this paperwork stage, can the potential employee expect better on the job?

Once the decision has been made to add an individual to the team, why not do a few things to make his or her first day easier? Discuss the dress code or provide any necessary uniforms. Talk about arrangements for eating lunch. Explain where to park. If the person is relocating from a distant city, it's a kind gesture to offer help in getting to know the new community and finding suitable housing.

It is imperative new hires be made to feel welcome. The first few hours and days are an important time. Be sure to introduce them around to coworkers, subordinates, their immediate supervisors, and other department heads. Assuming you're not large enough to have a separate personnel department, designate a friendly, long-standing employee to be a "buddy." Buddies take new hires under their wings, explaining the corporate culture and discussing the unspoken rules. They show where supplies are stored and reveal what the boss likes—and doesn't like. On a more professional level, a mentor might be appropriate to convey company expectations and pave the way for climbing the corporate ladder.

Perhaps you are small. Maybe this is only your first or second employee. Then it is vital you familiarize and educate the person *yourself.* This orientation is a fig leaf to a scared, new employee. It makes the person feel more comfortable, builds confidence, and lets the individual know what to expect.

Look at the big picture first. Explain your company's goals. By making your vision their vision, everyone heads in the same direction. Next, cover such details as when and where breaks are taken. Discuss any safety precautions—show where coat racks or lockers are located—tell a woman where to store her purse—point out the restroom.

Even small organizations can benefit from developing a general employee handbook or manual. It spells out company policy and outlines procedures for various tasks. This saves explaining the same thing over and over. It's also an invaluable reference to use in your absence.

Other helpful items for a new hireling include copies of your brochure, corporate profile, industry articles or books you've authored—any promotional materials. Do you have video or audio tapes that would be useful? Could the new person gain a better grasp of your industry by reading recent trade journals? Is there a seminar being sponsored soon that would provide supportive background information? Be creative in looking for ways to orient your new employee.

Why is this orientation process so important? On a personal level, it instills a sense of purpose in those who join your organization. They sense they are part of a professional and caring team. From a company standpoint, it makes good business sense. It is costly to replace a worker. When you lose good employees, you must expend dollars and time to replace them. Research shows employees often leave a firm within a year or two if they haven't been thoroughly prepared for the work there. You simply can't afford such turnover if you want to build a strong, expanding organization.

Showing You Care

Demonstrating to an associate that you really care is like giving catnip to a kitten. It's heady stuff. It is guaranteed to inspire your workers. How do you show you care?

One way is to pay attention to their working conditions. Is there good lighting? Have you made sure the heat and ventilation is adequate? Are safety measures taken to protect their well-being? Is furniture, such as steno chairs and desk heights, comfortable? Have you provided the office supplies, tools of the trade, and training needed so employees can reasonably proceed with their jobs? It is easy to take such details for granted. Yet an owner's or manager's lack of concern for working conditions can cause employee morale to plummet.

If you want worker loyalty, you have to earn it. Harping and sermonizing about employee loyalty is a waste of time. Allegiance is automatic when individuals feel they are given a fair shake. If you show you care, most people will respond in kind.

Your own attitude rubs off on those with whom you work. Especially in a small organization, the boss sets the pace. If you want a happy, responsive crew, behave that way yourself.

One sure method for setting a positive tone is to dispense praise and thanks generously. Be optimistic. Find constructive things to commend. It is easy to forget all the good things a person does when he or she makes mistakes. Yet dwelling on the mistakes seems to foster even more errors. Always praise in public; reprimand in private. When you must admonish someone, do so behind closed doors. Few things are more embarrassing—not only for the person being criticized, but for all within earshot—than listening to a coworker being severely chastised.

Listen to Liberate, Then Communicate

Contrary to what management typically believes, studies show employees most want recognition, interesting work, and a feeling of being *in on things*. They desire this even above good pay and a secure job. However, if we don't listen to our workers, we never hear the rumblings of "I'm always the last one to find out what's going on."

We spend more time at our job than doing anything else in our lives. Is it any wonder then that people feel isolated and left out when major changes occur around them they had no inkling about? Sharing information—up and down the ladder—is a powerful motivator.

We all think we communicate our expectations clearly. Do we? What happens if your service rep hears something other than what you meant? Or when your secretary interprets your words differently than the message you intended to convey? Problems, that's what! Even if you ask if they understand, most will say yes. People are generally too embarrassed to admit they didn't understand. An excellent way around this is to ask your subordinate to tell you what he or she is going to do. Close your mouth and listen. Then you can correct any misconception before it escalates into a major dilemma.

If the project is complex, you might want to pose a series of questions. "What will you do if X happens?" you might query. "Suppose

Y occurs. How will you handle things then?" you ask. When you listen, you help your employees to help you.

When working with professionals a different kind of problem can get in the way. These bright people sometimes tune you out, thinking they already know the question or where the discussion is leading. They mentally rush ahead and anticipate—often incorrectly. One tactic to use in this situation is to stop talking for a few seconds until they once again focus on the conversation.

Whether the discussion is with someone having only a high school education or a Ph.D., the approach is the same. The message sender should seek feedback from the receiver. Blindly assuming the other heard and understood what is wanted can be foolhardy.

It can also be rash to deprive yourself of input from your crew. They are in the best position to offer practical suggestions, because they do the work day in and out. (Not to mention, they will buy into ideas much more readily if they contribute to them.)

That's what Louise Rhodes discovered. She owns and runs a Rock Hill, South Carolina, janitorial service called Featherdusters. When Rhodes is faced with a big job and a tight deadline, she asks her workers to participate in coping with the situations. They may expend extra energy, effort, and commitment to meet the deadline. Or they may advise bringing in more help to get the job done within the time constraints. Because she encourages them and listens to them, her people often go the extra mile.

Another important time to pay close attention is when associates make special requests. Most people will not ask for unique treatment unless it is a major consideration to them. Really listen and sincerely try to accommodate their request. Don't reject unusual ideas out of hand. Give an employee a chance to explain why an unusual arrangement can succeed.

Journalists Margaret and William Freivogel proposed a job-sharing plan to their employer, the *St. Louis Post Dispatch*. In job-sharing, the two of them equal one full-time employee. With a large, active family, they needed a creative way to balance the conflicting demands of work and family life. Not only did they have to get the approval of the newspaper publisher, but also a skeptical bureau chief and the union. Everyone listened. Because they recognized the importance of these employees lives beyond the workplace, they were able to retain a productive and efficient team.

Listening can also lead to cost-cutting measures and greater customer satisfaction. In a hotel environment, a desk clerk suggested a change machine be installed in the game room so quarter-hungry teens didn't que up for change while hotel guests were trying to register.

Encourage employee suggestions. Their ideas won't always work. However, many a company has been saved thousands of dollars because a worker found a better way to do something.

You may want to give cash rewards for cost-saving or money-making suggestions. This gets people involved. They care much more about the company, because if they can make it more successful, they'll be personally compensated. Here again, no out-of-pocket expenses. You're only paying for something that will save or make you money—typically many times over. It's like having a staff of free consultants, each of whom has an intimate understanding of your business.

In Japan the average employee submits 800 ideas per year! Executives react quickly and respectfully to each suggestion. If we could get but 10% of Japan's participation, American capitalism would receive a tremendous boost. To encourage suggestions, have workers complete the sentence, "If I were the company president . . . "

Heed what subordinates say as they leave your employ as well. Exit interviews can provide a wealth of information. They often pinpoint problems workers were hesitant to discuss. This allows you to correct the internal difficulty and salvage future workers.

Involvement Equals Excellence

In the last decade many managers have become employee-centered rather than productivity-centered. They've discovered productivity comes automatically when workers are happy. In larger organizations, this has resulted in fewer levels of authority and more power toward the bottom of the pyramid.

Beginning entrepreneurs, on the other hand, tend to run benevolent dictatorships. In the start-up venture, their word rules. As the business grows, however, they must learn to coach a team of players rather than command a battalion of soldiers. It is important the person who began the business starts to let go and grooms others to carry part of the weight. They can help cover his or her blind spots. Key employees are the lifeblood of an expanding business. Sharp executives want to call some of their own shots. If the owner hires racehorses, then treats them like mules, all is lost.

People feel good when they are allowed to do their best. As Dr. Jay Hall points out in his excellent book, *The Competence Connection*, "People are inherently competent. Treat them like they know what they're doing and they will do what needs to be done." This precious, but neglected, resource is the bedrock upon which the achievement of excellence is built.

Cut your people loose to solve company problems. Expect them to use their own judgment and improvise solutions. When they realize you actually want them to become involved on more than a superficial level, they'll get excited about problem solving.

The surgical-service nurses in a Los Angeles hospital felt frustrated, because they were being used as servants instead of really helping patients to heal. When allowed to brainstorm about the problem, they came up with answers. The result was patients got their own snacks, helped each other, and ate together. This freed the nurses to provide the health care they were trained to administer and to really make a difference.

Mississippi Management Inc. is a hotel management company that believes in keeping its employees in the know. They hold annual seminars not only for managers and supervisors, but also for cooks, front-desk clerks, and housekeepers. The corporate trainer has maids play a version of "The Price is Right." There are two teams and two tables. One table contains items the maids use in their jobs—bars of vanity and bath soap, for instance. On the other table are price tags. One team tries to match the items with the right prices; the other team tries to correct any mistakes it thinks have been made.

Using this competition as a backdrop, the trainer explains how much soap costs. "If a facility has 200 rooms and you put in new soap each day 365 days a year . . . " The long and short of it is soap costs about $10,000 annually. The maids no longer see soap as an insignificant expense. Because they have been involved in the process, many of them will not throw away an open bar each day when a hotel guest stays on. They will leave it—plus a fresh, unopened bar. Most times the guest will continue using the open bar. Thus, a substantial savings can be realized over a year.

Before people can have an impact, they have to know what is going on. As in the case above, increased access to information paves the way for decreased spending. When you disclose company facts to associates, you demonstrate you respect them as people and want their contributions. Informed common sense is the underpinning people need to sort the worthwhile from the wasteful.

Employee and Volunteer Recognition Programs

What makes Johnny or Jenny run? A recent Public Agency Foundation survey of 845 random jobholders revealed their productivity is improved 58% by recognition for good work. Praise is a splendid antidote for apathy. It elevates employee enthusiasm or volunteer zeal even more when it takes the form of public recognition. Although everyone likes to be told he or she has done a good job, people *love* to be acknowledged in front of their peers. When doing so, you send a positive signal to all involved. One of the beauties of recognition programs is they usually produce exceptional results, yet cost little money.

If you have eight or more workers, consider starting an employee (or volunteer) of the month program. Spend 40 bucks and have a perpetual trophy made that passes to the new recipient each month. You'll see it proudly displayed on desks or counter tops or carted home to show off to family and friends.

Bring everyone together to announce the honors. Take the winner's picture and display it prominently. Write the chosen employee a special letter of commendation citing why he or she was selected for this honor or create a Certificate of Appreciation. Send a press release to local papers announcing the accomplishment. Consider awarding a small cash prize or bonus. Give recipients a half-day or full-day off. This doesn't cost you much and is greatly appreciated, especially by people with small children. If you produce an internal newsletter or other company-wide publications, do a feature article about the employee of the month. Include a photograph. Here again, it's low budget, but high reward.

Awards should not be monopolized by one or two people, but passed around. Naturally, you will be constantly on the lookout for deserving individuals. Maybe it's for working overtime to pull off a special project before deadline, maybe for being especially courteous with customers or coworkers, perhaps because someone's overall annual attendance is outstanding. Another time an award might be given because the salesperson did a phenomenal job that month. The reasons are as varied as the seasons. The point is you're giving people well-deserved recognition.

Of course, a natural corollary to the employee of the month is the employee of the year, chosen from the previous 12 contenders. The grand prize might include an all-expense weekend for two at a nearby resort.

But recognition need not cost anything. Consider designating an especially desirable parking space for the employee of the month, for instance. We noticed such a spot reserved for Top Associate at an ERA real estate office while in Denver recently.

Gainesville, Florida, has initiated a city employee of the month program. City Manager W. D. Higgenbotham wanted to modify existing employee behavior. City workers looked upon their livelihoods as a job rather than a career. They had an "It's not my job and I don't care" attitude. Higgenbotham decided to convert that into a new philosophy.

The program's slogan became "Ask me—I'll help." Teeshirts, buttons, stickers, stationery, hats, bumper stickers, business cards, and signs helped promote it to city workers. Seminars and rallies were used to boost morale. Employees were nominated for the community achievement awards by "Thanks for Helping" memos submitted by customers and coworkers. The final decision rested on a committee of city employees.

Transamerica Occidental Life established a different sort of award. They launched an "Effectancy Campaign" for ideas that are both efficient and effective. Winners receive buttons and are awarded prizes.

Although we'd all probably agree employee and volunteer recognition is a good thing, how does one go about pinpointing it? Watch for little things. Make a note when a worker does something good. (Unless jotted down, such gestures are usually forgotten.) Some supervisors even carry a pocket dictating machine to capture the moment when someone does something praiseworthy.

Of course, commendations needn't be limited to scheduled public displays. We write personal notes of appreciation when a person does an exceptional job. As the chair of a trade association, one of us penned a letter to a volunteer who had helped the organization for several years. He wrote back: "I appreciate your thoughtful words about my handling of the exhibit. I suppose that I'm like an old hound who hasn't quite collapsed far enough into senility not to prefer having its ears scratched occasionally rather than being kicked in the ribs."

In addition to increasing individual self-esteem, such activities establish an upbeat attitude in the workplace. Recognition pays big rewards for all concerned.

Versatile Employee Benefits

It isn't practical for small firms or associations to offer the extravagant benefit packages Fortune 500 companies dole out. However, that doesn't mean we can't do some exciting things for our people. Rather than all flying in a uniform "V" formation like a flock of migrating geese, let's spread our wings further and explore some innovative approaches to rewarding our associates.

In most cases they cost far less than traditional benefits. Yet the outcome—happy people and better productivity—can be much greater. Before this concept will succeed, however, we must break out of our stereotyped thinking. Desert the flock. Probe and scour and dig to discover nontraditional ways to add job value.

Space utilization is one consideration. Is your facility being used in the most intelligent way possible? Maybe you can condense storage areas or make other adjustments to allow room for a cheerful employee lounge. There workers can rest, talk, eat, and have a change of pace. By thinking imaginatively, we were able to turn a boiler room into a fitness center complete with a gym, treadmill, and exercise bike.

How about outside space? Is there room to play basketball or set up a volleyball court? Athletics foster a team spirit and relieve stress. What about using excess land for a company garden where you provide the space, seeds, fertilizer, and water? What a small price to pay for the camaraderie, goodwill, and tasty vegetables that result from such a community garden.

Here's an exciting idea for the jobholder involved in repair or production: when he or she meets an agreed-upon daily quota, that's it for the day. Go home early. This philosophy rewards results rather than time served. Although not a typical "employee benefit," word of this policy will soon guarantee you have the most conscientious workers on your payroll.

Why not help your employees save money on their personal purchases? Use your clout—and resale number—to buy items they need at reduced prices. You'd be surprised how many places will give you wholesale or jobber prices on such items as appliances, auto parts, electronic units, etc. Yes, it means a little extra paperwork for payroll deductions, but the goodwill far exceeds the effort. Look beyond the obvious. Passing along such savings provides employees with more spendable income without the need for a raise.

Although it should be self-evident, "'tain't necessarily so" that businesses allow their own workers to purchase, at rock-bottom prices, what they themselves sell. We've known retailers with a 50% markup who only gave their clerks 10 or 20% off. Yet this kind of employee perk costs the firm nothing and gives the individual real value.

There are also psychological rewards. These are things that make us feel good. Do you remember your employees' birthdays and company anniversaries? Most bosses don't. Yet this is such a simple thing. All you have to do is make a list of current employee dates, then put a reminder tickler on your calendar.

Birthdays and company anniversaries give you an opportunity to shine as an employer. Why not give your workers the day off in honor of the event? Anytime you can handle a benefit in this way, it helps your cash flow. Although no actual money leaves your corporate coffers, a tangible benefit is being given the employee.

Another nice way to celebrate is to have everyone sign a greeting card, then throw a surprise potluck lunch in honor of the occasion. In areas where businesses or agencies are bigger, this is often done on a departmental basis.

Do you have a mountain cabin, boat, snow mobile, travel trailer, time share, or riding horses that stay idle most of the time? You might consider favoring your employees with these items when you aren't using them. This costs virtually nothing, yet is perceived as a generous treat by other folks. Taking it a step further, you might also have some land that could be developed into a free recreational area for employee vacation getaways.

Now look within yourself, your relatives, your friends, and your business associates. More resources wait here to be tapped. Do you have a hunting guide in the family? Why not strike a deal with him or her to take a party of your employees out on an expedition.

How about teaming up with another local merchant for everyone's benefit? Let's say you own a restaurant. Maybe you could negotiate with the owner of a clothing store to offer each others employees a 20% discount on purchases. This is a win/win/win proposition. The workers of both firms have the benefit of reduced-cost clothes and food, while both companies have the opportunity for additional business.

Although certainly not new, covering the cost of employee personal and professional development often makes sense. The more educated and better trained your workers are, the more productive they will be. Encourage their participation in job-related courses and reimburse the fees. Consider footing the bill for them to attend seminars, conferences, or trade shows. If they indicate an interest, covering the costs of membership in trade organizations and subscriptions to professional publications is also a wise move.

A Charlotte, North Carolina, firm, Harper Companies International, has come up with an unusual benefit for their people. "We'll give an employee $500 if he or she will write and get a technical article published in a trade magazine," says Ron Harper. For more literary-minded types, this is an interesting possible perk.

Another creative idea is to begin a Wellness Program. Once thought of as faddish, today almost two-thirds of companies with 50 or more employees have such programs. (This has some definite advantages for the company, too. Healthy people are more productive, have higher morale, less absenteeism, and lower health insurance costs.)

Wellness Programs include everything from exercise and fitness classes to stress management seminars. They also encompass back care classes, hypertension control programs, stop-smoking clinics, and weight control assistance. Along with this, some firms cut down on absenteeism by rewarding employees who maintain excellent attendance records with either cash or time off.

The newest trend in employee rewards is termed "cafeteria style" benefit packages. This means just what it implies. Workers can choose from a menu of several options. Cafeteria programs aren't practical for small companies who don't have the economies of scale to offer various benefit options. For larger firms, however, the options save money, stimulate productivity, and make unions less attractive. In most cases the biggest cost is the courage it takes to do something different.

These adjustable plans give associates unprecedented say in how they're compensated for their work. Especially with more two-career families, this makes a lot of sense. When both husband and wife have health insurance, for instance, there is wasted duplication. How much better if a forward-thinking employer offers choices. One alternative would be a longer vacation period instead of health insurance. Another might be an allowance each month to be used toward child-care expenses instead of health benefits.

No, most small businesses can't afford elaborate employee perks. Free legal aid, company-funded child-care centers, and reimbursement for adoption or funeral expenses are out of our league. However, we can be inventive in offering our employees other things to make the workplace more humane. Some firms allow their people to work one (paid) day a month for their favorite charity.

In our organization, for example, associates get their birthdays as a paid holiday. We've also set up a fully equipped exercise room for their use. And we make our time-share available for vacations at our reduced cost. One of us is a member of the American Society of Journalists and Authors, which offers magazine subscriptions at greatly reduced rates. We pass these along. Because our aim is to develop a *work family* atmosphere, we also invite everybody to a social event at least quarterly. One year we took everybody river rafting; another time to the local melodrama. And because our people work hard, we also want them to play hard. We decided something we could afford to do was give generous vacations. Our policy is two weeks after one year, three weeks after three years, and four weeks after five years.

Options Within—and Without— the Typical Workplace

You can have a dramatic impact on your employees total quality of life. With so many two-career families, jobs wreak havoc on family schedules. Some companies are taking a personal interest in employees as individuals and designing flexible arrangements that allow people to customize their work arrangements.

If you're in an industry that doesn't mandate an 8 to 5 job, why require it? Flextime—where workers have a say about the hours they work and can adjust to family needs—needn't cost you a dime. Yet it can be a blessing for your employees. By permitting people to work staggered hours, it allows husbands and wives to cut down on baby-sitting costs and time away from their children. It also gives couples who have conflicting work schedules more time together if one of them has the latitude to adjust his or her hours. In a flextime program, one person may arrive at 7:00 A.M. and work until 3:00 P.M., while another might prefer to begin at 10:00 A.M. and wrap up at 6:00 P.M.

In a few progressive companies people participate in job-sharing. Under this arrangement, two individuals work part-time, dividing the responsibilities of one full-time job. They may do a morning/afternoon split or come in alternate weeks. Another choice is one works Monday and Wednesday, the other Tuesday and Thursday, and both of them work Friday morning.

A work-at-home arrangement is heralded by some. In our information age, many jobs can be effective accomplished via computer from the comfort of home. This is called telecommuting. It's ideal for those who must provide day care for elderly parents, for instance.

Sometimes employee leasing comes to the rescue. A few small firms have literally fired all their workers on Friday, then rehired them on Monday morning through an employee leasing company. That way workers can benefit from a package of fringe benefits superior to any the small company could provide.

A last elective is using peak-time employees. Banks, hospitals, and insurance companies find this holds down soaring payroll costs. These are top-quality people who are well paid to work only during the busiest times.

By sincerely seeking ways to motivate your employees, you'll likely build a reputation as a terrific place to work. In today's economy, that's like money in the bank. If you want associates who are outstanding, be an outstanding boss. Benefits given return manyfold. Now let's move into our final chapter where more exhilarating ideas await.

10

Other Techniques to Increase the Bottom Line

In this last chapter you'll find a collection of tips and techniques to make your job easier and your results excellent. We'll be exploring new ways to market via a computer and sharing facts about fax machines. The telephone is often an underused business tool. With it you can widen your horizons and save time. We will show you how.

What about putting a twist in the same old thing to gain greater exposure? We discuss this, plus details on how to establish a strong board of directors and where to locate your business. A grab bag of good ideas is also presented. Discover here why it's sometimes sensible to make your occupation your preoccupation.

Marketing via Computer

Once you have a personal computer, many new avenues are opened. You can customize promotional material, embark on desktop publishing, or create a database to track your prospects and customers. Additional uses include electronic mail and conducting sophisticated market research. Let's look at these various activities.

Word-processing allows you to create a standard form letter, modify it slightly to fit the occasion or person, then produce personalized correspondence. The same approach works for news releases. You can tailor them individually by simply altering the headline and first paragraph.

Some companies and nonprofit organizations have trimmed their promotional literature costs by as much as 50% by investing in desktop publishing. The other advantages are speed and flexibility. For this you need a personal computer (PC), appropriate software, and a laser printer. WordPerfect 5.1 can also deliver professional-looking typeset materials. And WordPerfect 6.0 is a dream.

What is often overlooked by proponents of desktop publishing, however, is that someone in your organization must know or learn a great deal about design and layout. The most sophisticated of equipment is still dependent on human knowledge to produce a suitable product. The operator must be proficient at creatively and effectively manipulating type and graphics. This issue of training should be addressed as part of the purchase decision.

Once you have desktop publishing capabilities, the uses for it are endless. Besides brochures, flyers, ads, and direct-mail packages, it is perfect for producing a newsletter. Other applications are proposals, training manuals, office forms, overhead transparencies, invitations, name badges, even signs.

In another dimension, a PC is handy for organizing and updating your list of publicity sources. This list maintenance is a useful feature that allows you to delete or revise names and addresses with the flick of a few keys. The tool for maintaining your list is a database management system (DBMS). The more information you want about each entry, the more sophisticated your database and the more powerful the database management software needed. We find Borland's dBASE IV, Version 2 to excel.

Even more vital to your success in today's competitive environment is detailed information about your current customers or clients. As we have determined, it is easier—and much less expensive—to sell two or three additional services to an existing customer than it is to acquire a new one. First, though, you must know about the activity of current accounts. A good DBMS details who bought what and when. It provides a sound foundation on which to build your communication program. Progressive financial service providers, for example, use databases to develop a strategy for cross-selling existing customers a new service.

A carefully designed database can also separate hot prospects from cold suspects. This helps you increase your hit rate, while decreasing the energy expended. You can analyze most profitable/least profitable contacts. In one instance a company narrowed down a field of 3,000 so-so possibilities to 600 valid leads.

This is accomplished by integrating information. The beauty of a good database is you can load different information from different sources, then target the right group by slicing and dicing it any way you want. DBMSs help you answer the following questions: Who am I trying to talk to? Where are they? How might I reach them? If you need help designing your DBMs, contact Tom for a bid.

Electronic mail, better known as "E-mail," is an innovative direct-marketing medium. With this computer wizardry, you leave messages in electronic mailboxes held by users of computer networks like the Source and CompuServe. Prospects who are interested spend between 20 and 40 cents to read and respond to your offer.

High-priced information is the most logical offering. Personal investing and financial management are ideal to merchandise in this manner. Immediacy is a major advantage. You can send E-mail out on Wednesday and have a sizable portion of your responses back by that Friday. It also allows you to reach prospects who are unresponsive to normal mail or telemarketing attempts.

By adding a modem to your personal computer, you can have the most comprehensive library in the world at your fingertips. This opens up market research in the pages of thousands of magazines, trade journals, newsletters, newspapers, and other resources. Those who subscribe to a database like the Source, Prodigy, DELPHI, CompuServe, or NewsNet have access to vast reservoirs of information.

As we've mentioned, a further computer-marketing possibility is "bulletin boards"—electronic rather than cork. With a modem you can communicate with diverse groups of people interested in specific subjects. They cover everything from sports to drama, sexual abuse to religion. Some are local, others national. No doubt there is a bulletin board devoted to your professional interests. For a paltry sum you can probably place an ad or carefully worded promotional listing on it. This method of "advertising" hasn't been widely discovered yet, so it offers fresh opportunities. Our advanced technology has made computerized marketing tools available and affordable for virtually any company.

And finally, computer *diskettes* can provide a big little marketing tool prospects can hardly resist. With more than 38 million computer users in America, using diskettes can be a practical way to reach this upscale segment of the population. "Customized diskettes are rarely thrown away," contends Jim Moreton, of Creative Disc, a diskette design and manufacturing firm. "Not only do they have value independent of their content, but human curiosity practically guarantees they will be reviewed. Ones that contain useful reference information or entertainment features are often copied and passed on to friends and colleagues. Thus you have an ever-growing audience."

A further advantage of this medium is that it gets the prospect involved. Research shows the average recipient of a diskette promotional program spends from 26 to 30 minutes interacting with it. This reinforces retention. If you offer a high ticket service, customized computer discs could well help you stand out from the crowd and cut through the customary clutter.

The Facts about Fax

Fax (a nickname for facsimile) machines are the current rage in business-to-business communication. If you and your client or prospective customer each have a fax, it's a simple matter to ask your machine to dial his or her machine's number. Within a few seconds whatever words, pictures, or signatures are involved will be transmitted over the phone lines.

Faxes now go anywhere a phone goes: in boats, cars, and airplanes. Some people find adding a fax board to their computers is a cost-effective alternative.

Why purchase one? Two prime reasons are prestige and timeliness. Businesses with fax communication are perceived as progressive. Their messages create a sense of urgency, receiving immediate attention. The only way to make a better impact is to have something delivered by personal courier. For home-based businesses, they create an aura of professionalism.

Fax transmission competes head-on with overnight express delivery services. Facsimile machines are fast, cheap to use (costing a little more than a first-class stamp in most cases), and easy. Some even double as primitive copiers. For those not ready to invest in their own unit, there are "for-hire" machines. Copy shops and office supply stores lead the pack in offering fax service.

Selective fax advertising is already being carried out by some firms. Those who have climbed on the infant fax advertising bandwagon claim it to be a professional alternative to conventional mailing methods. They reach hundreds in minutes. A test performed by a large publisher, using its own fax numbers, pulled over a 10% response. Direct-mail experts drool over such numbers.

If not done judiciously, however, criticism is heard from businesses who resent receiving unsolicited "junk fax." (Junk fax has already been outlawed in many states.) It is important prospects be carefully screened so only those *genuinely interested* receive transmissions. That this piece of office equipment will be abused as an advertising medium is a given. We already know of one Texas florist planning to wire ads to drum up corporate clients. If you decide to use it in this way, be sure you're not breaking any laws.

Telephone Tricks

For some businesses, the telephone is their lifeline. Even if your enterprise doesn't depend primarily on Mr. Bell's wonderful invention, we'll bet there are ways you can use a phone to be more successful. For important calls, always have a goal or desired result in mind. Make a brief list of points you want to cover.

When originating calls—especially sales calls or requests for donations—think through what you will say to launch the conversation. After you identify yourself, you have 15 to 30 seconds to convince the other person to stay on the line. Find a way to dramatize your reason for calling, devise a comment that ties your needs into something of interest to the other person. As we've said so often before, stress the *benefits.*

Suppose you need to get through to an important person—someone who is normally protected by an army of secretaries or assistants who carefully screen all calls. Mr. I. M. Notable isn't a personal friend, not even a business acquaintance. How will you ever penetrate the palace guard?

Using a "familiar" approach might be the open sesame. Say something like, "This is Jim Anderson calling for Ike." Your tone and manner suggest you've known Ike for years. (You never, however, lie and say that!) Chances are the secretary will tell you Ike is not available, whereupon you say, "Just ask him to call me please." Do *not* offer a number. That would blow your cover. Most efficient secretaries will ask you for one to save having to fish it out of the Rolodex. You then graciously provide it. This tactic usually gets your message placed in the "A" priority pile.

Another idea is to call after normal business hours. You can sometimes catch a busy executive working late and answering his or her own phone. A further suggestion is to try to track down a home phone number. Occasionally this can be accomplished by looking the person up in *Who's Who in America* or other directories. Some major libraries have street address cross-reference directories that also list phone numbers. If you have your target's address, this might help. Ask friends of friends if they can supply the needed information. If the person is an author, try calling their publisher for contact information.

If you do succeed in getting a personal number only to be greeted by an answering machine—leave just your name and phone number. By avoiding any further message, you will pique their curiosity and stand a better chance of getting a return call.

Dogged persistence has helped many scale the castle walls. When you realize only 17% of business callers reach their intended party on the first try, you know tenacity must play an important role. The higher the person is on the VIP list, the more phone calls you'll need to make. Calling, calling again, recalling—over and over—will eventually shake loose the desired response. One of two things will likely happen: The secretary will take pity on you and suggest to his boss she take the call. Or the VIP will say, "Oh, him again. Let me talk to him and get it over with so he stops calling."

Here are a few random tips for normal telephone situations. If someone wants to put you on hold, you might counter with, "I'll be happy to hold unless my other line rings. But please jot down my number in case I have to hang up." About half the people will call back *on their dime* if you do hang up. If you have a separate personal phone line, you may want to include the following message at the end of important business correspondence: "To get through to me directly without delay, use this personal number . . . "

If you do considerable phone business from coast to coast, instruct your secretary to always get the geographic location of the caller when taking a message. Then you can adjust for time zone differences when returning the call. By the way, depending on where you are located, you can save money by placing calls at the end or beginning of the work day. Here in Colorado, people can trim telephone costs by phoning the East Coast before 8:00 A.M. (it's almost 10:00 A.M. there). Call the West Coast just after 5 o'clock (it's barely past 4:00 P.M. there).

When your secretary announces callers with unfamiliar or foreign names, ask that the name be written out phonetically. Also consider teleconferencing when you need to get more than two individuals together. This often makes more sense than incurring travel expenses for several people. It is a prudent way to hold a group meeting and save both money and time.

Rather than play an indefinite game of phone tag, if you don't catch up with the proper person when returning a call, consider leaving a *time bomb* message. "Tell John, we'll go ahead with the plans we discussed unless I hear from him by 11 o'clock tomorrow morning." Another alternative is to send a fax.

Do you have a toll-free 800 number? Should you? Not only does this increase your lead inquiries, it allows you to upgrade orders and cross-sell other services. The average order by phone is 20% larger than by mail. Considering this statistic, shrewd marketers will do everything they can to make it easy for prospects to reach them via telephone.

Many companies assure their toll-free numbers are memorable by making them into a word. (800) FLOWERS, for instance, isn't just a gimmick. Memory research shows a catchy word or phrase is three to 10 times more likely to be recalled that its number equivalent. Especially if you use extensive TV, radio, or billboard advertising, a phone word tied to your company's service is smart. It is harder to dial, however. We get frustrated translating words into numbers. A way around this is to include the numbers in parenthesis. Look in Part III under Selected Suppliers for information on telephone companies to contact for 800 number particulars.

Location, Location, Location

Where you place your business can dramatically influence your success. Hotels and motels off the beaten track have a much more difficult job attracting guests. We know of a TV repair shop that moved from a dying downtown district to a thriving strip mall and tripled its business in a matter of weeks. If you depend on foot traffic to generate customers, be sure you locate in a well-traveled area. Also consider making your business portable. If this appeals to you, reread the section on "Take Your Service on the Road" in Chapter 5.

Many service businesses and professional practices begin in the owner's home. Because it keeps overhead to a minimum, this is very desirable for fledgling businesses. In fact, some entrepreneurs run substantial enterprises out of their residences. (Before you get too tempted, however, check zoning regulations; you may have to request a variance.)

A growing group of free-lance professionals are home-based and proud of it. These individuals—who have traded life in big cities and the corporate culture for building a solo high-tech businesses in the boonies—have been dubbed "Lone Eagles" by Phillip Burgess, president of the Center for the New West. Numbered among this group are writers, analysts, brokers, consultants, computer whizzes, and others who live by their wits. They connect with the outside world using PC's, telephones, faxes, modems, and airplane tickets. Living and working under the same roof, they serve their clients via electronic media.

The total number of full- and part-time home-based businesses should hit 24.3 million by the end of 1993, according to Link Resources Corp., A New York City-based research firm. That's an increase of 2.1 million people in 1992. As if that isn't impressive enough, it's estimated that a new home-based business starts every 11 seconds!

Professionals just starting out sometimes find sharing an office a simple and effective solution to office-space needs. Not only does this keep overhead down, you can provide client referrals to each other. This works especially well when the two consulting disciplines are complementary. An architect and an interior designer are a natural match; so is a management consultant and a marketing expert. What about a chiropractor and a massage therapist? Or a physical fitness specialist and a nutritionist?

Another option is called an *incubator*. No, we don't mean a toasty warm environment for hatching baby chicks. Incubators are facilities for bringing up baby businesses. And they're out there in record numbers. While only 50 existed in 1984, today there are more than 500. A business incubator houses from two to over 100 separate businesses. (The average number is 12.) Although each has its own unit, they share a common reception area, conference room, plus clerical and support services.

These support services can spell the difference between success and failure. Most small businesses are started by technicians. These people know their service inside and out—what they lack is experience in the day-to-day task of running a business. The Small Business Administration estimates that although nine out of 11 new firms fail during their first year, businesses that start in incubators have an 80% success rate. That is because they are given management and marketing guidance. This professional guidance is what nurtures them to success. An incubator gives a start-up a head start. Costs of photocopiers, fax machines, and postage machines are usually shared. So is the service of a receptionist and word processor. There are also excellent networking possibilities with other tenants.

While we're talking about location, let us mention a word about interior design. For some professional practices, this can have a huge impact. Take the case of a Denver, Colorado, children's dentist. Says Dr. Tim Adams, "Our patients seem to love this place as much as we do. We frequently have children who do not want to leave the office at the end of their visit."

Why are his young patients so enamored with Dr. Adams? His whimsical dental office is presided over by three-dimensional penguins. The reception area is a playhouse. To promote a sense of security, the treatment areas are open to the waiting room. Everything is carefully crafted to be comfortable, educational, and fun. (Now if we could just get *parents* to find dentistry an enjoyable experience!)

Establishing a Strong Board of Directors

Certainly not every service business needs a board of directors. As you grow, however, adding qualified outsiders to the brain trust relieves you of the sole burden of making decisions. By staffing your board with competent business leaders, you assure your company of strong, diversified advice. Something else you might consider: we're told many firms are going to boards of *advisors* rather than directors because this removes the risk of personal liability for those who serve.

It used to be corporate boards consisted of relatives or company officers—people who willingly rubber-stamped the CEO's wishes. Often a close advisor, like the firm's attorney or accountant, was also included.

Today the trend is toward including outsiders. According to a survey done by Growth Resources, Inc., two of the five directors on the average small company board now fall into this category. They are CEOs from related industries, professors from business and technical schools, and other professionals. Those in the know suggest starting with a small number of people. Large groups become mired too easily.

But before you can decide whom to invite to serve on your board, you need to decide what its function will be. While some boards are strictly window dressing to boost the company image, others are operational—involving themselves in day-to-day activities. Then there is the networking board, which is designed primarily to extend the number of contacts available to the firm's owners. More sophisticated corporations may want a board devoted to strategic planning. Their main function would be tackling issues such as succession planning and expansion. Perhaps the best approach is an all-purpose board that melds all of the above.

Sixty percent of the companies with boards compensate their directors. A recent study revealed fees range from $100 to $650 per meeting or are structured as annual retainers of $1,000 up to $6,500. If cash is not a possible reward, how about making your directors stockholders? Pay for their services with equity rather than money. Or you might do what a friend of ours did. She is a spa consultant who forged a win-win alliance. When Betsy called one of us and asked that individual to serve on her board of advisors, Betsy made a point of saying a free spa weekend was part of the deal.

A strong board of directors, based on a one-person, one-vote concept, helps a company stay dynamic. It can turn a business that borders on being a hobby into an aggressive enterprise. Possible candidates to staff your board include a marketing expert, public relations professional, an investment banker, a management consultant, or other CEOs. For more guidance, contact the National Association of Corporate Directors at (202) 775-0509.

Adding a Twist to the Same Old Thing

Oil Can Henry, a Portland, Oregon, quick-lubrication franchise, decided it needed a way to stand out from the crowd. The decision was made to create a different atmosphere, one that presented old-time values and established a feeling of trust. Consequently, customers are greeted by employees wearing clothes reminiscent of early 20th-century Americana. Attendants change their uniforms when they get dirty. Patrons are given a copy of *USA Today* to read while their cars are being serviced. Or they can watch the process on a TV screen positioned by their car window. Were the results worth the effort? Over a one-year period, business increased approximately 35%.

River-rafting, once perceived as high adventure primarily for macho men, today attracts families, seniors, even paraplegics and quadriplegics. The owners of rafting companies are adding a touch of luxury to this "rough-it" sport. Some lunches and dinners on the river provide better fare than many gourmet restaurants. Western outfitters even offer wine-tasting trips in Idaho and classical music trips in Colorado. That's definitely a twist!

Other businesses join forces with complementary companies to boost their bottom lines. By doubling up you can make more of a splash. The right partner is not a competitor, but rather is after your same type of customer. Be sure you don't lose your own identity in the process. If you twist and turn to fit into a shoe that really doesn't fit, you may cut off your circulation.

Another way to add a turn to the same old thing is to incorporate "bounce-back" merchandising. This is used more in wholesaling and retailing, but there are possibilities for some services. A bounce-back is an order received as a direct result of a promotional offer enclosed with a product shipment. The offer gets a free ride when enclosed with virtually anything mailed.

When a bank sends out monthly statements, what is to stop it from including a promotional flyer about another service? When an information management consulting firm mails out data to clients, couldn't it include details about a new peripheral service? A library sending out notices about reserved books being available could seize this opportunity to announce a story hour for children or a special summer reading program. A tax preparation service might mail a flyer about their monthly bookkeeping service with each tax return they do. This kind of back-end marketing builds upon the initial front-end sale.

Speaking of building reminds us of remodeling. Perhaps you should consider revamping your services—maybe even *narrowing* them. One of the restaurants in our town prospers because of its *limited* menu. It thrives because the owner only offers about six entrees. That way he can buy what he serves in quantity and doesn't have to cope with waste.

Remember we're looking at switching the tables now. Maybe it's time to think small. Perhaps your auto repair business would have more profit if you only worked on one make of cars, for instance. A janitorial service might specialize in offices rather than doing stores, warehouses, or whatever comes its way. A temporary service that provided only professionals could easily make a name for itself.

While you're analyzing your scope, also consider your hours of business. Banks have been very creative in establishing hours that serve their clientele best. If you run a towing service, should you be working a split shift to capitalize on morning and afternoon drive times? Wouldn't a music teacher have more students if he or she structured classes when children were out of school and adults off work? Likewise, a dating service should open in midafternoon and close in the later evening. Doctors, dentists, chiropractors, and other health professionals might do well to stay open on Saturday and take off Sunday/Monday. Altering your hours may be a smart way to fine-tune your operation.

A movie theater chain headquartered in Los Angeles added an angle and saved itself $750,000 a year. Instead of selling popcorn in cardboard containers, they package theirs in bags. They also push an array of gourmet popcorn flavors, which, in turn, push profits.

In Rye, New York, an interesting concept has developed. A hair salon located next to a boutique keeps its customers entertained with fashion shows. During slow times, boutique employees don newly arrived clothing and put on an impromptu fashion show for ladies under the hair dryers.

Only by being informed can you determine if there is a savvy way to add a twist here, subtract there for more advantage. Attack your lack. Educate yourself. Keep abreast of new trends, technologies, and techniques in your field. "Information is the manager's main tool," states noted management consultant, Peter Drucker.

A Grab Bag of More Good Ideas

Become active in appropriate trade associations. This doesn't mean simply join. It means serve on committees, run for office, and generally involve yourself. By doing so you get on the inside track. This gives you access to restricted information. It puts you shoulder to shoulder with the leaders in your industry, people who will prove to be valuable contacts. Larger associations also have unique reservoirs of specialized research facilities. Regularly reading industry trade journals and newsletters is another shrewd move.

So is acquiring a brainstorming partner. Why not approach someone whose opinion you respect and suggest getting together a couple of times a month to bounce around ideas? Done with honesty and tact, this kind of a support alliance can generate very meaningful thoughts and positive results.

Talking of support alliances, what about barter? In 1625, the Dutch traded the Indians $24 worth of trinkets for the island of Manhattan. (Naturally, we encourage more equitable exchanges.) A good trade has balanced merit for both parties. A maid service and a bookkeeping firm might barter their skills. A lawn service could spruce up the yard of a writer, who in turn might create a promotional flyer. An auto mechanic could repair the vehicle of a barber, who would provide several haircuts.

Or you might contact a local restaurant and cut a deal to bring your clients to lunch or dinner for nothing or at a reduced rate. Sell the proprietor by convincing him or her that you will be bringing a new customer to them. Given normal marketing costs, free meals are cheap advertising. We recently traded free entrance to an expensive three-day conference for our help with registration.

A nonprofit organization we know was sponsoring a fund-raising golf tournament with a $250 price tag. They gave free registrations to key members of the local media in exchange for plugs in print and on the radio. The possibilities are endless.

In 1992 an estimated $6.4 billion worth of goods and services were bartered globally. Through barter exchanges, some 200,000 companies rack up reciprocal "trade dollars." For a list of formal barter exchanges, contact the International Reciprocal Trade Association at (703) 759-1473.

Selling to the government is an option for some service providers. The federal government is the nation's largest consumer of goods and services. Of course, there are many books written on this subject, so check your public library. The U.S. Chamber of Commerce offers a free pamphlet on the subject. It is called *How to Sell to the Federal Government* (USCC-2002). You can order a copy by calling (800) 638-6582 [in Maryland, call (800) 352-1450].

Maybe instead of selling, you should be giving something away. That's what a faltering parking-garage management company in Baltimore did. Owner Lisa Renshaw decided to implement a low-cost marketing method to attract new customers from among the business travelers using the nearby Amtrak station. She devised a flyer that contained a coupon good for a free car wash after parking in her garage five times. Renshaw personally distributed them at the train station. Her scheme worked. By the time people had parked there five times it had become a habit. They not only came back to park their cars, but began paying for the $6 washes.

The service manager at Gafford Pontiac in La Mesa, California, prospects for business by sponsoring a free environmental and safety check for Pontiac owners. A letter announcing the inspection goes to appropriate car owners. It says the purpose of the inspection is to acquaint them with those conditions that affect their car's performance, efficiency, and safety. Might there be something in this for Gafford Pontiac as well?

When you are writing letters (or anything else for that matter), avoid using sexist language. Managers are not all "he" any more than secretaries are all "she." Sexism can't be skirted. It has to be addressed directly. By editing out inappropriate references, you are a lot less likely to offend people.

There are a lot of gender menders. Businesspeople replaces businessman, foreman becomes supervisor, chairman is replaced by chairperson or simply "chair." Often the he/she and his/her pronoun can be eliminated altogether. Try redoing your sentence without either. Another way around this problem is to speak in the plural. "All clients receive monthly printouts of their jobs" instead of "Each client receives a monthly printout of his job." You can also alternate using he/she and his/her so neither gender is slighted.

Now let's take a moment to explore another contrast: that of a fad versus a trend. Differentiating between them is about as easy and scientific as handicapping the ponies. It simply can't be done. Fads have included such things as the Hula Hoop, Pet Rocks, and Michael Jackson's spangled glove. Trends, on the other hand (not Michael's, mind you), have more staying power. You can lose your proverbial shirt by hooking up with a fad. By the time you discover it is a genuine fad, the craze is already on the way out. Aligning with a trend, however, can be an extremely clever marketing ploy. One trend we've seen develop over the last few years is a shift to small, fuel-efficient automobiles. Is there a trend on the horizon with which you might associate yourself?

Perhaps the best advice we can leave you with concerns not your business, but yourself: keep a sense of humor. In trying times, wit and buffoonery lighten the load. By allowing yourself to see the amusing side of things, you take the sting out of disappointments. And learn to enjoy the little things. One day you may look back and realize they were the big ones.

To be a consistently effective marketer you also have to recharge your own personal batteries. Can you relax? Really relax? Step off the fast track occasionally. Soak in a bubble bath. Listen to soothing music. Rest. Loaf. Let go. De-stress so you're not *dis*tressed. Small cooldowns prevent major meltdowns. Taking personal time allows you to increase the bottom line.

Part III

Sources and Resources to Help You Prosper

Marketing Plan Outline

A marketing plan is a realistic assessment of what you are selling, who your clients or customers are (or should be), and how you can best reach your most profitable markets. Developing it draws not only on your knowledge and experience, but also on your intuitive business sense. Here are some practical pointers to help you create an effective plan:

1. Make a list of *all* your options

2. Put yourself in your customers/clients' place

3. Define your markets

4. Segment your market into manageable units

5. Check out your competition

Now go back to the list you created in step 1. Choose the top 10 or 12 options that seem to make the most sense. When prioritizing them, keep in mind their relative profitability, ease of implementation, and if they fit with your current services and price points. Next, review the segments you identified in step 4, matching them with your new list of most promising options. Bingo! You've determined several potentially profitable strategies to use as your marketing bull's-eye.

Your marketing plan is a "working document"—one that is used to not only define goals and outline action to be taken, but also to chart marketing progress. It needn't be lengthy, cumbersome, or unfriendly. Six to 10 pages will be fine. Be sure to include specific costs and the length of time necessary to accomplish each phase. Going through the experience of creating a marketing plan is a wonderful growth opportunity. It stimulates lots of new thinking. (In addition to being your road map to success, this plan can also be included with your overall business plan if you are seeking financing.)

I. EXECUTIVE SUMMARY

This is a brief overview of the primary objectives, including planning factors involved in marketing your service in the target markets over the next year. (Ideally a 5-year overall plan is best, with particulars for the next year spelled out in detail.) Describe how the marketing objectives support the future company goals including increase in revenue, projected company size, additional staff, etc.

II. MISSION STATEMENT

This is a description of the philosophy of your service, the types of things you do, etc.

III. MARKET DEFINITION

Define the scope of your target markets. This definition includes as much information as possible about those markets: their size, growth potential, health, etc. It's sort of an industry profile for each target market.

IV. ANALYSIS OF CURRENT SITUATION

Description of the issues impacting your company's ability to compete in the target markets. The issues addressed are:

Internal strengths and weaknesses

Current market position (if any)

Client situation

Economic performance of the company in the past two years Competitive environment (Who is the competition and how can you position yourself to compete against them?)

V. GOALS AND OBJECTIVES

A list of the marketing objectives and specific goals to be achieved for the year. For example, you may want to commit to increasing sales revenues by 25%. Goals must always be *measurable*. Don't state something lofty like, "To become the best company in the world."

VI. ACTION PLANS

Taking into consideration all of the information gathered, what has to be done to reach your goals/objectives? Each marketing objective should have an action program.

Describe what you're going to do and by when (such as hire two outside sales representatives by December 15).

Identify all costs connected with each plan.

VII. BUDGET AND CONTROLS

This is your overall total budget for costs associated with implementing the action plans. Describe how you will monitor progress (such as sourcing every lead, creating a monthly marketing activity report, etc.) Remember that flexibility is a key ingredient. Review your marketing plan quarterly. Are you hitting that bull's eye you targeted? Should you make any adjustments or changes?

List of Service Businesses and Professional Practice Opportunities

Accountant
Actor
Adjuster
Adoption service
Adult day care
Advertising agency
Air charter service
Airline
Alteration
Ambulance service
Amusement park
Answering service
Apartment locator
Appliance repair
Arcade
Architectural service
Art gallery
Artist
Association

Athletic club
Attorney
Auctioneer
Author agent
Automobile repair
Aviation instruction

Bail bondsperson
Bakery
Band
Banking
Barber
Beauty shop
Bed & Breakfast inn
Bicycle repair
Boarding kennel
Bookmobile
Bowling alley
Butcher

Cabinet making
Cake decorator
Campground
Caterer
Charm school
Child care
Child clinic
Chimney-sweeping
Chiropractor
Church
Civic organization
Clinic
Collection agency
College and university
Computer-related service
Consultant
Convalescent home
Correspondence school
Courier service
Credit bureau
Credit union

Dance studio
Data-processing
Dating service
Dental clinic
Dentist
Detective
Diaper service
Dietician
Drama school
Dude ranch

Elementary school
Employment agency
Entertainer
Exposition
Exterminator

Family planning service

Financial planning consultant
Fortune teller
Funeral home

Golf course
Gunsmith

Health care maintenance
  organization
Heating and air-conditioning
  repair
Horseback ride
Horse shoeing
Hospice
Hospital
Hospitality
Hotel
Housekeeping and janitor
  service
Hunting guide
Hypnosis

Information management
Insurance
Interior decorator
Investment counselor
Karate instruction
Kayak and rafting instruction

Labor unions
Landscaping
Language instruction
Laundry and cleaner
Lawn service
Library
Limousine service
Loan company
Lobbyist
Locksmith

Massage therapist
Medical lab
Mobile home transportation
Modeling
Motel
Motion picture production
Moving and storage
Museum
Musical instrument repair
Musician
Music instruction

Nutritionist
Nonprofit agency
Notary Public

Office equipment repair
Optometrists

Paint and body repair
Pet grooming and boarding
Photographer
Photo lab
Physicians
Picture framing
Political organization
Printing service
Professional and vocational
school
Property management
Psychic
Psychotherapist
Publishing service

Race track operation
Radio station
Real estate appraiser
Real estate sales
Reducing salon
Refrigerator repair

Rehabilitation service
Religious organization
Research and development firm
Restaurant

Sailing instruction
Seamstress
Secretarial service
Security consultant
Security guard and patrol
service
Sharpening service
Shoe repair
Ski resort and instruction
Snow removal service
Social and fraternal associations
Stockbroker
Support group
Surveyor
Swimming pool maintenance

Tax return preparation
Taxidermist
Taxi service
Telegraph service
Telephone communication
service
Television and radio repair
Temporary service
Theater
Towing service
Trash removal
Travel agency
Trenching service

Upholstering

Veterinarian
Video

Weight control service
Welding
Well-drilling and service
Window-washing

Word processing service
Writer
Yacht club
Youth organization and center

Marilyn and Tom Ross

Governmental Sources of Special Interest

Government Agencies

For your convenience, listed below are main phone numbers for prime government agencies.

Department	Main Number	Public Affairs
Agriculture	(202) 720-2791	(202) 720-2798
Commerce	(202) 482-2000	(202) 482-3263
Defense	(703) 545-6700	(703) 697-5737
Air Force	(703) 695-4803	
Army	(703) 697-7589	
Navy	(703) 697-7391	
Education	(202) 708-5366	(202) 401-1577
Energy	(202) 586-5000	(202) 586-6827
Environmental Protection Agency	(202) 260-2090	(202) 260-3146
Farm Credit		

Administration	(703) 883-4000	(703) 883-4056
Federal Communication Commission	(202) 632-7000	
Federal Trade Commission	(202) 326-2222	(202) 326-2180
General Services Administration	(202) 708-5082	(202) 501-0705
Health and Human Services	(202) 619-0257	(202) 634-4140
Housing and Urban Development	(202) 708-1112	(202) 708-0980
Interior	(202) 208-7220	
Interstate Commerce Commission	(202) 927-7119	(202) 927-6050
Justice	(202) 514-2000	(202) 514-2007
Labor	(202) 219-5000	(202) 219-7316
National Aeronautics & Space Administration	(202) 358-0000	(202) 358-1898
National Labor Relations	(202) 632-4950	
National Science Foundation	(202) 357-5000	(202) 357-9498
Occupational Safety & Health Review Commission	(202) 606-5398	
Office of Personnel Management	(202) 606-2118	(202) 606-1800
Overseas Private Investment Corp.	(202) 336-8400	(202) 336-8634
Patent & Trademark Office	(703) 557-3080	
Securities & Exchange Commission		(202) 272-3100
State	(202) 647-4000	(202) 647-6575
Transportation	(202) 366-4000	(202) 366-5580

Marilyn and Tom Ross

US International Trade Commission	(202) 205-2000	(202) 205-1819
US Postal Service	(202) 268-2000	
Veteran's Affairs	(202) 233-4000	(202) 535-8300

Federal Information Centers

Each state maintains one or more Federal Information Centers that provide a source of free information on a wide range of government-related topics.

Alabama
Birmingham, Mobile
(800) 366-2998

Alaska
Anchorage   (800) 729-8003

Arizona
Phoenix   (800) 359-3997

Arkansas
Little Rock   (800) 366-2998

California
Los Angeles, San Diego,
San Francisco, Santa Ana
(800) 726-4995
Sacramento   (916) 973-1695

Colorado
Colorado Springs, Denver,
Pueblo
(800) 359-3997

Connecticut   (800) 432-2934
Hartford, New Haven
(800) 347-1997

Florida
Fort Lauderdale, Jacksonville,
Miami, Orlando, St. Petersburg,
Tampa, West Palm Beach
(800) 347-1997

Georgia
Atlanta   (800) 347-1997

Hawaii
Honolulu   (800) 733-5996

Illinois
Chicago   (800) 366-2998

Indiana
Gary   (800) 366-2998
Indianapolis   (800) 347-1997

Iowa   (800) 735-8004

Kansas   (800) 735-8004

Kentucky
Louisville   (800) 347-1997

Louisiana
New Orleans   (800) 366-2998

Maryland
Baltimore   (800) 347-1997

Massachusetts
Boston   (800) 347-1997

Michigan
Detroit, Grand Rapids
(800) 347-1997

Minnesota
Minneapolis   (800) 366-2998

Missouri
St. Louis   (800) 366-2998
Other locations (800) 735-8004

Nebraska
Omaha   (800) 366-2998
Other locations (800) 735-8004

New Jersey
Newark, Trenton
   (800) 347-1997

New Mexico
Albuquerque   (800) 359-3997

New York
Albany, Buffalo, New York,
Rochester, Syracuse
   (800) 347-1997

North Carolina
Charlotte   (800) 347-1997

Ohio
Akron, Cincinnati, Cleveland,
Columbus, Dayton, Toledo
   (800) 347-1997

Oklahoma
Oklahoma City, Tulsa
   (800) 366-2998

Oregon
Portland   (800) 726-4995

Pennsylvania
Philadelphia, Pittsburgh
   (800) 347-1997

Rhode Island
Providence   (800) 347-1997

Tennessee
Chattanooga   (800) 347-1997
Memphis, Nashville
   (800) 366-2998

Texas
Austin, Dallas, Fort Worth,
Houston, San Antonio
   (800) 366-2998

Utah
Salt Lake City (800) 359-3997

Virginia
Norfolk, Richmond, Roanoke
   (800) 347-1997

Washington
Seattle, Tacoma
   (800) 726-4995

Wisconsin
Milwaukee   (800) 366-2998

Census Bureau

The Census Bureau possesses a wealth of statistics and information useful in making marketing decisions.

Public Information Office
Building 3, Room 2705
Washington, DC 20233
(301) 763-4040
(General information and channeling of inquiries)

Census Service Industries
(301) 763-7039
(Five-year statistics)

Current Selected Service Reports
(301) 763-5528
(Various annual reports)

Department of Commerce

Expert help in navigating the maze of federal government information is available through the Department of Commerce.

U.S. Department of Commerce
Business Assistance
Office of Business Liaison, Room 5898-C
Washington, DC 20230
(202) 482-3176

(Call to get general information and the phone number of your nearest district office. Also request their *Business Services Directory*.)

Small Business Administration (SBA)

The SBA has numerous offices and programs to assist you. SCORE and ACE, for instance, offer free consulting help. Call the number listed here for more particulars on all their activities.

U.S. Small Business Administration
1441 L Street, NW
Washington, DC 20416
(202) 606-4000
8:30 A.M. to 5:00 P.M., EST, Monday through Friday

Small Business Answer Desk
(800) 827-5722

SBA Online

The SBA has established a toll-free electronic bulletin board to help small businesses find information and discover resources to help them start, maintain, expand, or operate their business. "SBA Online" offers SBA information and services, publications, files relating to business, and mailboxes for business-related topics. Many useful files are available for downloading. Call SBA Online at (800) 859-4636 if your modem operates at 2400 bps or (800) 697-4636 if your modem operates at 9600 bps.

SBA Regional Field Offices

REGION I
155 Federal Street, Ninth Floor
Boston, MA 02110
Tel: (617) 451-2023
* TDD: (617) 451-0491

REGION II
26 Federal Plaza, Room 31-08
New York, NY 10278
Tel: (212) 264-1450
TDD: (212) 264-5669

REGION III
475 Allendale Road, Suite 201
King Of Prussia, PA 19406
Tel: (215) 962-3700
TDD: (215) 962-3739

REGION IV
1375 Peachtree St. N.E.,
   Fifth Floor
Atlanta, GA 30367-8102
Tel: (404) 347-2797
TDD: (404) 347-5051

* Number for the hearing impaired.

REGION V
300 S. Riverside Plaza,
    Suite 1975S
Chicago, IL 60606-6617
Tel: (312) 353-5000
TDD: (312) 353-8060

REGION VI
9625 King George Drive,
    Building C
Dallas, TX 75235-3391
Tel: (214) 767-7633
TDD: (214) 767-1339

REGION VII
911 Walnut Street, 13th Floor
Kansas City, MO 64106
Tel: (816) 426-3608
TDD: (816) 426-2990

REGION VIII
999 18th Street, Suite 701
Denver, CO 80202
Tel: (303) 294-7186
TDD: (303) 294-7096

REGION IX
71 Stevenson Street, 20th Floor
San Francisco, CA 94105-2939
Tel: (415) 744-6402
TDD: (415) 744-6401

REGION X
2615 Fourth Avenue, Room 440
Seattle, WA 98121
Tel: (206) 553-5676
TDD: (206) 553-2872

Minority Business Development Centers

Atlanta Regional Office
75 Piedmont Avenue NE
    Suite 256
Atlanta, GA 30303
(404) 586-0973

Chicago Regional Office
55 East Monroe Street
    Suite 1440
Chicago, IL 60603
(312) 353-0182

Dallas Regional Office
1100 Commerce Street
    Room 7B23
Dallas, TX 75242
(214) 767-8001

New York Regional Office
26 Federal Plaza
    Room 3720
New York, NY 10278
(212) 264-3263

Oakland Regional Office
1212 Broadway, Suite 900
Oakland, CA 94612
(510) 271-0180

San Francisco Regional Office
221 Main Street, Suite 1350
San Francisco, CA 94105
(415) 243-8430

Washington Regional Office
2000 14th Street, NW
   Third Floor
Washington, DC 20009
(202 939-8740

U.S. Government Printing Office

Superintendent of Documents
Washington, DC 20402

U.S. Government Printing Office Bookstores

Alabama

Birmingham Bookstore
O'Neill Building
2021 Third Avenue North
Birmingham, AL 35203
(205) 731-1056

California

Los Angeles Bookstore
ARCO Plaza, C-Level
505 South Flower Street
Los Angeles, CA 90071
(213) 289-9844

San Francisco Bookstore
Room 1023, Fed. Bldg.
450 Golden Gate Avenue
San Francisco, CA 94102
(415) 252-5334

Colorado

Denver Bookstore
Room 117, Fed. Bldg.
1961 Stout Street
Denver, CO 80294
(303) 844-3964

Pueblo Bookstore
World Savings Bldg.
720 North Main Street
Pueblo, CO 81003
(719) 544-3142

Pueblo Distribution Center
Public Docs. Distribution
Center
P.O. Box 4007
Pueblo, CO 81003
(719) 948-3335

District of Columbia

Farragut Bookstore
1510 "H" Street, NW
Washington, DC 20005
(202) 653-5075

U.S. Govt. Printing Office
  (Main Bookstore)
710 North Capitol Street, NW
Washington, DC 20401
(202) 275-2091

Florida

Jacksonville Bookstore
Room 158, Fed. Bldg.
400 W. Bay Street
Jacksonville, FL 32202
(904) 353-0569

Georgia

Atlanta Bookstore
Room 100, Fed. Bldg.
275 Peachtree Street, NE
Atlanta, GA 30343
(404) 331-6947

Illinois

Chicago Bookstore
Room 1365, Fed. Bldg.
219 S. Dearborn Street
Chicago, IL 60604
(312) 353-5133

Maryland

Warehouse Sales Outlet
8660 Cherry Lane
Laurel, MD 20707
(301) 953-7974
(301) 792-0262

Massachusetts

Boston Bookstore
Thomas P. O'Neill Bldg.
10 Causeway Street
Boston, MA 02222
(617) 720-4180

Michigan

Detroit Bookstore
Suite 160, Fed. Bldg.
477 Michigan Avenue
Detroit, MI 48226
(313) 226-7816

Missouri

Kansas City Bookstore
#120 Bannister Mall
5600 East Bannister Road
Kansas City, MO 64137
(816) 765-2256

Marilyn and Tom Ross

New York

New York Bookstore
Room 110, Fed. Bldg.
26 Federal Plaza
New York, NY 10278
(212) 264-3825

Ohio

Cleveland Bookstore
Room 1653, Fed. Bldg.
1240 E. 9th Street
Cleveland, OH 44199
(216) 522-4922

Columbus Bookstore
Room 207, Fed. Bldg.
200 N. High Street
Columbus, OH 43215
(614) 469-6956

Oregon

Portland Bookstore
1305 S.W. First Avenue
Portland, OR 97201
(503) 221-6217

Pennsylvania

Philadelphia Bookstore
Robert Morris Bldg.
100 N. 17th Street
Philadelphia, PA 19108
(215) 597-0677

Pittsburgh Bookstore
Room 118, Fed. Bldg.
1000 Liberty Avenue
Pittsburgh, PA 15222
(412) 644-2721

Texas

Dallas Bookstore
Room 1C46, Fed. Bldg.
1100 Commerce Street
Dallas, TX 75242
(214) 767-0076

Houston Bookstore
Texas Crude Bldg.
801 Travis Street, Ste. 120
Houston, TX 77002
(713) 228-1187

Washington

Seattle Bookstore
Room 194, Fed. Bldg.
915 Second Avenue
Seattle, WA 98174
(206) 442-4270

Wisconsin

Milwaukee Bookstore
Room 190, Fed. Bldg.
517 E. Wisconsin Avenue
Milwaukee, WI 53202
(414) 297-1304

Government Document Depository Libraries

Alabama

Montgomery
Auburn University
  at Montgomery Library
  Documents Department
36193
  (205) 279-9110, ext. 253

University
University of Alabama Library
  Reference Department/
    Documents, Box S
35486
  (205) 348-6046

Arizona

Phoenix
Department of Library
Archives, and Public Records
  Third Floor State Capitol
  1700 West Washington
85007
  (602) 255-4121

Tucson
University of Arizona Library
  Government Documents
Department
  85721
  (602) 621-4871

Arkansas

Little Rock
Arkansas State Library
Documents Service Section
One Capitol Mall
72201
(501) 371-2090

California

Sacramento
California State Library
  Government Publications
    Section
  914 Capitol Mall
95814
(916) 322-4572

Colorado

Boulder
University of Colorado
  Norlin Library
  Government Publications
  Campus Box 184
80309
(303) 492-8834

Denver
Denver Public Library
Government Publications Dept.
  1357 Broadway
  80203
  (303) 571-2140

Connecticut

Hartford
Connecticut State Library
  231 Capitol Avenue
  06106
  (203) 566-4971
Note: Also serves as Regional
for state of Rhode Island.

Florida

Gainesville
University of Florida Libraries
  Documents Department
  Library West
  32611
  (904) 392-0367
Note: Also serves as Regional
for commonwealth of Puerto
Rico.

Georgia

Athens
University of Georgia Libraries
  Government Documents
    Department
  30602
  (404) 542-8949

Hawaii

Honolulu
University of Hawaii
Hamilton Library
  Government Documents
    Collection
  2550 The Mall, 96822
  (808) 948-8230

Idaho

Moscow
University of Idaho Library
  Documents Section
  83843
  (208) 885-6344

Illinois

Springfield
Illinois State Library
  Federal Documents
  Centennial Building
  62756
  (217) 782-5012

Indiana

Indianapolis
Indiana State Library
  Serials Section
  140 North Senate Avenue
  46204
  (317) 232-3686

Iowa

Iowa City
University of Iowa Libraries
    Government Publications
        Department
52242
(319) 353-3318

Kansas

Lawrence
University of Kansas
    Spencer Research Library
    Government Documents
66045
(913) 864-4662

Kentucky

Lexington
University of Kentucky
        Libraries
    Government Publications
        Department
40506
(606) 257-3139

Louisiana

Baton Rouge
Louisiana State University
Middleton Library
    Government Documents
        Department
70803
(504) 388-2570

Note: Also Serves as regional
for Virgin Islands.

Ruston
Louisiana Technical University
    Prescott Memorial Library
    Government Documents
        Department
71272
(318) 257-4962

Maine

Orono
University of Main
    Raymond H. Fogler Library
    Tri-State Regional
    Documents Depository
04469
(207) 581-1680
Note: Also serves as regional
office for New Hampshire and
Vermont.

Maryland

College Park
University of Maryland
    McKeldin Library
    Documents/Maps Room
20742
(301) 454-3034
Note: Also serves as Regional
for District of Columbia.

Massachusetts

Boston
Boston Public Library
  666 Boylston Street
  02117
  (617) 536-5400, ext. 226

Michigan

Detroit
Detroit Public Library
  5201 Woodward Avenue
  48202
  (313) 833-1409

Lansing
Library of Michigan
  Government Doucuments
  P.O. Box 30007
  735 E. Michigan Avenue
  48909
  (517) 373-1593

Minnesota

Minneapolis
University of Minnesota
  Wilson Library
  Government Publications
  309 Nineteenth Ave. South
  55455
  (612) 373-7813

Mississippi

University
University of Mississippi
  J.D. Williams Library
  Documents Department
  38677
  (601) 232-5857

Montana

Missoula
University of Montana
  Maurene & Mike Mansfield
    Library
  Documents Division
  59812
  (406) 243-6700

Nebraska

Lincoln
University of Nebraska-Lincoln
  D. L. Love Mem. Library
  Documents Department
  68588
  (402) 472-2562

Nevada

Reno
University of Nevada-Reno
  Library
  Government Publications
  Department
  89557 (Designated 1907)
  (702) 784-6579

New Jersey

Newark
Newark Public Library
   U.S. Documents Division
   5 Washington Street
   P.O. Box 630
   07101
   (201) 733-7782

New Mexico

Albuquerque
University of New Mexico
   General Library
   Government Publications
      Maps Department
   87131
   (505) 277-5441

Santa Fe
New Mexico State Library
   325 Don Gaspar Avenue
   87501
   (505) 827-3823

New York

Albany
New York State Library
   Cultural Education Center
   Empire State Plaza
   12230
   (518) 474-7646

North Carolina

University of North Carolina
   at Chapel Hill
   Davis Library 080A
   BA/SS Division Documents
   27514
   (919) 962-1151

North Dakota

Fargo
North Dakota State University
Library
   Government Documents
      Department
   58105
   (701) 237-8886

Note: In cooperation with University of North Dakota, Chester Fritz Library, Grand Forks.

Ohio

Columbus
State Library of Ohio
   Documents Section
   65 South Front Street
   43266
   (614) 462-7051

Oklahoma

Oklahoma City
Oklahoma Dept. of Libraries
  Government Documents
  200 NE 18th Street
  73105
  (405) 521-2502, ext. 252

Stillwater
Oklahoma State
  University Library
  Documents Department
  74078
  (405) 624-6546

Oregon

Portland
Portland State University
  Millar Library
  934 S.W. Harrison
  P.O. Box 1151
  97207
  (503) 229-3673

Pennsylvania

Harrisburg
State Library of Pennsylvania
  Government Publications
    Section
  Box 1601
  Walnut Street and
    Commonwealth Avenue
  17105
  (717) 787-3752

Texas

AustinTexas State Library
  Public Services Department
  P.O. Box 12927
  1201 Brazos
  78711
  (512) 463-5455

Lubbock
Texas Tech University Library
  Documents Department
  79409
  (806) 742-2268

Utah

Logan
Utah State University
  Merrill Library
    and Learning
  Resources Center, UMC-30
  Documents Department
  84322
  (801) 750-2682

Virginia

Charlottesville
University of Virginia
  Alderman Library
  Government Documents
  22903
  (804) 924-3133

Washington

Olympia
Washington State Library
  Document Section
  98504
  (206) 753-4027

West Virginia

Morgantown
West Virginia University
  Library
  Government Documents
    Section
  P.O. Box 6069
  26506
  (304) 293-3640

Wisconsin

Madison
State Historical
  Society of Wisconsin
    Library
    Government Publications
      Section
  816 State Street
  53706
  (608) 262-4347
Note: In cooperation with University of Wisconsin-Madison,
Memorial Library

Milwaukee
Milwaukee Public Library
  Documents Division
  814 West Wisconsin Ave.
  53233
  (414) 278-3017

Wyoming

Cheyenne
Wyoming State Library
  Supreme Court and Library
    Building
  82002
  (307) 777-5919

State Publicly-Accessible Databases

State-operated online electronic information systems (OEIS) allow you to capture little-publicized demographic files. Thirty-one states currently have such databases. They allow you to gain speedy access to such economic development data as population and income statistics in municipalities, counties, and states. In some states you can even find out about sales tax records and construction statistics. This is incredibly helpful to small businesses, not only in the initial stages but for future marketing decisions. Says one user, "Research that used to take me all day now takes me 20 minutes."

State	Contact	Agency	Phone
AK	William Paulick	Department of Commerce & Economic Development	(907) 465-2017
CO	Mark Krudwig	Colorado Division of Local Government	(303) 866-2156
DE	Judy McKinney Cherry	Delaware Development Office	(302) 739-4271
FL	Ed Perron	Florida Department of Commerce	(904) 488-4255
HI	Glenn Ifuku	Economic Planning Information Systems	(808) 586-2485
IN	Carol Rogers	Indiana Business Research Center	(317) 274-2205
IA	Steve Rosenow	Department of Economic Development	(515) 242- 4881
KY	Beverly Daly	Urban Studies Center	(502) 588-7990
LA	Rajiv Gupte	Northeast Louisiana University	(318) 342-1215
ME	Jean Martin	Maine Department of Labor	(207) 289-2271
MD	John Kozarski	Maryland Department of State	(301) 225-4450
MA	John Gaviglio	Institute for Social & Economic Research	(413) 545-0176

MI	Jane Benke	Michigan State University	(517) 353-3255
MN	Jim Ramstrom	Land Management Information Center	(612) 296-2559
MO	John Blodgett	Urban Resource Center	(314) 553-6014
MT	Dave Elenbaas	Department of Commerce	(406) 444-2463
NE	Tim Himberger	Center for App. Urban Research	(402) 595-2311
NV	Annie Kelly	Nevada State Library	(702) 687-5160
NJ	Doug Moore	New Jersey State Data Center	(609) 292-0076
NM	Juliana Boyle	Bureau of Business & Economic Research	(505) 277-2216
NY	Lenny Gaines	New York State Data Center	(518) 474-6005
NC	Joel Sigmon	State Library of NC	(919) 733-3270
OH	Mark Shaff	SOICC	(614) 644-2689
OK	Jeff Wallace	Commerce Dept. (SDC)	(405) 841-5137
PA	Erin Shannon	Pennsylvania State Data Center	(717) 948-6336
TX	Tom Linehan	Texas Department of Commerce	(512) 472-5059
VA	Sam Kaplan	Center for Public Service	(804) 924-4102
WA	Tim Norris	Employment Security Department	(206) 438-3163
WV	Ed McMin	Business Industrial Data Center	(304) 348-3810
WV	Linda Culp	The Center for Economic Research	(304) 293-5837
WI	Paul Voss	Applied Population Lab	(608) 262-9526

Source: *The Pennsylvania State Data Centers Second Annual National Survey on Publicly Accessible Online Electronic Information Systems.*

General Useful Resources

Entrepreneurial Organizations and Marketing Associations

American Marketing Association
250 S. Wacker Drive
Chicago, IL 60606
(312) 648-0536

American Society of Association Executives
Information Central
1575 Eye Street, NW
Washington, DC 20005
(202) 626-2723

American Woman's Economic Development Corp. (AWED)
71 Vanderbilt Avenue, Third Floor, Suite 320
New York, NY 10169
(800) 222-AWED; In NY: (800) 442-AWED

Center for Entrepreneurial Management, Inc.
180 Varick Street, Penthouse
New York, NY 10014
(212) 633-0060

Center for Entrepreneurial Studies
Babson College
Babson Park, MA 02157
(617) 239-4420

Center for Entrepreneurship
523 Zane Showker Hall
James Madison University
Harrisonburg, VA 22807
(703) 568-3227

Council of Better Business Bureaus, Inc.
4200 Wilson Boulevard, Suite 800
Arlington, VA 22203
(703) 276-0100

Direct Marketing Association
11 West 42nd Street
New York, NY 10036-8096
(212) 768-7277

Foundation Center
79 Fifth Avenue
New York, NY 10003
(212) 620-4230

Grammar Hotline Directory
Tidewater Community College Writing Center
1700 College Crescent
Virginia Beach, VA 23456
(Send SASE for free directory.)

Idea Exchange and Promotional Services
S. D. Warren Company
225 Franklin Street, 30th Floor
Boston, MA 02110
(A free source of over 100 categories of printing and promotional ideas.)

International Franchise Association
1350 New York Avenue, NW   Suite 900
Washington, DC 20005
(202) 628-8000

Marketing Science Institute
1000 Massachusetts Avenue
Cambridge, MA 01238
(617) 491-2060

MIT Enterprise Forum
Massachusetts Institute of Technology
201 Vassar Street, Room W59-219
Cambridge, MA 02139
(617) 253-0015

National Association of the Self-Employed
P.O. Box 612067
Dallas, TX 75261
(800) 232-NASE

National Association of Women Business Owners (NAWBO)
600 South Federal Street, Suite 400
Chicago, IL 60605
(312) 922-0465

National Business Incubation Association
One President Street
Athens, OH 45701
(614) 593-4331

National Federation of Independent Business (NFIB)
600 Maryland Avenue, SW, Suite 700
Washington, DC 20024
(202) 554-9000

National Small Business United (NSBU)
1155 15th Street, NW, Suite 710
Washington, DC 20005
(800) 541-5768
(202) 293-8830

National Women's Economic Alliance Foundation
1440 New York Avenue, NW, Suite 300
Washington, DC 20005
(202) 638-1200

Pattern Research
403 South Pennsylvania
Box 9845
Denver, CO 80209
(303) 778-0880

Small Business Administration
409 3rd Street, SW
Washington, DC 20416
Answer Desk: (800) 827-5722

Specialty Advertising Association International
Attention: Marketing/Communications Dept.
3125 Skyway Circle, N
Irving, TX 75038
(214) 580-0404

U.S. Chamber of Commerce
1615 H Street, NW
Washington, DC 20062
(800) 638-6582
(202) 659-6000
(Also talk with your local chamber.)

Washington Small Business Development Center
Washington State University
245 Todd Hall
Pullman, WA 99163
(509) 335-1576

Reference Books

Business Organizations, Agencies, and Publications Directory
Edited by Donald P. Boyden and Robert Wilson
Gale Research Inc.
Book Tower, Department 77748
Detroit, MI 48277-0748
(800) 223-GALE

Catalog of Federal Domestic Assistance
By the Office of Management and Budget
Stock No. 922-008-00000-1
U.S. Government Printing Office
Superintendent of Documents
Washington, DC 20402

Directory of Business Information Resources, The
Grey House Publishing
Pocket Knife Square
Lakerville, CT 06039
(800) 562-2139

Directory of Federal and State Business Assistance:
    A Guide for New and Growing Companies
(NTIS order No. PB88-101977)
National Technical Information Service
U.S. Department of Commerce
5285 Port Royal Road
Springfield, VA 22161
(703) 487-4650

Lesko's Info-Power
By Matthew Lesko
Information USA, Inc.
P. O. Box E
Kensington, MD 20895
(301) 369-1519

Small Business Sourcebook
Edited by Charity Anne Dorgan
Gale Research Inc.
Book Tower, Department 77748
Detroit, MI 48277-0748
(800) 223-GALE

Where to Find Business Information
By David M. Brownstone and Gorton Carruth
Marketing Department
John Wiley & Sons, Inc.
605 Third Avenue
New York, NY 10158
(212) 850-6000

Home-Based Business Information

For the work-from-home crowd, here are resources to make your heart race. With these associations, contacts, and newsletters, you need never feel isolated again.

American Home Business Association
309 Post Road
Darion, CT 06820
(203) 655-4380

Home Office Computing Magazine
P.O. Box 51344
Boulder, CO 80321-1344
(212) 505-3000

National Association for the Cottage Industry
P.O. Box 14850
Chicago, IL 60614
(312) 472-8116

National Association of Home-Based Businesses
10451 Mill Run Circle, Suite 400
Owings Mill, MD 21117
(410) 363-3698

National Home Business Report
Barbara Brabec
P.O. Box 2137
Naperville, IL 60567
(708) 717-0488

Selected Suppliers

Business Card Printers

Distinctive Cards

Perfect Image Graphics Co.
2429 West 12th Street, Suite 1
Tempe, AZ 85281
(800) 533-8732

Royal Publishing
P.O. Box 1120
Glendora, CA 91740
(818) 335-8069
(818) 335-6127 FAX

The Hirschhorn Company
P.O. Box 8848
New Haven, CT 06532-9986
(203) 562-5830

Mitchell Graphics
2230 East Mitchell
Petoskey, MI 49770-9604
(800) 841-6793

U.S. Toy Co., Inc.
1227 East 119th Street
Grandview, MO 64030
(800) 255-6124

Rolodex-Type Cards

Royal Publishing
P.O. Box 1120
Glendora, CA 91740
(818) 335-8069
(818) 335-6127 FAX

PromoCards
8829-D5 Kennedy Boulevard
North Bergen, NJ 07047
(201) 869-1721

Gentile Brothers Folder Factory
116 High Street
P.O. Box 429
Edinburg, VA 22824
(800) 368-5270

Standard Cards

High Tech Printing
1400 Southwest 1st Street
Miami, FL 33135
(800) 323-8324

Stationery House
1000 Florida Avenue
Hagerstown, MD 21741
(800) 638-3033

Parrot Printing, Inc.
2525 West Euclid
Des Moines, IA 50310
(515) 277-2400

Walter Drake & Sons, Inc.
Drake Building
Colorado Springs, CO 80940
(719) 596-3854

Clip Art Sources

Art Direction Book Company
10 East 39th Street, 6th Floor
New York, NY 10016
(212) 315-1989

The Printers Shopper
111 Press Lane
Chula Vista, CA 91910
(800) 954-2911; in CA: (800) 522-1573

ArtMaster * Art-Pak
500 North Claremont Boulevard
Claremont, CA 91711
(714) 626-8065

Dynamic Graphics, Inc.
6000 North Forest Park
Peoria, IL 61614-3592
(309) 688-8800

Clipping Bureaus

Bacon's Clipping Bureau
332 South Michigan Avenue
Chicago, IL 60604
(800) 621-0561

Burrelle's Press Clipping Service
75 East Northfield Avenue
Livingston, NJ 07039
(800) 631-1160

John P. Stewart Newspaper
Clipping Service
233 Dupras Avenue
La Salle PQ H8R 3S4, Canada
(514) 366-8410

Luce Press Clippings
420 Lexington Avenue
New York, NY 10170
(800) 528-8226

Packaged Facts, Inc.
581 6th Avenue
New York, NY 10011
(212) 627-3228

Pressclips, Inc.
One Hillside Boulevard
New Hyde Park, NY
(516) 437-1047

Novelties

Best Impressions Company
345 North Lewis Avenue
Oglesby, IL 61348
(815) 223-6263

Build Your Business
Box 999N
Lake Forest, CA 92630
(800) 886-6448

U.S. Toy Company, Inc.
1227 East 119th Street
Grandview, MO 64030
(800) 255-6124

Video News Releases

J-Nex Satellite News Services
5455 Wilshire Boulevard
Los Angeles, CA 90036
(213) 934-4356

Medialink
708 Third Avenue, 21st Floor
New York, NY 10017
(212) 682-8300

Reuters Television International
630 Fifth Avenue, Suite 700
New York, NY 10111
(212) 698-4500

Worldwide Television News
Corp.
1995 Broadway
New York, NY 10023
(212) 362-44401

Miscellaneous Vendors

Accelerated Business Images
P.O. Box 1500-BI
425 Cedar Street
Buena Vista, CO 81211
(719) 395-2459
(The authors' PR/advertising
agency.)

Harrison Publishing Co.
624 Patton Avenue
Asheville, NC 28806
(704) 254-4420
(Clever greeting cards for business purposes.)

Ornaal Glossies, Inc.
24 West 25th Street, 3rd Floor
New York, NY 10010
(800) 826-6312
(Inexpensive quantity photo
supplier.)

Computer Information Services

America Online
8619 Westwood Center Drive
Vienna, VA 22182
(800) 227-6364

CompuServe
5000 Arlington Centre Blvd.
P.O. Box 20212
Columbus, OH 43220
(800) 848-8199

DELPHI
1030 Massachusetts Ave.,
4th Floor
Cambridge, MA 02138
(800) 695-4005

Dialog Information Services, Inc.
3460 Hillview Avenue
Palo Alto, CA 94304
(800) 334-2564

Dow Jones News/Retrieval
P.O. Box 300
Princeton, NJ 08543-0300
(609) 452-1511

Genie
401 N. Washington Street
Rockville, MD 20850
(800) 638-9636

NewsNet
945 Haverford Road
Byrn Mawr, PA 19010
(800) 345-1301

Prodigy Interactive Personal
Service
P.O. Box 8667
Gray, TN 37615
(800) 284-5933

Though not exactly like the big consumer information services listed above, another option is Internet. This is a collection of more than 11,000 computer networks: a doorway to a whole new universe of information and resources. It includes state and federal government institutions, universities, libraries, museums, businesses, etc. More than 10 million users around the globe use this information superhighway—for as little as $1 a hour! To get more particulars about where to locate public access to the Internet, call the InterNIC Information Services' Referral Desk at (800) 444-4345, extension 1.

Toll-Free 800 Phone Number Options

To set up an in-house 800 phone number, call one of the following telephone companies:

AT&T
(800) 222-0400

MCI Telecommunications (TeleCom)
(800) 888-0800

US Sprint
(800) 877-2000

Recommended Reading

Did you enjoy this book, but have a taste for more? Let us help in your search for greater success. We offer a small business "emporium." Each of these books and tapes has been personally screened by us. They offer real value for your investment. And for your convenience, **all are available from us by mail order.** Perfect for anyone with an entrepreneurial spirit, these tools will guide you toward greater profits.

And there's no risk. If you're not satisfied with any item, it may be returned for a refund—for up to a full year! (Tapes are guaranteed against any defects.) What an easy, one-stop shopping opportunity. All you have to do is complete and return the order form on the page following this list, or call our toll-free phone number (800-331-8355, ext. BI) and use your VISA, MasterCard, American Express, or Discover Card.

ANATOMY OF A BUSINESS PLAN: A Step-by-Step Guide to Starting Smart, Building the Business and Securing Your Company's Future is guaranteed to give you access to capital and keep your small business profitable. Why pay huge fees when everything you need is right here? Benefit from Linda Pinson and Jerry Jinnett, who have 35+ years of experience helping thousands of small business owners. They've refined forms, checklists, and worksheets to give you all the financial documentation you need for lenders. You can be up and running quickly with this great tool kit, $17.95.

ATTITUDE CONNECTION, THE: Focus on Quality gives testimony through true-life stories that our attitudes drive our "success engines." This is especially true in the small business sector. Keep this wonderful little volume handy to give yourself a regular *attitude checkup*. Attitudes are contagious. Are yours worth catching? This Joe Black offering will help you make sure they are! (And it also makes the perfect gift.) $14.95.

BACON'S NEWSPAPER/MAGAZINE DIRECTORY puts accurate print media contacts at your fingertips. Considered the "bible" of the industry by most publicists, Volume I lists 8,400 U.S. and Canadian magazines—with up to 13 editorial contacts. Volume II covers newspapers. And does it ever! There are 8,100 weeklies and 1,700 dailies with up to 31 department editor names. Everything you need to put together a spectacular print media campaign, $270 for the set.

BACON'S RADIO/TV/CABLE DIRECTORY is the most complete reference available for broadcast planning. Information on networks, cable satellite systems, superstations, syndicated shows, news/talk programs—everything you need to put together a dynamite media campaign! You'll find staff names and content profiles to help you target all the right shows. Just $270 for the set.

BEST HOME BUSINESSES FOR THE '90s is by Paul and Sarah Edwards. Here is the inside information you need to know to select a home-based business that's right for you. These self-employment experts profile 70 top businesses. They reveal how each works, what you can earn, start-up costs, where to get customers, plus how much to charge. Dynamite stuff if you're not sure which way to go, $10.95.

BIG IDEAS FOR SMALL SERVICE BUSINESSES Get a copy of the book you're reading for a colleague or loved one! Details 283 innovative strategies ideal for any businessperson or professional. Jay Conrad Levinson, author of *Guerrilla Marketing Attacks*, declares: "jammed with useful, practical, helpful, and profitable ideas for any right-thinking entrepreneur . . . I recommend it without a moment's hesitation." A terrific business start-up tool or refresher course for those who seek cost-effective business builders, $15.95.

CASH COPY: How to Offer Your Products and Services So Your Prospects Buy Them ... Now!!! When writing promotional copy, you'll want to refer to this book time and time again to reinforce the often overlooked point that one's job is to *sell*, not just create pretty prose. This 480-page handbook addresses it all, as only Jeffrey Lant can, $35.00.

CATALOG OF CATALOGS, THE: The Complete Mail-Order Directory is edited by Edward L. Palder. It's the ultimate catalog resource. This indispensable reference lists more than 5,000 catalogs. Both the ordinary and unusual are covered in 850 categories ranging from automobiles to water skiing. Fun to browse through, it makes ordering virtually *anything* easy. (And what an extraordinary place to prospect for sales outlets if you have a product to sell!) $19.95.

COMPLETE GUIDE TO SELF-PUBLISHING, THE: Everything You Need to Know to Write, Publish, Promote, and Sell Your Own Book is also by Tom and Marilyn Ross. Planning to write and publish books or booklets? Then you need this resource! Full of practical and innovative advice, it's considered the "bible" on this subject. Over 400 information-packed pages tell you everything about successfully creating, selling, and profiting from books, $18.95.

CONSULTANT'S KIT, THE Jeffrey Lant again doles out a healthy portion of proven advice—this time for establishing and operating a successful consulting business. Recommended by the Small Business Administration, it's a must for anyone just entering this field. An excellent self-training program for those living in remote areas, $35.00.

COUNTRY BOUND!™ Trade Your Business Suit Blues for Blue Jean Dreams™, by Marilyn and Tom Ross, helps people realize their dream of escaping the big city rat race and experiencing enhanced quality of life. A business book as well as a lifestyle guide, this unique resource shows how to earn a good living in small town America. Hundreds of practical, thought-provoking ideas for prospering in paradise. Readers discover ways to turn avocational interests into paying profits—telecommute to an existing job—set up an Information Age home-based business—buy an existing rural enterprise—or create their dream job in the country. Dozens of quizzes, checklists, maps, and tables to make your rural relocation easy, $19.95.

COUNTRY BOUND!™ Now this rural relocation classic is available on audio cassette. Sit back and listen as you drive, fly, or relax. You'll discover how to make a peaceful exodus to the country, open your own business by "countrypreneuring," and prosper in paradise. You're in for a treat as you hear Emmy Award winner Steve Johnston tell you how to find a fulfilling life in the country, $59.95.

EDITING YOUR NEWSLETTER Design and produce an effective publication using traditional tools and computers—on schedule and within budget. This excellent third edition, by Mark Beach, helps you manage all aspects of production from planning through distribution. If you publish a newsletter—or contemplate doing one—get this book! $18.95.

FINDING YOUR NICHE . . . MARKETING YOUR PROFESSIONAL SERVICE is by Brad Brodsky and Janet Geis. The authors cover everything from exploring career options to organizing your business, client profiles to researching your market, promotion and marketing to publicity and advertising in the mass media. A terrific value for the money, $15.95.

FUNDAMENTALS OF COPY & LAYOUT If you do a lot of print advertising, here's everything you need to know to prepare better ads. A special section highlights creative philosophies of six advertising giants. Authors Albert C. Book and C. Dennis Schick cover all the basics. Self-quizzes provide creative challenges, $19.95.

GETTING IT PRINTED is a superbly useful book. This reference work is a must for anyone who plans, designs or buys printing. Written by Mark Beach, it show you how to slash printing costs, understand the process, maintain quality, and work effectively with vendors, $29.95.

GOVERNMENT GIVEAWAYS FOR ENTREPRENEURS, by Matthew Lesko is a practical, comprehensive road map for those who want to start or expand a business. Perfect for anyone who lives in a remote area, Lesko does Uncle Sam's job and shows taxpayers where to tap into 9,000 sources of free help, information, and money. Be one of the over 150,000 businesses that will get money from the government to begin operation! $33.95.

HABITS OF WEALTH are ones we all want to develop. Without them we tend to be "also rans." This book is an incredible tool for any entrepreneur. Since it's written as snippets of wisdom, it's perfect for quick reading. Bill Byrne, a self-made millionaire, has used these habits to guide him to the top. Now you can too! $21.95.

HANDBOOK FOR PUBLIC RELATIONS WRITING Geared for the PR practitioner, this handbook of business communications is easy to read and relevant. The chapters include writing for electronic media, press releases and backgrounders, print advertising, collateral information pieces, newsletters and house publications, speeches and presentations, even the basics of grammar and style, $29.95.

HOMEMADE MONEY: The Definitive Guide to Success in a Home-based Business was written by Barbara Brabec. Recommended by SBA and SCORE specialists across the country, this is a wonderful nuts and bolts book. It includes an A-to-Z legal financial section and a 500-listing resource chapter of free and low-cost sources of information. The author is a leader in the home-based business field and offers many savvy marketing tips as well, $18.95.

HOW TO BUILD & MAINTAIN YOUR OWN PART-TIME/FULL-TIME CONSULTING PRACTICE, by Howard L. Shenson, the consultant's consultant. Want to turn your know-how into ready cash? This superb 3-tape cassette album includes a workbook and an action plan that helps select the most promising prospects, cause these potential clients to seek you out, and build a substantial referral and retainer business, $89.00.

HOW TO CREATE SMALL-SPACE NEWSPAPER ADVERTISING THAT WORKS, by Ken Eichenbaum, specifically deals with the over 70 percent of all newspaper ads that are less than one-fourth page in size. Here you learn how to design, write, and maximize your small-ad space. Over half of the book reproduces actual winning small-space ads. Available for $24.50.

HOW TO MAKE AT LEAST $100,000 EVERY YEAR AS A SUCCESS-FUL CONSULTANT IN YOUR FIELD is by Dr. Jeffrey Lant. Though the title smacks of hyperbole, the contents are exceptional. This is the last word on succeeding in the advice business. Lant shows consultants sophisticated ways to profit from providing problem-solving information.

Like all the others in his series, it's stuffed with practical, precise ideas that help you turn your expertise into cash, $35.00.

HOW TO SET YOUR FEES AND GET THEM So you've decided to become a consultant. Do you know what to charge? How much will your chosen market bear? What are you really worth? Seldom-seen information by Kate Kelly on how to set appropriate rates for your consulting services awaits you in this book, $17.50.

HUDSON'S NEWSLETTER DIRECTORY can open tremendous new sales avenues for you. We've sold thousands of dollars worth of books solely through reviews and mentions in newsletters! No publicity anywhere else; no paid advertising. Just newsletter exposure. Published by newsletter guru Howard Penn Hudson, the directory is out in a new edition and lists 3,000 subscription newsletters all over the world, $128.

IS THERE A BOOK INSIDE YOU? This revised third edition by Dan Poynter and Mindy Bingham offers a step-by-step approach to writing your book—alone or with help. A boon for anyone struggling with the writing process. Chapters include topic choice, revising and editing, working with collaborators, writing and your personal life, self-quizzes and more, $14.95.

IS THERE A BOOK INSIDE YOU? (audio cassette program) This complete and unabridged album contains over five hours of the above book on tape. A great way for busy professionals to digest this important information (also includes a copy of the book), $69.95.

LOOKING BACK ON THE FUTURE: A Quality Foundation is from the insights gained by the internationally-known firm, Executive Quality Management, which works with Fortune 500 companies around the world. What's the core message of Joe Black's excellent book of "down home" truths? Professional quality cannot exceed personal quality: We're only as good at work as we are at home. Discover here how to balance *overall* quality in your life. $16.95.

LOOKING GOOD IN PRINT Desktop publishing design know-how and inspiration par excellence! In this new third edition, Roger C. Parker talks about avoiding the 25 most common design pitfalls—typography tips—enhancing documents with boxes, screens, rules and more—using illustrations, charts, and graphs to communicate your message—all the elements of outstanding computer design. Invaluable advice no matter what software you use, $24.95.

MAKING IT ON YOUR OWN: Surviving and Thriving on the Ups and Downs of Being Your Own Boss is by experts Sarah and Paul Edwards. Being your own boss can be the greatest . . . or the pits. This book helps you master the psychological side. Oodles of tips to take the stress out of your path to success, $10.95.

MAKING MONEY WITH YOUR COMPUTER AT HOME also by Paul and Sarah Edwards, is hot off the press. It shows how to take advantage of computer technology to produce full-time, part-time, or add-on income at home. Choose from 75 computer-based businesses, some so new or specialized you haven't even heard of them yet! This hi-tech book also gives you instant online access to strategic information and contacts only a highly-paid research staff would normally be able to find. No businessperson should be without it, only $10.95

MARKETING WITHOUT ADVERTISING is a treasure-trove of creative strategies for small businesses. Instead of throwing good money after bad in an expensive effort to hype your business, Michael Phillips and Salli Rasberry show you how to use creative promotional techniques to generate sales, $14.

MEDIA POWER: How Your Business Can Profit From the Media is by master promoter Peter G. Miller. It reveals insider information on how the media works—and how you can get it to work for you. Proven strategies and common sense advice galore. Here you'll discover how to deal with reporters, find the best media outlets, handle a crisis, and get solid coverage year after year, $19.95.

MONEY MAKING MARKETING is another winner by Dr. Jeffrey Lant. Gives detailed instructions on how to find the people who need what you're selling—and make sure they buy it. Both informational and inspirational, it contains Jeffrey's usual practical advice, $35.00.

NATIONAL DIRECTORY OF NEWSPAPER OP-ED PAGES, THE is edited by Marilyn Ross. Op-ed (opposite editorial) page essays focus attention on industries, issues, and ideas. This one-of-a-kind resource benefits publicists and authors alike. It pinpoints the needs of scores of newspapers. Each listing contains the paper's name, address, phone, fax, editorial contact, fees paid, preferred length, copyright policy, and residency requirements. It also includes valuable individual editorial comments, plus insider instructions on how to penetrate this ideal publicity medium, only $19.95.

NATIONAL HOME BUSINESS REPORT is edited by Barbara Brabec. Written in a breezy, informal way, this newsletter contains a smorgasbord of information for home-based businesses. There's plenty of experienced advice from the editor, plus articles from accomplished contributors in the field. Imaginative, low-cost marketing strategies—money-saving tips—hard-learned success secrets—it's all here, $24 per year.

NEW MARKETING OPPORTUNITIES: The Business and Trade Directory for the New Age/Metaphysical Marketplace is a 418-page indispensable sourcebook for anyone wanting to reach this niche market. The third edition by Dr. Sophia Tarila has over 7,000 listings and is a great helping hand for those involved with holistic health, recovery, self-help, consciousness exploration, etc. Divided into three sections—The Products, Creating the Market, and Reaching the Public—it's a practical do-it-yourself kit, $89.95.

NEW TOOLS OF TECHNOLOGY, THE: A User Friendly Guide to the Latest Technology is by Daniel Burrus and Patti Thomsen. A terrific product idea-generator and futuristic problem-solver, this book has been called the businessperson's guide to the next century. It pinpoints 20 key technologies entrepreneurs and managers need to know about for short- and long-term planning, $24.95.

NEWSLETTER ON NEWSLETTERS is a welcome reference for anyone wanting to prosper in the lucrative newsletter publishing field. This 24-times-a-year publication is truly *the* reference in the newsletter industry. And no wonder: it's by Howard Penn Hudson. Each issue contains case histories, the latest on promotion, tips on writing and editing, plus management advice, $120 per year.

NEWSLETTERS FROM THE DESKTOP: Designing Effective Publications with Your Computer has a whopping 200 illustrations and offers a solid introduction into newsletter design. By Roger C. Parker, it explores the best layout possibilities, the nameplate, the most impressive typefaces, the integration of text and graphics, and more. Before and after makeovers stimulate a wealth of ideas and provide inspiration, $23.95.

NO MORE COLD CALLS This is Lant's newest—a whopping 680 pages to show you how to find clients and close those prospects. If you sell a service you need this course-in-a-book. It's made more than one multi-millionaire. Avoid the 30 major mistakes, turn your computer into a client-centered marketing department, learn how to upgrade prospects, plus generate all the low-cost leads you need, $39.95.

1001 WAYS TO MARKET YOUR BOOK Don't be deceived by the title, this is must for *every* hungry entrepreneur—and any author who wants to boost sales on his or her book! John Kremer outdid himself on this new, revised edition. It contains extremely creative ideas and real-life industry examples of shrewd marketing ideas, all organized in an easy-to-scan way. Highly recommended at $19.95.

PEOPLE SMART: Powerful Techniques for Turning Every Encounter into a Mutual Win is just that—a powerful tool. Your professional and personal success can be amplified by knowing how to relate better with all kinds of people. This book explains the different personality types. Being able to recognize them puts you a leg up on the competition. Learn how much more effective and profitable you can be by using "The Platinum Rule." A great offering by experts Tony Alessandra, Ph.D., and Michael J. O'Connor, Ph.D., with Janice VanDyke. $24.95.

POWER PUBLIC RELATIONS: How to Get PR to Work for You offers a short-cut to public relations literacy. By Leonard Saffir, it details how to win maximum exposure and awareness among target audiences. Covers influencing public opinion, championing popular or controversial causes, and managing crisis. Included are checklists, forms, letters, releases, and planning documents you can put to immediate use, $39.95.

PROFESSIONAL SPEAKING: Increase the Speed at Which You Succeed is by international speaking pro Patricia Fripp. She put this audio cassette program together for people who want six hours worth of advice when she only has five minutes. The program includes all aspects of speaking and is a boon to CEOs who find themselves asked to talk in public or those wishing to pursue a professional speaking career. Practical, powerful stuff to make you comfortable and unforgettable, $55.00.

PUBLICITY HANDBOOK, THE: How to Maximize Publicity for Products, Services and Organizations details how to produce big results. Why learn the hard way when expert David R. Yale can show you how to initiate and administer a publicity program that puts you in the right place at the right time—and pays big dividends? Includes advice from working journalists. This is an indispensable tool for those who are serious about getting more than their share of media attention, $39.95.

PUBLICITY MANUAL, THE is by Kate Kelly. Written by a practicing PR pro, this book tells how to develop good publicity relationships and write compelling news releases. All the hows and whys are covered here, $29.95.

QUEST FOR SERVICE QUALITY, THE is filled with dynamite ideas for improving the quality of service in any business, small or large. Whether we admit it or not, our level of profit is directly proportional to our quality of service. At last there's a book that offers practical and proven guidance for being the best you can be. Let Phillip S. Wexler, W.A. (Bill) Adams, and Emil Bohn, Ph.D., lead you on a successful "Quest for Service Quality." $24.95.

QUICK SOLUTIONS TO GREAT LAYOUTS contains 100 "swipeable" answers to the dilemma of creating effective layouts. By Graham Davis, it covers everything from ads to newsletters, brochures to letterheads. Core techniques are covered, as well as the reasoning behind what is recommended. Often several solutions are given for the same problem, illustrating that there is more than one design solution, $24.95.

SENIOR MEDIA DIRECTORY Others have tried to imitate this collection of senior-specific media. They don't come close. It includes national publications, regional ones by state and province (yes, Canada is included too), newspaper supplements for seniors, syndicated columns for older people, plus TV and radio for seniors. Information includes frequency of publication, circulation, editorial profile, key personnel and advertising information. A dynamic resource if you target older Americans! $90.

SMALL TIME OPERATOR: How To Start Your Own Small Business, Keep Your Books, Pay Your Taxes, & Stay Out of Trouble! Want to stay clear of the I.R.S.? Seek help setting up your books? Need to know the bottom line on the new tax laws? This excellent business book—written and revised annually by CPA Bernard Kamoroff—tells all. It's a great start-up tool and also offers many useful tips for established business barons, $14.95.

SUCCESSFUL DIRECT MARKETING METHODS is by guru Bob Stone. A classic 575-page book on marketing, this fourth edition is *the* definitive book on direct mail selling. If this is how you plan to market your services, you need Stone's professional advice to keep you in the forefront of the direct marketing revolution. This all-inclusive reference answers questions you never thought to ask, $34.95.

SUCCESSFUL TELEMARKETING Crammed with proven ideas to increase your sales and profits and decrease the cost of generating those sales! Written by marketing masterminds Bob Stone and John Wyman, this book gives you step-by-step techniques to effectively, yet not impertinently, win more clients or customers. A fantastic tool for speakers, consultants, and entrepreneurs who want to "reach out and touch" more business, $39.95.

TALKING WITH YOUR CUSTOMERS: What They Will Tell You about Your Business When You Ask the Right Questions shows how to improve customer and client satisfaction and at the same time measure and evaluate your firm's strengths and weaknesses. Discover how to design your own survey to glean the information you need to be more successful. From Mike Wing you'll learn about easy ways to get information from competitors, what actions to take to please current customers and attract new ones, plus how to measure your company's responsiveness to feedback, $19.95.

UNABASHED SELF-PROMOTER'S GUIDE, THE is by Dr. Jeffrey Lant. We can unabashedly say this is one great book. It reveals what every person or organization needs to know about getting ahead by exploiting the media. Seldom-told tips and imaginative ways to focus attention on yourself, your service, and your company, $35.00.

WHICH AD PULLED BEST? Want to learn precisely what makes ads work and how to create better ones yourself? This is the book. The new seventh edition has 50 all-new matched pairs of ads plus analysis of which one worked—and why. Uncover the winning combination of headline, copy, and position strategy that moves readers to action—and gives you or your clients greater profits, $16.95.

WINNING WITH THE POWER OF PERSUASION: Mancuso's Secrets for Small Business Success shows you how to convince anyone to do anything. Lessons on entrepreneurship you've seen nowhere else wait here in Joe Mancuso's superb book. Master the art of persuasion as you blend the classics of selling, negotiating, and motivating into your own powerful entrepreneurial combination. Rollicking anecdotes make it fun reading too. A truly unusual book to help you grow your business, $19.95.

WORKING FROM HOME: Everything you Need to Know About Living and Working Under the Same Roof Paul and Sarah Edwards again team up here to offer their perceptive business advice. You'll learn about solving zoning problems—juggling family, friends, children, and work—managing self-discipline—and combatting the isolation factor. Loaded with useful nuts and bolts tips for anyone contemplating a home-based business, only $14.95.

WORKING SOLO is a practical guide to freedom and financial success in your own business. It's an essential transitioning resource for choosing the business that's perfect for you, turning your computer into a money-making assistant, getting money without going to a bank, joining forces with other independents, and painlessly managing bookkeeping, taxes, and insurance. The book is divided into four information-packed sections: The Dream, The Decision, The Details, the Delight. Author Terri Lonier includes over 1,000 solo business opportunities to stimulate the thinking of new-breed entrepreneurs who will create the services, products, and markets for the 21st century, $14.95.

Recommended Reading Order Form

Yes! I want to become a more savvy and profitable entrepreneur. Please send the books or tapes listed below. I understand if I'm not satisfied with any book, it may be returned for a refund—up to a full year! Ship to: (*please print*)

Name _____

Company _____

Address _____

City/State/Zip _____

Phone (____) _____ Signature _____

□ Check or money order payable to Communication Creativity enclosed
Please charge my: □ Visa □ MasterCard □ American Express □ Discover
Card # _____ Expires _____

Qty	Title	Price
_____	_____	_____
_____	_____	_____
_____	_____	_____
_____	_____	_____
_____	_____	_____
_____	_____	_____
_____	_____	_____
_____	_____	_____
_____	_____	_____

Shipping and Handling: ($3 per item) $ _____

Sales Tax: (Colorado residents please add 7%) $ _____

TOTAL (Thanks for your order!) $ _____

If a price has been raised by the publisher, please:
□ Send the item, bill me the difference. □ Cancel my order.

U.S. currency only. Prices and availability subject to change and slightly higher in Canada. Allow 3-4 weeks for delivery. For faster special handling please call us at:
Credit Card Orders: (800) 331-8355, ext. BI
(Please have your credit card handy)
8 A.M. - 5 P.M. Mountain Time
You may fax credit card orders to (719) 395-8374
Or mail to: Communication Creativity, P.O. Box 909-BI
Buena Vista, CO 81211-0909

Index

Bold page numbers indicate the primary reference for a subject.

Tom and Marilyn Ross

The Rosses are the principals of Accelerated Business Images, a public relations and advertising firm that specializes in helping service businesses on a "Spot Marketing Alternative" basis. Rather than demanding expensive monthly PR retainers, they develop individualized shoestring promotional campaigns that get results. These veteran entrepreneurs use creative strategies to help their clients build profits through greater visibility and credibility in the marketplace.

Marilyn and Tom are members of the National Speakers Association. They're frequently called upon to give their unique team seminars and workshops to organizations, associations, and corporations from coast to coast. They speak on such topics as "Unabashed Power ProMOTION," "Top Drawer Marketing Strategies for Bottom Line Results," and "Country Bound!™ Trade Your Business Suit Blues for Blue Jean Dreams™."

In 1993 the Rosses were invited to be Senior Associates of the prestigious Center for the New West, "A think tank that casts its visionary net over the vast economic and cultural landscape . . ." according to *The Christian Science Monitor*. They are both listed in the 24th edition of *Who's Who in the West*. And between them, this dynamic pair is also included in *Who's Who of American Women, The World Who's Who of Women, The International Businessmen's Who's Who* and *Men and Women of Distinction*.

Their writing careers are detailed in *Working Press of the Nation, Who's Who in U.S. Writers, Editors & Poets, The International Authors and Writers Who's Who* and *Contemporary Authors*.

Both also belong to the Authors Guild and Marilyn is a member of ASJA. This is their seventh book collaboration. They can be reached at the address below.

Accelerated Business Images
P. O. Box 1500-BI
Buena Vista, CO 81211-1500
(719) 395-2459

Give the Gift of Business Success to Your Colleagues and Friends

CHECK YOUR LEADING BOOKSTORE OR ORDER HERE

☐ **YES**, I want ___ copies of *Big Ideas for Small Service Businesses* at $15.95 each, plus $3 shipping per book (Colorado residents please add $1.12 state sales tax per book). Canadian orders must be accompanied by a postal money order in U.S. funds. Allow up to 30 days for delivery unless special arrangements are made.

☐ **YES**, I may be interested in having Marilyn and Tom speak or give a seminar on marketing to my company, college, university, or organization. Please send information.

My check or money order for $_____ is enclosed.

Please charge my ☐ Visa ☐ MasterCard ☐ Discover ☐ AmEx

Name _____ Phone _____

Organization _____

Address _____

City/State/Zip _____

Card # _____ Exp. Date _____

Signature _____

Make your check payable and return to:
Communication Creativity
P. O. Box 909
Buena Vista, CO 81211-0909
Fax credit card orders to (719) 395-8374

Call credit card orders to: (800) 331-8355, ext. BI
between 8:00 A.M. and 5:00 P.M. Mountain Time